FURTHER PRAISE FOR *TEACHER AS TRAVELER*

"Kenneth Cushner has infused his immense experience as a global ambassador and advocate for globally competent teaching into the new edition of his book. By sharing his perceptions, and those of teacher candidates with whom he has worked over the years, Cushner shows readers how to prepare for international teaching experiences in ways that foster the development of global competence. This book provides a solid foundation for rich and meaningful experiences teaching abroad. I highly recommend it to anyone preparing to teach abroad and to those who prepare them."

—Sharon Brennan, PhD, professor and director of field experiences, University of Kentucky

"There is nobody more qualified to write a book such as this than Kenneth Cushner, who has spent his career advocating for the importance of integrating international and intercultural experiences into the education of young people. Taken together, the well-organized and timely collection of chapters in this new edition represents the most comprehensive guide available for designing and implementing impactful learning experiences abroad. The narratives are captivating and the advice—learned through decades of first-hand experiences—is priceless!"

—David M. Moss, PhD, director, Global Education, and associate professor, Neag School of Education, University of Connecticut

"As international study-travel gains popularity in at all levels of education, Kenneth Cushner reminds us that mere placement in another country does not necessarily result in students' intercultural development or expanded worldview. Cushner provides a framework for impactful international immersion experiences defined by meaningful preparation for the trip, scaffolded on-site requirements, thoughtful guided reflections, and post-trip follow-up, which together, launch participants on a trajectory of lifetime growth and development. His penchant for story-telling, including stories in the words of students for whom he has facilitated such experiences, brings to life the learning that can take place when international study-travel is done the right way. If you are new to the field of intercultural experiential learning, or you are seeking to strengthen programs you already offer, Dr. Cushner's book is for you."

—Laura L. Stachowski, PhD, director, Global Gateway for Teachers, Indiana University

Teacher as Traveler

Teacher as Traveler

Enhancing the Intercultural Development of Teachers and Students

Kenneth Cushner

Second Edition

ROWMAN & LITTLEFIELD
Lanham • Boulder • New York • London

Published by Rowman & Littlefield
An imprint of The Rowman & Littlefield Publishing Group, Inc.
4501 Forbes Boulevard, Suite 200, Lanham, Maryland 20706
www.rowman.com

Unit A, Whitacre Mews, 26-34 Stannary Street, London SE11 4AB

British Library Cataloguing in Publication Information Available

Library of Congress Cataloging-in-Publication Data Available
ISBN: 978-1-4758-3822-0 (cloth : alk. paper)
ISBN: 978-1-4758-3823-7 (pbk. : alk. paper)
ISBN: 978-1-4758-3824-4 (electronic)

Contents

Preface

Increased attention has been given to the internationalization of education, both for children in K–12 schools and for those in teacher education, since the first edition of this book appeared in 2004. A major component of this activity has focused on study and/or travel abroad. More and more secondary students are traveling internationally as part of their regular schooling or in specialized summer experiences, and there has been a corresponding almost meteoric increase in the number of university students studying abroad. This has been accompanied by an increase in the number of professional associations that have begun to consider ways to enhance the international dimension of their various disciplines.

One of the often-stated goals of all of these efforts is to enhance people's intercultural effectiveness. Those working in the field of study abroad, however, know that it is one thing for people to have an international experience and yet another for that experience to be interpersonal in nature and ultimately enhance one's intercultural competence. The essence of this book is to increase the potential to turn these international experiences into meaningful interpersonal encounters that form the basis for intercultural learning.

I have been traveling with students of all ages and writing about these experiences for more than forty years—long before it was common and relatively easy to do through prepackaged programs offered by third-party providers. The change of title of this second edition reflects the more recent international experiences I have had as well as what we are learning from the research undertaken in this field. One thing we know from the field of intercultural education and training is that most people have not had significant experiences across cultures from which they can draw upon to enhance their learning. Hence, stories are often used as a foundation to build upon in an attempt to ground subsequent concepts and content.

In the first edition, I used my personal travel experiences with students as the foundation to introduce concepts related to intercultural interaction and to point out some of the important concepts and strategies educators can employ to enhance intercultural learning. Although not common in academic presentations, this edition continues in this vein, relating much from the first-person perspective, not only my own, but that of student participants as well. In chapters that are interspersed with academic content (chapters 1–7), the first-person voice is set in italics. Because the majority of chapters 8, 9, and 10 are told from the perspective of participants, I have retained standard text formatting.

This second edition contains substantial additions and modifications. This edition reflects the considerable amount of research that has occurred in recent years that has helped us to better design international programs with an intercultural emphasis and to understand their impact. Thus, the research base in most of the chapters has been updated.

An increasing number of preservice teachers are taking advantage of the opportunity to complete their student teaching abroad as the culminating experience in their teacher education program. A new and updated look at the international student teaching experience is presented in chapter 8, coauthored by Dr. Martha Lash, a faculty colleague at Kent State University, and Justine DeFrancesco, a recent overseas student teacher currently completing her master's degree in early childhood education with a concentration on globalization and intercultural competence.

The previous edition of this book ended on a tragic note—the death of a student on a program in Kenya. I have wrestled with the decision of retaining this experience or not, choosing to keep this as a part of the study-abroad experience that we can all learn from. However, rather than end chapter 9 and the book on such a sad note, I challenge the reader to recognize that even in the face of extreme challenges, we must continue to move forward if we are to achieve the ultimate goals and objectives we seek. I continue to be engaged in schools in East Africa and share these more recent experiences and how I have worked to build mutually beneficial connections between Maasai children in Tanzania and young students in Ohio.

In the years since the first edition was written, I have had the pleasure of teaching numerous times with Semester at Sea, a globally focused study-abroad program that takes university students around the world on board a ship. This one-of-a-kind program enables students to complete a semester's worth of courses while acquiring a comparative look at various practices across multiple countries and cultures. Chapter 10 introduces readers to a number of these young students as they reflect upon the experiences they are having in various ports of call as well as adjusting to the life and culture of a shipboard community.

The body of the book concludes with chapter 11, which looks closely at the critical role that experience plays in facilitating intercultural growth and development. A substantial amount of research has been undertaken in recent years assessing the impact of study and travel abroad as well as the program qualities that seem to facilitate intercultural learning. This forms the basis of the chapter, providing a theoretical and research-based foundation that grounds this work.

This book includes an appendix that provides an array of resources and other considerations to make one's travel meaningful, safe, and rewarding. I welcome your insights and recommendations and encourage you to communicate with me as your ventures unfold.

Chapter 1

Teacher as Traveler—Travel as Teacher

Do not go where the path may lead; go instead where there is no path and leave a trail.

—Ralph Waldo Emerson

When I was younger, I wanted to be an adventurer. I'm sure this notion began as a result of all the time I spent scanning the pages of old National Geographic *magazines and then reading the Johann David Wyss novel, and later watching the Disney film,* Swiss Family Robinson, *countless times. If this was the beginning of my interest in places far away, I can blame Joy and George Adamson's account of raising Elsa the lioness in their books* Born Free *and* Living Free *for furthering it along and giving it context. From my early days, I envisioned myself as the Adamsons, working in the African bush, saving and protecting vulnerable wildlife, helping to raise and teach the young, and then setting them free to encounter the world on their own.*

During my undergraduate college years, I must have written to more than forty game parks, from Kenya to South Africa, seeking work of almost any kind. I even studied Kiswahili, the language spoken throughout East Africa, as my undergraduate foreign language requirement. At the time, I was the only student to have taken the full two-year cycle of Kiswahili, learning from Meki, my teacher and mentor, who had come from Tanzania to Ohio to pursue his PhD. Talk about assumptions and stereotypes. The bureaucracy of the African Studies Department at the time assumed I was an African American student. Every six months, they would send me a postcard reminding me that it was time to get my blood checked for sickle cell anemia.

But I'm white and Jewish, and not a likely candidate for sickle cell anemia. And inexperienced game wardens from outside the continent weren't

1

particularly wanted in the late 1960s and early 1970s, especially at a time when most African countries were busy nationalizing themselves and struggling to dispose of any reminders of their colonial past. So I became a teacher instead. I can barely recall any of the Kiswahili I learned at the time and never did fulfill my dream of reaching East Africa until the late 1990s. But I have been fortunate since then to have gone on multiple safaris and to have spent significant time working with young people and teachers in schools in Kenya and Tanzania.

Most teachers do for children many of the things the Adamsons did for the young, vulnerable, and orphaned animals they nurtured and returned to the natural habitat. Teachers are entrusted with helping raise the young of our species by providing them with some of the specialized skills, guidance, nurturance, support, and experiences that might "set them free," so to speak, to become functional adults ready to face a complex society composed of our own producers and consumers, predators and prey, vultures and other scavengers, and for what some might consider, a "dog-eat-dog" world. And like the Adamsons, most teachers help others in many ways that they, nor those on whose behalf they are working, could ever imagine.

Opening up new horizons and providing novel opportunities for others comes naturally to all good teachers and underlies much of what they do. Today, if young people are to be adequately prepared for the future, these horizons must reach well beyond the traditional three Rs of *Reading, 'Riting, and 'Rithmetic*, to include a fourth R—*Relations*—or intercultural relations that embrace the broader world and take account of the intercultural realities in which teachers and their students live.

Globalization, although not really a new phenomenon because it has been occurring ever since Columbus ventured across the oceans, links people in myriads of ways never before imagined. From the tragedies that unfolded on September 11, 2001, when people from more than seventy countries were lost, to the increasing threat of global pandemics, environmental stresses, and the almost inexplicable ways in which world economies intersect, we are reminded daily of how all lives across the planet are inextricably woven.

To continue to teach from a relatively narrowly focused or traditional orientation will do little to move us forward as individuals, as a nation or as a world. Like it or not, education, as life today, is a global concern, and we are remiss if we do not educate all of our students to be competent, global citizens who not only understand others but who have the skills and dispositions required to collaborate across cultural boundaries to solve some of the world's complicated problems. The problems faced across the world today are so complex and interconnected that they will be solved only by the concerted efforts of people from a variety of backgrounds who have the skills and willingness to collaborate with one another—or they will not be solved.

Teachers must also be futurists. That is, they must project and anticipate the future needs of society and, with that in mind, develop educational experiences for their students that achieve the goals and objectives determined to be of most need. But teachers must themselves be citizens of the world if they are to guide their students in this direction. If teachers are not skilled at reaching out across the cultural divide and do not learn how to bridge cultural gaps, and if they do not consider their global citizenry and do not take their own risks, then it will not be possible to adequately prepare their young students with the kinds of skills they will need to be born free in the twenty-first century. Teachers, thus, are central to the process of intercultural development, and they must model such an orientation for their young students as well as for their communities.

And many students are aware and concerned! Read the words of a sensitive and future-oriented fifteen-year-old student from Australia who challenged her teachers, asking whether they possessed the ability to prepare her for her life as a global citizen. Although speaking of her life in Australia, it is clear that her reality and concerns apply to all. Her thoughts, modified and updated from the original (Tudball, 2012), are paraphrased below.

"I want you to understand how I think about my future and my world. Wherever I live and work, I will certainly be mixing in a multinational, multifaith, multicultural setting. During my lifetime, a planet-wide economic system is likely to operate, controlled not so much by big nations as by big business networks and regional centers of trade like Singapore, Los Angeles, London, Tokyo, and Sydney. By the time I am thirty-five years old more people will live in Shanghai, just one city in China, than in the whole of Australia. Most people will be working across national borders and cultures, speaking more than one language—probably including an Asian language. That's the kind of job for which I must be prepared.

"Because I am growing up in Australia, the Asia/Pacific area will be a strong focus of my world. There are three billion people in Asia alone—and that number will certainly continue to grow. The Asian continent (from India to Japan) already accounts for half the world's population. And the world's largest Muslim country is here too, in Indonesia, just north of Australia, with a population of over 220 million—larger than that of Japan and Russia. People the world over will have to learn about Islam at school and to respect Muslims—even in the face of all the challenges present today.

"But it's not only happening to those of us in Australia. More than half of the population in many of the world's developing countries is under the age of twenty-five—think about the consequences of that! These are all our potential partners and competitors—and they'll all want the good things they see that life has to offer. It will not matter what nationality any of us have because our world is smaller, people move about, and most workplaces will

be internationalized. Our world is likely to be borderless. We are more than likely to be employed in an internationally owned firm, and it is likely that in our homes someone will speak Japanese, Korean, Spanish, or Chinese.

"Our environment, too, will continue to be changed—and challenged. In the 1950s, when my grandparents were born, only two cities in the world, London and New York, had more than 8 million inhabitants. In 2016, there were forty-two such cities—more than half of them in Asia. Environmentally what happens within the border of one country is no longer solely that country's business. Environmental responsibilities will have to be enforced internationally. By the time I am fifty, the world could be threatened by 'green wars' or 'water wars' unless my generation learns to do something to balance the unequal access to clean water, good soil, food distribution, and climate change."

Sophie is like every child sitting in every classroom today, growing up in a world that is vastly different from that of most of their parents and teachers. They need to be prepared for the inevitabilities of a globally and interculturally connected future. Yet most of our schooling, from the way people look at things to many of the textbooks in use around the world, are relatively narrow in their thinking and orientation and, in many ways, out of date. Schooling today must teach young people about living comfortably and successfully in an intercultural world.

What skills and understandings will people living and working in the near future need? Do we know what an international curriculum looks like and how it can be taught? Most schools today say that students need to be global citizens. But do teachers know what to teach? Do they know how to teach? Are teachers confident that they can design and deliver a curriculum that will equip young people to live in a complex, intercultural world? These are our challenges as teachers today.

An overriding objective of this book is to inspire educators and others to include international as well as domestic intercultural encounters as an increasing part of the education of young people. In no other time in human history has it been more essential that individuals develop an intercultural perspective and reach a certain level of comfort in their intercultural interactions.

But not only is it necessary that individuals develop this broader understanding of the world; it is becoming increasingly possible to do so. Through sensitive and well-designed experiences, students can move along a continuum of intercultural development from a monocultural, ethnocentric mindset to one that is intercultural and ethnorelative, from being rather inexperienced in terms of intercultural sensitivity and competence to possessing an ability to think more broadly and interact more effectively with people different from oneself.

Essential to this development are the impactful, firsthand, interpersonal encounters that travel brings and that serve to make many of the abstract concepts of intercultural understanding practical and real. This book thus is part autobiography of a traveling teacher and teacher educator, part travelogue, part lessons learned, and part guidelines for those interested in developing meaningful travel experiences or who are simply interested in getting the most that they can from their own travel. I welcome you on this journey.

Travel, while enriching, engaging, and educational for the individual or group, is rarely easy. Educators committed to developing and delivering thoughtful curricular experiences designed to achieve certain goals and objectives related to travel and intercultural learning must understand the reasons that may underlie people's desire to travel as well as some of the obstacles that may be encountered along the way.

It is interesting to consider that the derivation of the word *travel* is from the word *travail*. Its root, however, is ironically from the Latin *tripalium*, referring to a medieval torture rack, implying bodily or mental labor; toil, especially of a painful or oppressive nature; exertion; hardship; suffering; a journey. A surprising relationship perhaps, yet similar to how some people may recall their years of schooling. And as many have experienced, and Cosineau (1998) reminds us, there are moments when traveling that are difficult and demanding—perhaps like being "on the rack."

What is a bit surprising is that people often recall the more difficult and demanding moments of their travels—the times they were sick, got lost, had something stolen, or met a "shifty" local. Yet people tend to feel a sense of accomplishment and pride when they report that they have "survived" the ordeal. This may appear a peculiar and non-commonsense finding, but it seems to be a rather common part of the process.

With preparation and guidance, the challenging and difficult moments of travel can be reduced, eliminated, or at least managed and serve as a foundation for learning. But we need to be a bit cautious in this regard. Some would say we are fortunate today because the modern travel industry has removed much of the risk and difficulty from traveling. Much of group travel or tourism can be experienced in a somewhat protected and sanitized context. It is only through direct personal encounters with other people and the environment, however, that true culture learning and intercultural growth can occur. Nevertheless, whether we are on vacation, traveling with students, or on our own far-reaching adventure, we can look at the demands along the road as either torment or opportunities to stretch and grow.

We might ask, "Why do people continue to invest an incredible amount of time and money to move themselves and their belongings over vast distances, uprooting themselves from the surroundings they have become accustomed to, and exposing themselves to potential dangers and certain discomforts?" Obviously, there are many reasons people travel, some of which are personal, some of which are for one's livelihood, and some of which are involuntary as with refugees from the many war-torn regions of the world.

Increasingly, the business community demands continual movement of people, goods, and services. Accounting for much of the travel people do today, the business executive can move with relative ease between the cultures of the world's multinational and international corporations. Well over 6,000 international firms have offices in the United States, and an equally high number of American corporations have an overseas presence. Globalization of the world's industries accounts for a significant amount of world travel today. This represents one of the reasons young people should learn the art of travel—many will eventually join the global workforce.

For many, travel represents a vacation or an opportunity to experience something different in another part of the world. For others, it has become a hobby, and in this day of excesses and expendable income, they travel the world collecting passport stamps just as stamp collectors accumulate philatelic mementos or as any other hobbyist amasses the artifacts of his or her pastime. Travel in this sense provides an escape from one's daily routines by offering relaxation and possibly fresh, albeit brief, encounters and new experiences that could not be found at home.

The travel industry continues to grow faster than most sectors of the global economy, contributing more than US $7 trillion to the global economy, supporting an estimated 300 million jobs, and employing one in ten people worldwide (WTTC, 2016). Travel and tourism will continue to outpace the global economy in the coming decade, fueled in large part by this type of recreational traveler. This is another reason young people should learn the art of travel—to be good stewards of the Earth and its people by traveling responsibly and in a sustainable or ecologically sound manner.

With increased internationalization, we have witnessed a homogenization of much of the travel experience. For many people, travel consists of taxi or Uber rides between rather similar international airports to familiar and comfortable brand name and chain hotels. Many find themselves so uncomfortable when they are out of their familiar surroundings that they become critical of the local's way of life, and the travel industry has gone to incredible lengths to provide such travelers with accommodations that, behind the facade of difference, are designed either to replicate what one would find at home or to mask the reality of where one is.

One must keep in mind, however, that a foreign country is not designed to make the visitor comfortable—it is designed to make its own people comfortable. For this type of traveler, who typically wants the comforts of home, it may not matter where they are—just that they are somewhere else enjoying that to which they have become accustomed. They don't really want things to be different; they just want or need to be elsewhere. Herein lies another reason we should teach the art of travel—to help people learn to see beyond their own frame of reference and to be comfortable and welcome the differences they will encounter in the world.

Some people may travel to avoid a problem or an uncomfortable situation at home, to escape a struggling marriage, a stifling career, or dissatisfaction with self, only to find that the problem cannot be avoided and that it accompanies them wherever they go. Being away from one's familiar context and support groups then exacerbates the problem they tried to avoid in the first place. One soon finds that it is easier to change one's surroundings than it is to change one's heart and mind. There is a truism here—no matter where you go, you too will be there—you simply cannot escape yourself. Herein lies another reason to teach the art of travel—to help people understand what it can and cannot accomplish.

Evolutionary biologists and anthropologists might argue that travel is in our nature and that people really have no choice but to constantly be on the move. The hunting and gathering way of life, they contend, is what is natural for humans; it is hardwired into our systems and, if fully embraced, would guarantee the sustainability of the planet.

In his book *Ishmael*, Daniel Quinn (1995) proposes that the invention of agriculture marked the beginning of the environmental decline. He argues that some 12,000 years ago, when people stopped wandering and became relatively stationary, they assumed the role of God, determining which species of plants and animals lived and which would not be tolerated on land designated as cropland. We have witnessed an increase in the number of extinct and endangered species as well as global threats of pollution ever since we became stationary and stopped our hunting and gathering ways.

One can find evidence of the tensions that might have developed in our evolutionary past if we listen to the words or observe the behavior of some of the world's indigenous people. A Caribou Eskimo, for instance, once told Dr. Knud Rassmussen, "What can we do? We were born with the Great Unrest. Our father taught us that life is one long journey on which only the unfit are left behind" (Chatwin, 1987). Or, in Turi's *Book of Lappland*, we learn that Lapps consider themselves to have the same nature as reindeer—in the springtime they long for the mountains; in the winter they long for the woods.

Chatwin (1987) also pointed out the strong need for human mobility. Day in and day out, he says, a baby cannot be walked enough, suggesting that if babies instinctively demand to be walked, the mother on the African savanna must have been walking too, from camp to camp on her daily foraging round, to the waterhole, and on visits to neighbors. Evolutionary evidence does support this contention, suggesting that it may not have been the development of tools that prompted early humans to venture out of Africa as first believed. Rather, simple wanderlust may have been part of Homo erectus's personality encouraging it to change its range and habitat—perhaps in pursuit of game (Lemonick, 2000).

One might even trace the human drive for movement to others in the animal kingdom. In *The Descent of Man*, Darwin points out that in certain species of birds, the migratory impulse may be stronger than the maternal instinct, stating that "late in the autumn swallows, house martins and swifts frequently desert their tender young, leaving them to perish miserably in their nests" (Darwin, 1874, p. 108). He cites other examples, including Audubon's goose, which, deprived of its pinion feathers, started out to walk the journey on foot. He goes on to describe the sufferings of a bird, penned up at the season of its migration, which would flail its wings and bloody its breast against the bars of its cage (Chatwin, 1987).

To counter this, some Western psychiatrists, politicians, and tyrants have tried to convince us that the wandering life is an aberrant form of behavior; a neurosis; a form of unfulfilled sexual longing; a sickness which, in the interests of civilization, must be suppressed (Chatwin, 1987). Nazi propagandists, for instance, claimed that Roma (referred to by some in a derogatory manner as gypsies) and Jews—people they assumed to have wandering in their genes—could find no place in a stable Reich. They thus become the target of persecution because they were considered so different.

Yet, in the East, people still preserve the once universal concept, that wandering reestablishes the original harmony that existed between humans and the universe. For some, travel provides answers to questions they cannot find at home. *Solvitur ambulando*, it has been said—"it is solved by walking." And Guatama Buddha's last words to his disciples reportedly were, "Walk on!"

But perhaps not all of the answers to one's questions can be found on the road. One must consider carefully that some travel the world over in search of what they need, only to find it at the home they had left. Perhaps internal travel, as in meditation, prayer, and other forms of introspection, is a more fruitful means to satisfy one's desires and needs in this realm.

Finally, some travel as a means not only to learn but also as a means to teach—to help open up worlds for others that they may not readily do by themselves. Before the development of tourism, travel was conceived to be like study, and its fruits were considered to be the adornment of the mind and the formation of judgment (Fussell, 1987). The traveler was a student of what he sought. In such a case, travel can be accompanied by intellectual or spiritual growth, a sense of connectedness with something greater than oneself and one's immediate surroundings be that nature, people, or both. Read of the first student travel excursion I made with students and decide for yourself, which if any of these outcomes were realized.

It was beginning to get colder, windier, the rain was picking up, and there I was one night, searching the island for a fifteen-year-old student who, at the moment, was missing and nowhere to be found. Who would have thought that just three months after graduating from college and beginning a career in teaching that I would be traveling to Greece and worrying about losing a student? Most of my peers were in the United States, teaching in schools quite similar to one's they had gone through themselves. And most of them wanted nothing more than to return to their home community and teach in their alma mater, as many young teachers, unfortunately, still desire today. Not me. I didn't even have a passion for teaching when I first went to college. I disliked my own school experience so much that returning to the classroom as a teacher was absolutely the last thing I ever thought I would do.

That was, until I found myself at the American School in Zurich doing my student teaching. It was here where I found what an education might really be. This school was an exciting, engaging environment that young people wanted to be part of—as did I. Perhaps, I thought, that I could be a different kind of teacher, one who would create an environment where young people wanted to be. Teaching, for me, as I was soon to learn, would become a way to learn and to expand my horizons as well as those of my students.

I had been in my first official teaching job for no more than three months when I embarked on a rather ambitious adventure. Having just completed my student teaching and remaining on staff teaching biology on a part-time basis, I wanted to see as much of the world as possible. Not really having the necessary resources to fund such escapades, I looked to my students and their supportive parents for the opportunity. Perhaps, just perhaps, I could recruit a large enough group of students who would be interested in traveling to Greece over our spring break that I could cover my expenses. It seemed worth the effort.

To my surprise, fourteen students and their parents expressed interest—and more surprising, trust. They allowed me to take their children, most of them between the ages of fourteen and seventeen, by train from Zurich to the port town of Brendisi, tucked away in the heel of Italy's boot. From there, we would catch an overnight ferry to Greece and spend the better part of two weeks traveling between Athens and the islands.

Now, this was not going to be first-class travel by any stretch of the imagination. We would be traveling like most student backpackers—staying in youth hostels, using public transportation in and around Athens, and traveling third class by ship between the islands of the Aegean wherever possible. That was the only way I knew how to travel, having Arthur Frommer's "$5-A-Day" as a mantra in my head. Any "real" traveler, I thought, had to remain within *such a budget, and I would guide my students with this strategy. The highlight of our trip would be a one-week stay on the island of Santorini, or Thera, as it is known locally, in five homes I was able to rent through a contact in Zurich.*

It was not easy traveling to Santorini, but it was an adventure for each of us on many levels. My young students were surprisingly comfortable carrying their belongings in backpacks, staying in inexpensive student-oriented accommodations, and sailing south to Crete, where we stayed for three days learning about the ancient Minoan civilization.

A short four-hour, but very choppy ferry ride on stormy seas, took us north to Santorini. I never expected to meet so many locals on such a brief trip, but I seemed to be the only one who had any seasickness remedies on hand. Suddenly, the most popular person on the ship, I passed out pill after pill of Dramamine as we swayed from side to side, clutching our bags out of fear that they might fly overboard, and our bellies as they, for many, were relieved overboard. Half of the people on ship were ill by the time we arrived in the tranquil port—and I was out of Dramamine.

Some believe the island of Santorini to be the legendary Atlantis, blown apart by the volcanic eruption some 4,000 years ago that sent a tidal wave rushing to destroy the Minoan civilization in Crete. Today, the only habitable portion is a crescent-shaped ridge that rises some 1,000 feet from the water and a few hundred meters from the still active volcanic cone. Ships enter through a channel, with the volcanic cone on one side and the remaining landmass on the other, and see the sparkling white buildings atop the island that characterizes many popular photos of the Greek Islands. One could, at the time of our venture, reach the villages only by taking a burro or walking up approximately 600 broad zigzag steps from the "old" port to the town of Thira on the top of the island. Today, as the world of travel continues to change, a cable car whisks visitors from the port to the top with little effort.

Our homes were well situated, about one-half kilometer from the center of town, making it easy to get around. It was a safe community, and after our daily excursions to archaeological ruins, volcanic sites, and general jaunts around the island, I felt comfortable allowing the students to explore on their own.

This was my first exposure to Greek folk traditions, as it was for my students. Night after night, we would find ourselves in local restaurants, cafés, and nightclubs to observe, and ultimately participate, in local song and folk dance. This was also my introduction to the tradition of men dancing with other men—something quite foreign to me at the time. Although initially reluctant, I soon learned to join in the fun, and I began to look forward to those evenings. Besides, how could I expect my students to embrace new experiences if I was reluctant to do the same?

We were welcomed wherever we went—in small villages, in people's homes, in their churches, and of course, in their shops. Greeks by their nature are quite open to outsiders, more so than they may be to other Greek nationals to whom they are not related. Many visitors to Greece quickly find themselves included in the ingroup and leave the country with fond memories of the warmth and hospitality of its people.

Why should I have worried about the evenings? Where else could my students go? The entire island encompassed twenty-nine square miles and was populated by fewer than 500 people. But there I was, worrying, not only about the one student that night but also about my entire teaching career. Why travel in the first place? What was I doing here? What brought me to this point? The questions never seemed to end.

About 10:00 that night, about five days into our stay on Santorini and toward the end of our trip, I was making the rounds between the houses to check that everyone was accounted for. I came up one student short and, after rechecking all the houses, was certain that Irene, a rather quiet girl of fifteen who had been a pleasant, but somewhat detached participant, was missing. Nevertheless, I was worried and really did not know where to begin. I was especially concerned because the weather had been getting worse as the night progressed. I called together the other two chaperones, and we planned our strategy. Linda would head toward town—perhaps Irene was in one of the nightclubs or cafés. I would head toward the waterfront, and Barb would stay near the homes in case Irene returned.

It was getting windier by the hour, and it was pretty evident that a storm was approaching. By the time I started out, the gusts of wind were so strong that the branches of the few trees that remained on the island appeared as if they would be gone by morning. I walked through the coming storm and down the 600 steps toward the port area in search of Irene. Where could she be? What could have happened to her? I didn't know, nor did I really know where I was going, but I had to do something. Myriads of possibilities floated through my mind, none of which I really wanted to entertain at the moment.

As I reached the waterfront, I noticed a form hunched over in the darkness. There, all alone, was Irene, sitting crouched over on the pier with her head hung between her hands. She was cold, wet, and bawling her eyes out. I approached, anxious and cautious, but quite relieved to have found her.

What the problem could be, I couldn't have guessed. And it wasn't forthcoming—at least not at first. We walked back the long way up the steps and toward our houses, initially in silence. I wasn't quite sure what to say to a young, crying girl, but I had to know what had happened and what had brought her to tears. Breaking the awkward silence, I simply came out and asked, "What happened?"

"I was going to go with him … I wanted to be with him," she blurted out between tears.

"Go with who?" I asked. "Be with who?" I wanted to know.

It seems that Irene had met a Greek sailor earlier in the day and, as she put it, had fallen in love. She told me that she had thought seriously about joining her new friend and running away with him! A fifteen-year-old in love with one day's meeting? Was it possible, even without a working knowledge of the other's language? I guess, at least for the moment, that was a reality I had to accept.

Now, I really began to worry. Here I was, a new teacher having just begun my career. Irene had supposedly fallen in love with someone she had just met earlier in the day. What had transpired throughout the day I did not know, but I instinctively began to count the months. If anything had happened and she became pregnant, she, her parents, and the school administration would know in about, say, three to four months. The school year would be over, and I would have returned to the States. If she was pregnant, was I liable? Would this end my teaching career? The possibilities were endless as I waited, and waited, and worried.

Fortunately for all, Irene did not become pregnant, and I was able to pursue a very fulfilling career of teaching. Although at times the travel experience did seem tortuous, at least emotionally for me as well as Irene, we all learned a tremendous amount as a result of the trip.

Aside from concrete experiences interacting with present-day Greek society, touring through early Greek ruins, and studying ancient Minoan civilization, the students developed a sense of independence and group identification that could not have been achieved in the traditional classroom. And I learned that group travel with students, although stressful at times, has a much bigger payoff than most anything else a teacher might do in school. What better way is there to learn to trust oneself, one another, as well others in the world? In travel, teacher and student go forward, ideally with open arms and an open mind, to embrace the world. Young people can be trusted to be conscientious members of a traveling group and can take responsibility and look out for others. This was something I was certain I would be doing more of in the future.

Chapter 2

Get Ready; Get Set: Before You Go

The day on which one starts out is not the day to start preparation.

—*Nigerian folk saying*

The field of cross-cultural training has developed significantly over the past forty years, drawing upon the knowledge and research findings from such interrelated disciplines of study as anthropology, communication, education, psychology, and sociology. It has found practical application in a variety of fields, including but not limited to community and global health, conflict and mediation, diplomacy, international business, K–12 and higher education, mission work, and study abroad.

I was like a fish out of water when I began some forty years ago to consider ways in which I, as a teacher of children with an eye toward the future needs of an emerging global society, was convinced of the importance of integrating international and intercultural experiences in the education of young people. I traveled regularly with my young students, as you will read about in the pages to come. But when I began doing this there was little information available to guide my efforts. I "shot from the hip" on more than one occasion but continued to delve further and further into these fields, recognizing the value and potential impact that significant intercultural experiences can have on young people, ultimately pursuing a doctorate in curriculum and instruction with an emphasis in multicultural education and cross-cultural psychology.

I share some of my early travels with children—some as young as nine and ten years of age—in chapters 2, 3, and 4. A number of these experiences and strategies I employed set the stage for my further activities and investigations into this field.

"Do you know what I think I'll have a really hard time with?" Maria reflected during the debriefing session. "When you men have to blow your nose, you walk over to the water's edge, block a nostril, exhale really hard toward the water, repeat the procedure with your other nostril, wipe your nose with your hand, and then rinse your hand off in the water. UGH! How disgusting!"

"And do you know what really bothers me about you Americans?" was the quick reply. "When you have to blow your nose, you pull a handkerchief or tissue out of your pocket or purse, blow your nose into it, roll it up in a ball, and then put it back and carry it around with you for the rest of the day. And some of you then go and wash the handkerchief with your other clothes. UGH! How disgusting!"

Good teachers are constantly on the lookout for the teachable moment, and Maria's reaction presented an invaluable opportunity to discuss and learn about the concept of ethnorelativity. What appears to be healthy and appropriate from one perspective may be seen as dirty and disgusting from another. Cordial and formal through one's eyes becomes cold and stuffy from another's. Tactful and polite may seem overbearing and insincere.

People, both as individuals and as groups, are conditioned to see the world from one particular point of view. Another's perspective, belief, point of view, and ways of doing things may as a result be viewed as suspect, inferior, or just plain wrong. For the most part, people do not embrace such an attitude out of maliciousness. Rather, it is a consequence of ethnocentrism that people adopt as a means of protecting their own worldview and the considerable amount of time and energy they have invested to understand and maintain that reality. After all, one of the main purposes of culture is to pass on to the next generation those aspects that are deemed important.

Ethnocentrism, or the tendency to view the world and evaluate others from one's own perspective, thus becomes an important element of group survival. It can also become an obstacle to the attainment of an ethnorelative orientation and thus intercultural sensitivity.

Greg Trifonovitch, a former intercultural specialist at the East-West Center in Honolulu, spent many years preparing American teachers and administrators, like Maria, to assume visiting teaching assignments in various South Pacific nations. Constructing a simulated South Pacific village setting on about twenty-five acres on the Hawaiian island of Molokai'i, Greg would invite groups of would-be teachers, administrators, and their families for two-week orientation experiences. Here, in the safety of this constructed environment, Maria, and others like her, would have the opportunity to sample a bit of what life might be like for them once they arrived at their final destination, be it the islands of Tuvalu, Kapingamarangi, Kwajelein, or any of the hundreds of other inhabited islands scattered throughout the South Pacific.

Assisting with the orientation of the new recruits would be a number of Pacific Islanders, who would serve as trainers and consultants, helping to create a simulated island setting. For the first week, the trainers would speak only in their native language, thus adding to the range of factors to which the trainees had to adjust. In such a setting, people like Maria could project themselves into the future, and if they felt that the subsequent real-world adjustment in the islands would be too challenging or something they no longer wished to undertake, they could decide now before they made a significant overseas transition and remove themselves from the project.

People would typically voice a range of questions, worries, and concerns during the debriefing sessions that followed these orientation experiences. Some would ask whether there would be flush toilets once they get out to their island? A somewhat tongue-in-cheek reply to such a question would rather matter of factly be, "Yes, about every six hours the tide comes in, and every six hours the tide goes out again." At least one doesn't have to clean toilets on a regular basis.

People would also practice gathering food resources as many of the locals might do. They soon found that it was rather time consuming and quite difficult to gather coconuts from palm trees and break into them without destroying much of the contents as well as to fish from the local waters to gather enough sustenance for just one meal. After a few days, participants would discuss what it might be like to eat the village dog—a frequent visitor in the village site. People soon discovered the first of many disconfirmed expectations—that paradise may not be the idyllic place it is made out to be and life may be more challenging for some than anticipated. It was during one such debriefing exchange where Maria's reaction to nose blowing was discussed.

Information taken for granted and perceived one way in one cultural context may mean something significantly different in another. Three psychological phenomena frequently intersect that help to explain this—perception, categorization, and attribution. *Perception* refers to what people immediately report on their senses—what they think they have heard, seen, tasted, felt, and smelled. *Categorization* refers to the process that enables people to simplify the world around them by grouping similar items together. Culture teaches people how to categorize the objects they encounter in particular ways depending upon the cultural group to which they belong. *Attribution* refers to the judgments people make about others based on the behavior they observe, judging them to be honest, hard-working, well-intentioned, and so forth.

Stop for a moment and consider the relatively simple example of the common dog. All people perceive the animal in the same way and would objectively describe it in a similar manner—a small mammal with fur, four legs, a tail, barks, and so on. What people do with this information may differ, however, depending on how one was raised. In the United States, as in many countries around the world, the dog is often thought of as a member of the family, "man's best friend" some would say, and may be found eating in the kitchen or sitting on the couch or bed. From a traditional Muslim perspective, the dog may be viewed as a filthy animal, one to be avoided at all costs—as some would classify an animal such as a rat or a pig. In yet other parts of the world, dog may be considered a preferred part of one's diet and be eaten—not eating—in the kitchen.

There is nothing inherently right or wrong about any of these practices; it is simply that one's culture has exerted such pressure on its members that most don't even consider the possibility that alternative ways of thinking and behaving can exist. What can be problematic in intercultural interactions are the negative judgments or attributions that are often made about those who do things in a different manner. Thus, some would consider the dog eater as cruel and barbaric—"how could that disgusting person eat my dog?" Therein lies one of the dangers of ethnocentrism—people have a tendency to judge others not only in a negative manner but also as inferior simply because they operate from a different cultural context and view life from their own culture's point of view.

But understanding and accommodating these differences are two distinct skills that cannot be accomplished nor sufficiently achieved from a cognitive-only approach to learning. Literally, thousands of good books have been written, hundreds of films and videos produced, and countless effective speakers can present hours of relevant and interesting information about culture and intercultural contact.

Unfortunately, the link between simply having knowledge and subsequently feeling different about others or behaving more effectively in an intercultural situation is weak at best. People really must engage in significant firsthand intercultural experiences as travel provides or as illustrated by Greg's use of simulated cross-cultural experiences if they are to become more effective in their intercultural interactions and truly functional in a cross-cultural setting.

There may be nothing more critical to a successful international or intercultural encounter than that of preparing for the experience one is about to embark upon. For the solo traveler who is off on her or his own adventure, this may mean gathering maps, guidebooks, lists of possible accommodation, means of travel, and so forth. When organizing travel where the major purpose is enhancing intercultural sensitivity and competence, in addition to the nuts and bolts of daily living, one must focus attention on such things as cross-cultural differences in communication, behavior, attitudes, and values.

When working with groups or educational programs, attention must be given to pointing out for participants the processes involved in culture learning—that of understanding oneself as a cultural being; unlearning some of what they have spent their entire lives learning; guiding them to become less ethnocentric in their orientation; and then relearning new knowledge, insights, and skills that will enable them to function effectively with a new mindset and within a new context.

A comprehensive orientation program prior to an international experience can provide opportunity for people to do just this while considering how they might respond and react in a new setting. The skilled and artful teacher, or cross-cultural trainer, is thus more of a creator or an engineer, constructing an environment with forethought in such a manner that a particularly desired outcome is achieved and has real meaning for the learner. Overcoming ethnocentrism and one's own prejudices, then, becomes one of the critical dimensions of this effort.

Young people have always enjoyed communicating with their age mates in other countries whether through traditional letter writing or more recently via e-mail or through any of the increasing number of Internet-based sites designed to link classrooms around the world in joint educational activity. Early in my teaching career, after I had transitioned from teaching high school biology to elementary and middle school, I encouraged my students to engage in such activity as part of integrated language arts and social studies activities.

Each week, we would write letters to other young people around the world describing our way of life and inquiring about such issues as the daily activities of children, the environment, local culture, cultural conflict, and global news events that could be examined from each of our different perspectives. And each week, my students would eagerly await the mail, anticipating replies from around the world. They regularly wrote to students in such countries as the Soviet Union (this was pre-Perestroika), Liberia, Japan, Israel, and Belize and actively exchanged photos, school artifacts, and other kid-related memorabilia.

One particular February afternoon, a package from our pen pals in Belize arrived that was literally overflowing with letters, stamps, stories, artwork, seashells, and a promise of larger artifacts that were to arrive in a separate mailing. In the letter from the teacher was a request that we consider hosting a small group of his students. If possible, he would like to bring some students to visit us during the month of June. It was our luck and his good fortune that because we were in a laboratory school affiliated with a university, we were in fact in session for half days from mid-June to mid-July. That was how it all began. We invited our pen pals from Belize to spend a few weeks with us during which they would stay with local host families, attend school in the mornings, and participate in a number of cultural and recreational activities in the afternoons and on weekends.

It was with this in mind that James Ramos brought four young students from the village of Dangriga in the southern part of Belize to our school in northeastern Ohio. The differences between the two settings, the United States and Belize, at the time were quite extreme. Most people know of Belize as a tiny country that lies just east of Guatemala, south of the Yucatan Peninsula, and with the Caribbean to its east. In 1979, when we first connected with the school, Belize had no building taller than four stories and hence no elevator in the nation and only one hotel that could be booked from abroad through a standard travel agency. Belize was often spoken of as "well off the beaten track" and, as the guidebooks were quick to say at the time, potentially a dangerous place, frequented by drug runners and others escaping the law from somewhere else.

Primarily a fishing village and citrus fruit processing center, Dangriga, formerly known as Stann Creek, is the largest city in the southern part of the country. At the time, Dangriga boasted a population of about 5,000 people, mostly of Gurifuna heritage, an ethnic group who trace their roots to West Africa. The village had no paved roads, a couple of dozen telephones, only a few televisions that would on occasion receive broadcasts from Mexico or Guatemala (Belize had no television station of its own), and one VCR that was owned by a businessman whose brother had brought it from New York. Although the country's infrastructure has certainly developed in recent years, it remains an adventurer's delight.

Mr. Ramos and his students, Leroy, Nikita, Louise, and Anna, departed Dangriga for an adventure of a lifetime. This was their first trip out of the country, and they must have spent $50 in quarters in the Miami airport while waiting for their connecting flight to Ohio, this also being their first exposure to video game technology. This really was to be an intercultural educator's delight.

Talk about assumptions and disconfirmed expectations. Not wanting to overwhelm the children with a large reception when they arrived in Ohio, the four host families met their students at my home the day the group arrived from Belize. Assuming that children growing up along the shores of the Caribbean would be natural swimmers, if for no other reasons than they were active in fishing or simply for safety purposes, I encouraged the students to go for a swim in our apartment pool.

It was a good thing I went along! My students, eager to swim and needing to burn off a bit of their own anxiety and excitement, began running toward the pool from quite a distance away. Throwing their towels to the side as they ran, they plunged into the water. Nikita, Louise, Anna, and Leroy followed suit, although a bit less enthusiastically than my students. But in they went, one right after the other, laughing and frolicking about. Looking toward one end of the pool, I saw Leroy, still at the bottom, arms flailing about underwater and going nowhere. Realizing that he was not about to rise to the surface, I jumped in and lifted him up until he could breathe.

In all the excitement of the moment, Leroy simply followed suit and joined the activity, either not wanting to be left out, assuming the water was shallow, or not thinking about it at all. Another lesson to be learned—many Belizean children are rather afraid of the water and spend little time if any actually swimming in the sea. This would not be the last time we had to look out for our inexperienced visitors. Crossing busy city streets, an everyday occurrence for our students in Ohio, was another new experience to which our guests had to become accustomed.

Throughout their stay, students and their families were eager to share all that they could and to spend as much time as possible with the visitors. There were constant battles over who would go home with whom, who might be able to spend the night or weekend, who was invited to dinner, and so forth. The children all seemed color-blind and eagerly engaged with one another in a variety of ways, and we all learned a considerable amount from one another.

There was real surprise and disappointment at the end of the experience with another disconfirmed expectation. James had gone away for a weekend to visit some friends from his village who were living in Detroit. When he hadn't returned on Sunday as planned, I began to get a little worried. The following afternoon, he telephoned and informed me that he would not be returning to Belize, let alone our school, because he had decided to stay in the United States and affiliate more closely with his church—they would take care of him and support his desire to study in an American college. "Oh, and by the way," he went on to say, "I have the students' passports that they need in order to return home next week, and I don't know how to get them back to you."

It was obvious that James had no intention of returning the passports to us. After countless telephone calls, a three-hour drive across the state to rendezvous with him, and a very cold and angry goodbye between the two of us, I retrieved the passports and returned home. The following week, we said our goodbyes, and I accompanied the children to their connecting flight in Miami. All in all, even with this recent challenge, the impact on all participants—the Belizean children, my students, and their families as well—was extremely positive. This was the first of many intense international, interpersonal relationships I would develop for young people over the years.

One might ask, "Why would anyone want to travel overseas with a group of young children?" Talk about student-directed learning—my next group travel experience unfolded at the request of the students themselves.

After the children went back, unaccompanied, to Belize, my students asked, "Gee, Mr. C. (it was Mr. C. then), can we go there?" Not having really thought about it, I followed up their request with a letter to parents informing them that their child had expressed an interest in going to Belize to visit their newfound friends and, if there was sufficient interest, I would pursue the possibility. To my surprise, seventeen students came back with letters from their parents saying something to the effect of "You want to take my child to Belize for a few weeks at Christmas time? By all means, P-L-E-A-S-E do!" That was all I needed to hear—the kids were willing to travel, their parents were eager to send them away for two weeks, and I was off making plans.

But making plans for this coming venture was not easy. As had already been discovered, there was very little tourist information available about Belize and only one hotel that could be booked from outside the country, and no one seemed willing to arrange group travel programs to a place labeled at the time as a "hideout for criminals." It really was surprising that so many parents entrusted their children to me given how little we really knew about the country. I can only assume that they knew even less than I did—but trusted in me nonetheless. It was an awesome responsibility.

I wrote to numerous international social service agencies; the Peace Corps; the Usher family, whose son, Nikita, had been with us in the summer; and anyone else I could think of in an attempt to find out how to travel with a group of seventeen children and five adults from Ohio to Belize. Most of the replies yielded little hope, except from Hubert and Aura Usher, Nikita's parents. They were willing to assist and would make all the local plans for our upcoming visit provided that we could get to the border between Mexico and Belize. They asked me to send a check for $800, which would pay for a bus to take us from Chetumal on the Mexican border to Dangriga. The check was sent, fingers crossed, and plans begun. We now had to go, if for no other reason than to track down my money in case we were stood up.

I was planning to fly into Merida, the capitol of Yucatan, where we would spend a few days visiting Mayan ruins and other local sites. With any luck, time would be spent visiting a Mexican school. I wrote to the American consulate in Merida, an appropriate place to begin I assumed, seeking assistance in locating a school we might visit. No response. No problem. A few days of sightseeing in the region would keep us busy and fulfilled before departing by public bus from Merida to Chetumal on the Mexican–Belizean border. Here, we would rendezvous with our hoped-for bus and travel the remaining distance through Belize to Dangriga—assuming all went well. The plans finally came together. All that had to be done was to stay on top of things to be certain all was in place in time for our departure in mid-December.

Next was the task of preparing the students, none of whom had ever traveled outside the United States before and many never having been on an airplane to boot. I really was at a loss as to what to do to best orient the children because there were neither materials nor information readily available to help us understand what to expect in terms of either the country or culture.

And because we hadn't considered traveling ourselves until after our visitors left, we never really used their expertise to prepare for a return visit.

Belize is different from all of its neighboring countries, being the only English-speaking former British colony amidst the Spanish-speaking Latin-oriented Central American region. I knew we would be spending a few days in Mexico and assumed, wrongly so I would later learn, that many Belizeans would speak Spanish because Spanish-speaking people and nations surrounded them on all sides. And I knew we would encounter many surprises along the way that neither the children nor I could anticipate with any specificity. Nevertheless, I wanted the kids to be as prepared as possible, but really, I could not anticipate with any specificity what they would find in terms of host families, housing, foods they would eat, activities in which they would participate, and so on.

The field of cross-cultural psychology and the applied field of intercultural training initially were established to assist businesspeople, diplomats, scholars, missionaries, and Peace Corps volunteers to better understand and successfully adapt to the experiences that occur when people from two or more cultures interact. Today, given the increasing diversity found in schools and communities in many nations, the rapid rate at which globalization has impacted the movement of people and goods and the realization that many of the issues we face are global in nature, concepts and strategies found in the interculturalist's toolkit are of increasing importance.

Certain goals and objectives are common to all intercultural training programs. In general, intercultural training attempts to assist people to communicate more effectively, both in verbal and nonverbal modes; develop effective and meaningful interpersonal relationships; and reduce the stress that accompanies most intercultural experiences (Cushner & Brislin, 1996). Intercultural training also seeks to help people reduce their ethnocentrism, guiding them to become more ethnorelative in their judgments about others. These all, incidentally, benefit the goals and objectives of domestic multicultural as well as international or global education programs—all of increasing relevance and practice today.

Attaining intercultural competence is a developmental process that evolves over a significant period of time as a result of a series of guided interpersonal interactions and opportunities that are reflected upon and analyzed. Although traditional schooling may be good at imparting a significant amount of knowledge using such approaches as lectures, books, and film, there is a weak correlation between the simple acquisition of cognitive knowledge and the subsequent achievement of the goals of intercultural training. Culture learning thus requires a long-term, experiential approach—the very thing that travel provides—coupled with the knowledge or cognitive inputs that the classroom can offer. It is the blend of experience and knowledge that is critical.

The intercultural orientation of sojourners—temporary travelers entering a new society—can be approached from two possible vantage points. A culture-specific approach provides a significant amount of information that is unique to a target cultural group or destination. A culture-general approach focuses on the commonalities in the intercultural experience that people are likely to encounter, such things as communication or value differences and confronting personal prejudice as well as dealing with disconfirmed expectations.

Good intercultural training integrates culture-specific as well as culture-general concepts and strategies—both having value. In this specific circumstance, preparing children to travel to Belize, however, was not possible because there were no culture-specific materials available to help prepare us for our experience in Belize. At the time, I really did not know much about the field of intercultural training anyway because I had only my own travel experiences to draw upon. So I punted, and armed with the best of intentions, made it up as we went along. Little did I know that this would lead in large measure to the future direction of my own career.

Seventeen committed student travelers met for one hour after school each Monday to participate in a number of group-building activities and to prepare us for what we might encounter. One advantage of having a school near a university was that I could offer a field placement site for university students interested in gaining experience teaching introductory Spanish language to children. Although no one expected the children to learn the language with any degree of fluency in just a few short months, they could at least develop some basic familiarity.

Preparation for the other eventualities, however, was another story. It is pretty certain in any travel experience that people will encounter all kinds of differences—they may just be difficult to predict. While in Mexico, our group would be staying in a small hotel in town, a "culture" with which most were familiar. While in Belize, however, accommodation would be with host families.

Everyone wants these experiences to be as positive as possible, avoiding those embarrassing moments when a child, responding to someone's hospitality, screws up his or her face at some new food or unfamiliar behavior and lets out a groan of utter disgust. Not knowing what food practices would be encountered on the trip, I would bring new and different-looking, but edible, food each Monday and provide it for the afternoon snack. This seemed to be a pretty good approach to "getting the yucks out" in the safety of the classroom before venturing into a new and unfamiliar family while encouraging the development of new eating habits.

Each week the children would be presented with something they had never seen before—Middle Eastern dips that were unfamiliar, a variety of Mexican sauces that were not available in the local Taco Bell, that notorious Australian yeast extract Vegemite, and bottled gefilte fish usually eaten during the Jewish holiday of Passover. This seemed to work fairly well—there were lots of "yucks" shared each Monday—most going home hungry each day.

Chocolate-covered ants brought to class one Monday became the basis of a contest to see how many each student could eat. Only a few brave students would compete—most not willing to even touch the stuff. John, a rather tall twelve-year-old who put on an air of machismo, was quite the show-off and proceeded to devour ant after ant, consuming at least twice as many as any other student. He won the competition, but to his embarrassment, he quickly ran off and vomited in the restroom across the hall. He had to withstand weeks of ridicule after that.

During these sessions, time was also spent discussing safe eating habits while on the road, such standard things as avoiding water or ice in beverages; not eating fruits and vegetables that had not been peeled or cooked; and not having cream-based foods that may have been sitting, unrefrigerated, for some time. Perhaps I overdid some aspects of this, raising everyone's anxiety, but at the time, I thought it better to be safe than sorry. It was only many years later that I learned that a certain amount of anxiety is not only to be expected but actually beneficial to cross-cultural adjustment.

Travel, as well as planning for travel, demands that one be flexible and able to accommodate most any circumstance that is confronted. And here was one of our first—just weeks before our departure. Current events can have a major impact on people's perception of a particular place. Five days before a parent orientation meeting I'd scheduled, four nuns from northern Ohio were taken hostage and killed in El Salvador.

What incredibly poor timing not only for the nuns but also for our group. I was certain, especially with all the publicity the story was receiving in the local papers, that most of the parents would pull their children from the experience. In preparation for the evening, one of the parents telephoned the US Department of State for a travel advisory. He shared with the group the relative lack of concern on the part of the government and that Belize was considered a safe place to travel, being not too heavily engaged in the Central American political conflicts of the time. I guess those modern-day pirates I had read so much about in the travel guides really didn't amount to much—at least from the perspective of the State Department.

We were off in just a few short weeks, busy now with last-minute planning meetings with the school principal and parents, making certain all our travel documents were in order, planning for our stopover in Mexico, and deciding what kinds of gifts and cultural artifacts we would bring along. All went well in this regard as we patiently waited for our departure day to arrive.

Chapter 3

Traveling with Class: The Trip Begins

"Haba na haba hujaza kibaba." Little by little we fill the bucket.

—Swahili proverb

Intercultural orientation in general is designed to prepare one for the inevitable adjustment challenges, often referred to as culture shock, that people encounter as they travel to new destinations and make the transition to a different cultural context. Although people generally expect to encounter differences in the objective, visible aspects of culture, such as language, food, and dress, they are often surprised and caught off guard by how quickly and strongly their own emotions are aroused.

The real test of the effectiveness of intercultural orientation can be seen almost immediately after departure—especially with children. Tears flowed among our travelers to Mexico as children and parents said their goodbyes to one another, each knowing that this would be their first Christmas away from one another. Unfortunately, I hadn't given this as much forethought as I should have. Here I was, a Jewish teacher in a non-Jewish community, focused on intercultural and international activities, giving scant attention to the meaning of the holiday in the lives of these children. Oh, what I was to learn!

The plane ride was, as most are, thankfully, uneventful. This group of young travelers felt quite comfortable, and mature, as they moved freely among the passengers and crew on the plane, proudly telling others of the adventure they were embarking upon. They were the center of much attention from the flight attendants and passengers throughout the entire trip as we made our connection in Miami for our final destination, Merida, capitol and largest city in the Yucatan Peninsula.

25

I was not prepared for our arrival with seventeen children and five adults into the crowded, noisy Merida airport, filled with people coming and going as the holiday season approached. My wife, Hyla, instinctively knowing what to do, stepped into action once we cleared customs, herding children, parents, and baggage into groups while I went about searching for the transportation we had arranged to take us to the hotel.

"Excuse me," someone said as he tapped me on the shoulder.

"I don't need your help," I blurted out, anticipating an onslaught of taxi drivers and other locals who would, like vultures circling overhead waiting for an animal to finally give in and die, see me as the vulnerable newcomer that I was. I wasn't about to relent so early in the experience; we hadn't even left the airport yet!

"Are you Ken Cushner?" the voice asked.

Okay, now, he caught my attention.

The soft-spoken man speaking perfect English continued, "My name is Enrique, and I am the head of the English Department at Colegio Peninsular Rogers Hall School. The American consulate sent me your letter a few weeks ago. I'd like you and your students to come to our school tomorrow, spend the last morning before the holiday break with us, and then we'll take you to some of the Mayan ruins in the region. If it's okay with you, we'll pick you up at your hotel at 9:00 a.m."

If it's okay with me, I thought? Some behind the scenes work must have taken place that I was not aware of.

"What a pleasant surprise," I responded, not quite convinced that he was for real.

I couldn't have wished for anything more—a chance to spend a day in a school and share in some social time with local Mexican students! This was a dream come true. I shared this information with the group once we were on the bus and on our way to our hotel.

As we checked into our city hotel, I told the children to meet me in the hotel restaurant in about an hour for a light meal. This would give everyone a chance to unpack, explore his or her new surroundings, and give Hyla and me a bit of time to unwind.

The kids were talkative and energetic as they came running down the stairwell toward the lobby and into the café. I gathered them at a few tables in a far corner along a wall. There was a wine cart in the corner. Amidst the bottles of wine on the cart was a can of Raid insecticide. That didn't bother me as much as the sign on the cart that said, "The manager has personally passed all the water used in the hotel." Now wasn't that comforting. I knew then that we were in for more than a few surprises.

Hyla and I listened in on some of the conversations of the children as they settled into their chairs.

"Do you believe it's all in Spanish?" laughed Julie. "I tried to turn on the air conditioner and the dials were all in Spanish. How am I supposed to make it work?"

Confronting disconfirmed expectations is quite a common occurrence for travelers, especially in the early phases of an experience when one's emotions are highly engaged (Cushner & Brislin, 1996). In this case, it was equally evident for the students as well as for me. During preparation for travel, people tend to construe certain images and expectations of what the new setting will be like as well as how they will respond in this new situation. And these expectations are generally positive and exciting. The reality of what is encountered, however, is oftentimes inconsistent with the image conjured up in the mind. The ability to reconcile this difference is one key to a smooth transition in the early stages of an intercultural experience.

It was suddenly apparent that all the orientation and language training we had undergone may not have done the job as assumed. Julie acted as if the fact that everything was in Spanish came as a complete surprise. This was really disturbing and confusing because we had spent four months studying Spanish during our weekly orientation sessions. For Julie, there seemed to be no connection between what had been done in the classroom and the reality that she now faced.

Intercultural researchers have discovered a few unanticipated and non-commonsense surprises in the intercultural transition experience, and this was one of them. That is, cross-cultural orientation, at least at the onset, may not be as meaningful to participants who have not had direct and personal intercultural experiences from which to draw upon. This is supported in the research literature by learning theorists and cognitive psychologists who suggest that a significant portion of what people learn in any learning situation—up to 80 percent—may be directly dependent upon what they already knew before they ever began the learning process (Bransford, 1979).

One of the major tasks of any good educator or trainer then is to stimulate prior knowledge of the student so new information can be added to the preexisting foundation. If people do not have prior knowledge—or in this case cross-cultural experiences—new concepts may "come in one ear and go out the other," so to speak. Those who have had little if any significant intercultural experiences are thus at a disadvantage when it comes to cross-cultural orientation. Julie was demonstrating this reality.

Research suggests that intercultural training may be most effective after people have embarked on their sojourn and have some direct experience with which to fall back upon—not necessarily before they depart. Therein lies the dilemma. How do people who have had little intercultural experience best prepare for the eventualities they are certain to encounter? Perhaps it would be now, once the children had begun having some direct experiences, that cross-cultural training would be most meaningful. But in this particular situation there was little time in the schedule to accommodate classroom-oriented instruction. These issues would have to be addressed as best they could as the days unfolded—on buses, in waiting lounges, over common meals, and the like.

Susan, who had skipped a grade early in her schooling, was the youngest of the children traveling with us at nine years old—pretty impressive that a child as young as Susan would venture away without her parents for so long. She was in tears though when I approached her table after ordering her first meal.

"I can't eat this stuff," she cried. *"You told us not to eat mayonnaise. And look at this. My sandwich has mayonnaise all over it."*

"No problem," I said. *"Just send it back and tell the waiter you don't want anything on your sandwich."*

Sounded simple enough. I helped Susan communicate this, or so I thought, as we spoke slowly to the waiter in English and very broken Spanish. Five minutes later, I looked back and Susan was in tears again.

"All he did was change the bread," she cried. *The mayonnaise is still all over the meat! And what is this stuff?"* she yelled, pointing to a side dish of refried beans that had been placed in front of everyone. *"It looks like I got sick right here on the plate. How disgusting!"*

"I can't eat this, Mr. C. I want to go home." And she continued to cry.

One day into this trip, and I was confronting the beginnings of culture shock and homesickness with these young students. Rather early in the trip, I thought, but nevertheless, real and something to contend with.

As long ago as 1960, the anthropologist Kalvero Oberg coined the term *culture shock* to refer to the anxiety and stress that results when people living or working in a new overseas context lose many of the familiar signs and symbols to which they have become accustomed while trying to satisfy their everyday needs. It is a rather generalized description of the responses people experience when things do not go as expected in a new cultural setting, when there is a general inability to make sense of the new stimuli to which one is exposed, or when one's own behavior does not produce the expected results.

Culture shock, perhaps more appropriately termed adjustment or transition shock, is not a disease or something that only unsuccessful people experience as is often thought. It is a perfectly normal response and an ongoing process that in many ways is essential to learning in the new setting.

Transition shock is the rather broad construct experienced when people encounter differences in such things as verbal and nonverbal communication; in the varying orientations people have toward time and space; and to the more subtle and intangible aspects such as differences in attitudes, behavioral norms, and the underlying values people defend as fundamental to their lives. Other differences too, such as those in the physical places one encounters while traveling; in the technologies used; in the power, structure, and support people have; and in what is seen, heard, felt, and even smelled and tasted, can provide aspects to which one must adapt and which thus affect the traveler. Such is the essence of what contributes to the range of transition challenges one should expect to confront.

How one responds to and accommodates these experiences, however, is critical. If people react negatively, common responses such as alienation, anxiety, resentment, a high degree of stress and anger—none of which facilitate adjustment—may result. If the individuals can anticipate some of the differences they are likely to encounter ahead of time and develop a range of strategies to respond to such challenges, they are less likely to be debilitated during the process. Such is the role and function of good orientation and training programs.

Culture-specific training is successful when preparing people for interactions that will be restricted to one culture or when a significant amount of information is known about a particular target group. In most instances, particularly in contexts that are as culturally diverse as American schools and communities, people encounter a wide variety of cultures on a fairly regular basis. Even in settings that may at first glance appear to be rather homogeneous in makeup, a wide range of diversity is possible that may include gender, religion, socioeconomic status, ability/disability differences, and so forth. Additionally, people today are likely to encounter a wide diversity of difference throughout their professional and adult life that simply cannot be anticipated. Culture-general training, or developing an understanding of a number of concepts and constructs that are common across the intercultural exchange, thus has much to offer educators.

Over the years, a number of cross-cultural training strategies have been developed, many of which have proven to have varying degrees of positive impact. Among the most extensively researched and useful of cross-cultural training strategies is the culture assimilator, or intercultural sensitizer (Cushner & Landis, 1996). In this approach, trainees or students read a number of critical incidents or short stories that depict individuals from different cultures who encounter some problem caused by miscommunication or misunderstanding. The reader is then asked to select from four or five alternative choices the one that best explains the problem from the other culture's perspective.

Intercultural sensitizers were initially developed for culture-specific situations, for instance, to prepare Australian bankers to live and work in Thailand or American adolescents to work with Honduran villagers in Amigos de las Americas volunteer programs. Although extremely beneficial, their use is rather restricted because of their cultural specificity and lack of widespread availability, usually having been developed for relatively small and role-specific groups.

A culture-general sensitizer or assimilator was later developed to prepare people for the kinds of experiences they are certain to encounter in their intercultural interactions (Cushner & Brislin, 1996). Similar in structure to the culture-specific forerunner, this tool uses the critical incident format to introduce people to eighteen culture-general themes that people are certain to encounter regardless of their background or with whom they will interact.

The eighteen themes are categorized into three general categories. Knowledge Areas introduce readers to eight themes that all cultures define and learn, albeit differently, and includes work orientation, time and spatial orientation, roles, communication, group versus individual orientation, rituals and superstitions, class and status, and values. The Bases of Cultural Differences encompasses five themes that address the manner in which people process information and includes categorization, differentiation, ingroup and outgroup distinction, learning style differences, and attribution formation. Finally, five themes under Experiences that Engage the Emotions include anxiety, the need to belong, ambiguity, confrontation with prejudice in self and others, and disconfirmed expectations—all of which seemed at play at the moment with my young travelers on this first day!

Early the next morning, Hyla and I went from room to room knocking on doors reminding the children to meet in the lobby at 7:00 a.m. so we could have breakfast before our bus arrived. Venturing down the street, we found a suitable restaurant. Susan was a bit more relaxed as she sat with Hyla and me and ate her first breakfast of huevos rancheros, a tortilla topped with fried egg and a mild sauce. I noticed she left the beans untouched on the side of her plate, as did most of the children. At least there were no more "yucks" coming from the group.

Not wanting to miss our 9:00 a.m. bus, I rushed the kids back from the restaurant to the hotel. The kids were running up and down between the lobby and their rooms while I paced back and forth looking for our bus. Fifteen minutes passed, with no bus and no Enrique. Thirty minutes later, and still no bus! Now, I was really getting worried, and I continued to pace back and forth between the lobby and out the door to the street, hoping to catch a glimpse of a bus. The kids were almost impossible to control, running throughout the lobby, in and out of the café, and up and down the stairs, going just about anywhere their little legs would carry them. Oh, what would they be like in the school, I wondered, if we ever got there? Forty-five minutes, and still no Enrique. I had no idea what to do. I couldn't call the school because I'd hardly recalled the name of it. So I continued to pace and worry.

Finally, after more than an hour, a bus weaved its way down our winding street and pulled up in front of the hotel. Enrique climbed down from the bus, greeted me with "Hola" as if we'd been long lost friends, and mumbled something quickly about being a bit late. A bit late, I thought. This was more than an hour after he said he'd pick us up.

"Remember, this is Mexico," he said, as I confided that I had been getting a bit impatient. "Time takes on a new meaning here, and you'd better get used to it."

My American, or better yet, my "United States" culture, was operating in full force, as I, like my young students, fell victim to our own cultural conditioning. This would not be the first instance where a difference in time orientation would cause me to feel those strong emotions associated with anxiety and ambiguity.

Our day at the school was far more than we could have hoped for. This was the last day of school before the holiday break, and we spent the morning attending a variety of classes and joining in on holiday celebrations. The most fun for all was the breaking of piñatas, and the kids got quite involved. Blindfolded and swinging away, they seemed like naturals while displaying an openness and willingness of spirit that endeared them to all in the school. I was quite pleased and proud of our group of young travelers.

Enrique invited a number of his students to join us for lunch, followed by an outing to Uxmal, one of the largest of the ancient cities of the Yucatán peninsula. Located about an hour south of Merida, Uxmal was home to about 25,000 Maya, flourishing between 600 and 900 CE. Carvings most commonly found at the site include serpents and latticework along with masks of the god Chac, the god of rain, who was greatly revered by the Maya because of the lack of natural water supplies in the city. It was to Chac, Enrique would tell the group, that human sacrifices were performed at the highest temple of the site—the House of the Magician. With the victim still alive, the priest would rip out the heart of the sacrificed soul with a flint knife and throw the body, allegedly still moving, down the steep steps. It was thought to be an honor to have been chosen for this rite.

My students were fully engrossed in Enrique's storytelling, and perhaps grossed out by the detail and gruesomeness of the stories. But it was certainly a motivator to encourage them to want to learn more. Our adventure in Mexico far exceeded my expectations. And I truly enjoyed getting to know Enrique. This relationship alone developed into an exchange between our two schools that lasted for three years. Each year, I would take up to forty students to Merida, and Enrique would bring an equal number of his students to Ohio. But for now, it's on to Belize—and other cultural surprises.

Chapter 4

The Power of Travel Occurs Off the Beaten Track

Keeping to the main road is easy, but people love to be sidetracked.

—Lao Tze, 6th century BCE

The kids were understandably getting a bit bored and tired from traveling by bus for six hours by the time we reached Belize City, and they were begging for some free time to explore and move their legs. But given all I'd read about Belize City, this bastion of crime, criminals, and drugs, I was not about to let them out of my sight to go traipsing around a strange city—even if they did feel confident and sure. We were able to busy ourselves in and around the bus station where we stopped for a break. I couldn't figure out what was happening at first. The kids kept running in and out of the restrooms the whole time we were there. It wasn't until I went into the men's room to investigate that it all became comically clear.

Another difference to get used to—toilets! The kids, it seemed, had discovered that an open sewage system was in use and went about creating their own amusement. One by one, each child would sit on the toilet, release yesterday's lunch, flush it down the toilet, and then everyone would run outside to see whether they could beat their business before it dropped into the open sewer that ran alongside the station. And this was in the largest city in the country! I really began to worry about what we'd find once we arrived in a small village.

We spent the previous day in Chetumal, a rather drab and seemingly lifeless town on the Mexico–Belize border, without much of a problem, having traveled from Merida for six hours by public bus. I was quite relieved when the bus driver found us at the agreed upon hotel. And what a surprise it was to find that our bus was nothing more than an old retired yellow American school bus that had found its way to Belize to serve as major transportation throughout the country. And what a sight we must have been, twenty-two of us rolling along the countryside as if on a field trip from school. It was—of sorts—but not like one most children, or adults for that matter, would ever have back home.

We left Chetumal early the next morning for our long journey south that would take us through most of Belize. The driver could only guess at how long it might take to reach Dangriga, our destination, some 120 miles away, estimating anywhere from ten to fourteen hours. One hundred twenty miles in ten hours—and that was the quickest route! What could he be thinking?

Driving time in Belize, our driver informed us, depended on a number of factors, including how often and for how long we needed to stop and the conditions of the road along the way as well as a bit of luck that we would make the trip without breaking down. As we would soon find out, our driver was correct, and we had all those things to worry about. The roads in Belize leave much to be desired. We would dodge pothole after pothole along a road that looked to be not much different from the surface of the moon as we zig-zagged our way along at a top speed of twenty miles per hour. But we could never maintain that speed for long.

Our route took us south through the towns of Corozol, Progresso, Orange Walk, and then into Belize City. From this former capital, we continued on to the new capital, Belmopan, the smallest capital city in the continental Americas, established inland in 1970 when people grew tired of cleaning up after hurricanes.

We continued south toward Dangriga, traveling through rainforests and citrus groves on roads that grew increasingly bumpy and narrow the farther south we drove. At one point, we approached a one-lane bridge, so narrow that the driver, fearing we might get wedged along the road and then unable to exit using the door, had us all get off the bus while he maneuvered, inch by inch, to the other side. Mark, one of the parents traveling along with us, was a psychologist who worked with people's phobias. He ran off the bus with camera in hand, photographing the entire ordeal, planning to use the photos as a means to help some of his patients overcome their fear of small spaces.

We arrived in the village just before the sun was to set. About 100 people followed along as the bus pulled into town, with Nikita, Leroy, Louise, and Anna leading the crowd. General introductions were made, children were matched with host families, and all went to their respective homes for their first encounter with their new friends. The adults were taken to the one hotel in town that would serve as a base. We had the only available phone, and the children knew where they could find us if they needed anything. We would have a formal program of introductions and a presentation in the morning.

Today, numerous companies exist that provide group travel experiences for school students, enticing teachers to recruit students by offering free travel for every six to ten participants they can enlist. Such organizations can make it easy for teachers and students to travel to many countries in the world for sightseeing to enjoy some of the world's most spectacular sights.

There is a downside to such trips, however. Groups of teachers and students, encapsulated in buses and tourist-class hotels, visit museums, monuments, and mansions, often at the expense of having meaningful, in-depth contact with host nationals. Any cross-cultural experience that is encountered tends to be at the surface, or tourist level, often referred to as objective culture. Intercultural experiences that impact the more profound levels of culture learning, however, do not simply happen—they evolve slowly over time and involve long-term engagement with people on a much deeper level, allowing people to gain an understanding of people's attitudes and values. This deeper level of culture is referred to as subjective culture.

There is a critical distinction between objective and subjective levels of culture that is essential for the educator to understand (Triandis, 1972). Objective culture, sometimes referred to as "big C" culture, refers to the visible or tangible elements of a culture, such things as the artifacts people make, the clothing worn, the foods eaten, and sometimes the names given to things. Objective cultural elements are easy to see and touch, and people generally agree upon what it is that they can observe. Such elements, however, are not the aspects of culture that are most critical and meaningful nor are they the ones that lead to the problems people generally encounter in intercultural interactions.

The more profound and meaningful levels of culture operate at the subjective level and exist beneath the surface. Subjective culture, sometimes referred to as "little c" culture, refers to the intangible, invisible aspects of a people—such things as the attitudes people bring with them to any interaction; the expectations they have of others; and the values they may hold about such things as education, elders, or another group of people. Examples of subjective culture are many of the concepts introduced in the eighteen-theme cultural general framework (Cushner & Brislin, 1996). These aspects of culture are much more difficult to put on a table to see and discuss; yet they are at play in all interactions.

In addressing subjective elements of culture, people learn about such things as people's historical experiences and prior interactions with other groups and the expectations they may have of others. They begin to understand why people do the things they do, why they communicate in the manner in which they do, and why they behave in ways that may appear, at the outset, to be quite different and perhaps confrontational. Such an understanding and orientation allows people to get beyond the initial and oftentimes negative reactions to meeting someone new and different, thus encouraging continuation of a relationship.

The iceberg is often used as an analogy to explain the distinction between objective and subjective culture. Typically showing about 10 percent of its mass above the surface of the water, this portion of the iceberg can be likened to objective culture. It is the tangible and visible elements of people that are easy for all to see.

Ninety percent of the iceberg, however, is invisible to the naked eye, lying beneath the surface of the water. This is the portion that is of most concern to the ship's captain and can do the most damage to the ship. So too it is with subjective culture. These deeper elements, such as the assumptions people make and the attitudes they hold, are not readily visible to the casual observer but are operating at all times. Understanding this is fundamental to the success of any intercultural interaction. It is at the level of subjective culture that good intercultural education and culture learning must focus. It is through impactful and meaningful travel experiences that subjective levels of culture can be encountered and analyzed.

The children really had no idea what they were in for when they agreed to go on this venture. Coming from their comfortable middle-class community, they had most of the comforts and privileges anyone could have wanted—most had private bedrooms, fully equipped kitchens, well-stocked refrigerators, and the like. In Dangriga, they had the opportunity to experience, firsthand, many of the things that they could only read about in their textbooks back home.

Our hosts opened up their lives and homes, providing their guests with all the comforts that they could. Even though most families had comparatively little, they were more than willing to share it all, such is the nature of Belizean hospitality. Most of the homes, for instance, consisted of no more than two or three rooms, and in many cases, two or three children shared a bed. Our hosts vacated these beds so our kids could have a bit of the comfort they assumed they would need.

Children in many of the families were given the opportunity to assist with meal preparation. Many, for instance, had the chance to point out the chicken from under the house that they wanted for dinner—and then help with its preparation. Or going to the river, children could help in the hunt for "bamboo chicken"—iguanas that grow much larger than the typical pet-store variety and considered a local delicacy. The kids certainly had plenty of opportunity to experience things they would rarely have the chance to do elsewhere. I'm not sure how many became vegetarians during their stay, but I'm sure it prompted some serious contemplation.

John, the young, boastful boy who had eaten all those chocolate-covered ants during orientation, was staying with a family not too far from the hotel. *Late in the afternoon of the second day, after our morning welcome session at the community center and after the kids had gone back for time with their families, his host mother came to us worried because he had been complaining of stomachaches. Here we go, I thought, already having to deal with problems caused by food, and we'd been in town for only one full day.*

Hyla and I went to see John. Sure enough, he was doubled up in pain, complaining about his stomach and asking whether he could come spend the night with us. The family gave us some private time with him. After a while, John relaxed. His real problem, it seemed, was not food related at all but rather a psychologically oriented adjustment problem. This rather macho young man of twelve years had been placed in a family of five young girls. Aside from the father, there were no other males in the family, and he was just uncomfortable with the entire situation. Once this was established and communicated, we were able to make the necessary change of families—and all were happier as a result. Subjective cultural differences of another kind were certainly at work here.

Even though it was school holidays, our days were filled with immeasurable educational activities. We would meet each morning at the community center for some kind of collaborative activity that differed each day. On the first day, we presented brief plays about life in Ohio to the children. It was awkward, to say the least, to dramatize snow on stage to an audience who, for the most part, had never actually seen or felt the stuff—and all this in seventy-plus degree weather and a backdrop of the Caribbean!

On the next day, we participated in a broader community ceremony attended by many of the village elders that included the mayor and all the school officials as well as many children and their families. It was quite a moving experience. We presented the school with a world atlas signed by all the children in our school in Ohio, including those who could not travel with us. This gift, it turned out, represented the first book owned by the school—something that my students just could not understand.

Each of these mini-adventures presented opportunities for all to grow. One day, we ventured out to one of the nearby islands for lunch and to snorkel along the northern hemisphere's largest barrier reef—second in size only to the Great Barrier Reef in Australia. What an exhilarating day we all had as we stopped for lunch and walked along the shoreline of a nearby uninhabited island amidst the coral and colorful fish.

At one point, Karen, a young, adventurous girl of eleven, had strolled quite a distance from shore. We weren't sure what could have been wrong, but there she was, yelling to us to come and save her—yet she was standing in only ankle-deep water. Hyla went out to her as quickly as she could, stepping carefully so as to avoid damaging the coral. When she reached her, Karen grabbed onto Hyla's arm as tightly as she could. There was no apparent danger—Karen, it seemed, had simply panicked. Focusing at her feet and walking amidst a new environment consisting of fish, coral, sea urchins, and other marine life, she simply became overly anxious about her surroundings as well as her ability to manipulate through the maze of activity teeming underfoot.

Christmas in Belize, the children soon realized, was celebrated quite differently than back home. The students were accustomed to lavish holiday displays and huge trees adorning each and every home. In Belize, the celebration was much more low key—something that was not anticipated by the children. Trees, if they were displayed in the homes at all, were never more than two or three feet tall, looking more like a small bush than the tree to which they were accustomed. And there were few if any presents lying beneath waiting to be opened—and none, it seemed, for those over twelve years of age. What a disappointment for my students.

And with that realization, the tears began to flow—for two days. Sometimes, it's difficult to differentiate culture shock from homesickness, and in this case it didn't really matter—one just led to the other. For the next two days, all we had were miserable children, moping around, dreaming of sugarplum fairies and whatever other holiday memories were on their minds. This didn't happen all at once, mind you. Children seemed to ebb and flow in and out of their moodiness. But once one or two became emotional, it caught on like wildfire, and we had to deal with everyone all at once. It eventually became nonstop tears and a losing battle.

We finally hatched a plan. Because we were the only ones who had a telephone in our hotel, we would allow each child to make a five-minute call home from our room, basically as a way to reassure them that their Christmas presents would be waiting for them upon their return. Some even begged their parents to keep the Christmas tree until they returned home. This seemed to do the trick. Everyone was reminded that they were still loved, that they too were missed, and that they would celebrate upon their return. And Hyla and I vowed that the only children we would take on any future trip at Christmastime would be Jewish children to Israel or others to the North Pole.

Although traditional educational efforts tend to be rather slow at bringing about the needed shift in one's thinking, travel affords the opportunity, and often forces one, to see and confront the world from another perspective. We all left this experience renewed and refreshed, having learned an untold amount, much of which would not even be known until long after our return. We also left committed to maintaining our relationship with the community.

The experience of giving the school its first book, for instance, made an enormous impression on the children, none of whom could fathom that a school could exist without books. Even before we left Dangriga, the students had decided to do something they thought might change the situation that they had encountered. When they returned home, the students started an after-school snack bar that raised enough money to ship over 500 donated books to the school! This is exactly the kind of social action response any teacher would hope to see—that people become involved in ways and in activities where they feel they can make a difference. And this as a result of a firsthand travel encounter, thus reinforcing the important role of lived experience in the attainment of a global perspective and commitment. But more on the impact of travel later in the book.

Chapter 5

Learning to Travel Is Learning to See: Developing Intercultural Sensitivity

The real voyage of discovery consists not in seeing new landscapes, but in having new eyes.

—Marcel Proust

The lessons learned while traveling are often unanticipated and quite profound and can have an unexpected impact. For the open minded, travel affords the opportunity to see the world from another perspective. But these lessons don't always jump right out at you. More often than not, they are missed because of one's inability to perceive what has gone on from the local perspective or because time may be needed to step back and reflect upon the situation.

Good teachers make it a priority to take the time to reflect upon what their students are encountering, to discuss with them their reactions, and to help them to find new meaning in the experiences. When it happens by oneself without others helping guide reflection, it may take time for the lessons to become evident if they do at all. Such is the nature of intercultural learning— it is evolutionary not revolutionary, developing slowly as a result of repeated experiences that are reflected upon through the guidance of a good teacher.

It is only in the past twenty years that we have begun to investigate and understand the notions of intercultural sensitivity, awareness, and competence and the mechanisms that facilitate intercultural development. This chapter begins to consider the importance of direct experience as an essential element in the foundation of intercultural learning.

Hyla and I had been planning our first trip to Kenya as preparation for taking a group of teachers on safari following an international conference the next year. We had done our homework before leaving and knew the areas of the country that we wanted to visit. We did not want to be too prescriptive or packaged with our plans, allowing many of the day-to-day details to unfold once we began our travels. After an initial week in Nairobi beginning to familiarize ourselves with the people and collecting the necessary gear, we rented a jeep and began our own self-guided safari that would take us around the country to such areas as the Maasai Mara, Samburu, and Amboseli game reserves.

Prior to leaving Nairobi, we were warned about travel around Nakuru, Kenya's fourth largest town, located halfway between Nairobi and Kisumu on Lake Victoria. Travelers, it seemed, were the object of numerous scams whereby unsuspecting drivers passing through town would be motioned by numerous people pointing to the front of their car. After pulling over and being told there was something wrong—smoke was visible or something like that—they would be directed to a local garage, which just happened to be operated by a friend of your new "savior." The garage would, of course, repair your car—the bill totaling many hundreds of dollars for what ended up being unnecessary repairs. Oh, for the blessings of a new friend.

But we were ready. This would never happen to us. We were aware and would have our guard up. Trusting as we were, we wouldn't be taken by any novice criminals.

We were driving south on our way to Amboseli National Park and Mt. Kilimanjaro after three glorious days of photographing wildlife in the desertlike environs of Samburu National Park when we came upon Nakuru. A bit hungry, but not wanting to stay long, we decided to stop at the Kenya Coffee House on the corner of Moi Road and Kenyatta Avenue. Our guidebook suggested that this was the best place in town to get a good cup of coffee.

After considerable negotiation of the local streets, we finally found the Kenya Coffee House, near the center of town. We parked along Moi Road, just around the corner from the coffee shop, feeling lucky not to have confronted any auto hustlers along the way. In front of us were a number of small shops—a pharmacy, a seamstress, a fruit stall—and what seemed like hundreds of people milling about.

"I don't feel right about this place," Hyla cautioned, grabbing my hand as we got out of the vehicle. "I don't think we should stay here."

"Oh, don't be silly," I replied. "We're only going to stop for ten minutes to get a cup of coffee. Let's lock the jeep. Now, walk with intention, letting others think we know where we're going." The phrase "walk with intention" had become a mantra I found myself repeating quite often on this trip, hoping that if it looked as if we knew where we were going, we would have fewer encounters with shady characters.

"I don't know," Hyla said, "I just don't feel right." I grabbed my back-pack, which held our passports, tickets, and camera; locked the vehicle; and off we went.

It was hardly ten minutes later when we left the coffee shop to return to our vehicle. Upon rounding the corner, I noticed the doors of our jeep wide open. My stomach knotted as I grabbed Hyla's arm and told her I thought we had been robbed. Sure enough, every door was wide open—and all of our luggage was missing. We frantically checked all around, hoping that somehow we'd overlooked something. No luck; everything was gone. We began asking those standing in the doorways of the shops and on the walkway if they'd seen anything. Not a word! A hundred people stood around and watched as our vehicle was cleaned out, and no one saw a thing! How baffling.

We were angry, to say the least. Not knowing what to do, we began driving around town, hoping that perhaps we might see our bags being shuffled off by someone. No luck. We wanted—no, needed—our luggage. I, at least, had left a suitcase back in a hotel, and we could continue on our trip going back through Nairobi to pick it up. Hyla, on the other hand, had all of her belongings in the jeep, and they were nowhere to be found. I could hear it all now. "I told you so! I didn't feel right about this place! Walk with intention???" Thankfully, none of that was forthcoming.

We drove to the market thinking that perhaps we'd see our things already on display and being sold in some used clothing stall. Again, no luck. What we really did not want to lose were the twelve rolls of exposed film that documented our adventures and the notebook that contained the names and addresses of people we met along the way who would help to put our group together the following year. Before leaving town, we wrote a brief classified ad and left it with the local newspaper asking—no, pleading—for the return of our film and notebooks. And we filed a report with the local police.

We were furious and felt violated when we left Nakuru, angry with our-selves for trusting enough to leave our belongings unattended. But that was our nature. We had been in Kenya for almost two weeks and had developed a certain level of trust and comfort. Even with all the warnings about theft and muggings in Nairobi, or "Nairobbery" as it is sometimes called, and espe-cially the warnings about Nakuru, we should have been more careful. And I should have listened to Hyla's gut feelings.

In between bursts of anger, we left town—without a plan. And wouldn't you know it? Just when we got to the outskirts of town, young men and boys started pointing frantically at the front of our jeep. No way were we going to succumb to that game! This helped to turn our anger into laughter as we drove as fast as we could from town. We did, however, stop to check the front of our vehicle every now and then, just as a measure of safety.

What to do? We couldn't continue as planned because neither of us had anything to wear. We decided to return to Nairobi, pick up my remaining suitcase, and see about picking up some new clothes. We called ahead to our lodge in Amboseli and postponed our arrival by one day. We also called to the hotel we had used earlier in Nairobi to see about staying the night. No problem. Both places were understanding, accommodating, and apologetic. At least we found the caring human spirit once again.

Our shopping spree was like nothing we had ever done before. We were not certain of what we should buy. Most of the clothes were not of a style we would wear at home. The pants, underwear, and even the socks seemed to fit differently. We decided on a few T-shirts—at least we'd have some souvenirs when we returned home. We also grabbed a few pairs of pants, shorts, running shoes for Hyla, and other things we thought we'd need for the remainder of our trip. Our credit cards came in quite handy, and a nice dinner at the hotel helped us make the transition to the return to the road. The remainder of the trip was pleasant and, thankfully, uneventful.

We never did recover our belongings, see the photos we had taken, or retrieve the names of the people we had met along the way. We did learn some valuable lessons that became evident not long after we returned home. There are some incredible inequities on the planet, and they had just been pointed out to us. Thus, we found it difficult to continue to hold onto our anger. We had been violated—there was no doubt about that. But we had not been phys- ically threatened. We had traveled through a country where the majority of the people live at or below the poverty level, many subsisting from day to day on whatever they are able to gather from their immediate surrounding.

Perhaps it is a carryover from our hunting and gathering days that what- ever is available in the surroundings and not rooted to the ground or bigger or stronger than you becomes fair game. Our luggage certainly fit that cat- egory. So be it. We represented wealth beyond most people's imagination, carrying in our suitcases more clothes and belongings than many would have in their lifetime. Those who took our belongings did so without putting us in harm's way. In our entire trip, we never felt threatened. Most people were gracious, if not interested and inquisitive, as were we.

And it was embarrassingly easy for us to replace our lost items. Thanks to the plastic in our pockets, we were given endless credit to purchase whatever it was we wanted. And to top it off, upon our return home, we were able to recoup 90 percent of our loss on our homeowner's insurance policy.

Questioning what is fair and equitable in a global society, one must ask, "Who are the criminals? What is to blame for these incredible global imbalances? How does a lifestyle and behavior in the North, or developed world, contribute to the poverty and behavior of others in the South, in a country like Kenya—even the auto scam artists?"

These are questions and issues that most people never confront. Yet these may be the very questions that lie at the base of much of the social unrest and discontent experienced by people across the planet. Who is responsible for the refugee crisis encountered across Europe and the Middle East, and how should others respond? What of the climate refugees that are predicted to be on the move in the not-too-distant future? In some small way, perhaps we contributed to the welfare of a few, who now having our belongings, might otherwise have very little. And in one major way, this engaging experience taught us much more than any classroom lesson could ever accomplish. That was a small price to pay for an important lesson. Can we help our students grow from similar experiences?

An archaeologist sifts through layer upon layer of soil in an attempt to better understand the patterns that reflect the progression, development, and impact that have occurred at a given site over time. In a similar manner, interculturally skilled teachers look for patterns that emerge in their students' behavior, thoughts, perceptions, and dreams as they learn to reinterpret and then redefine their understanding of another's reality. Opening up the means of perception so people are able to see and interpret things differently than they were able to do prior to an intercultural experience becomes one of the long-term goals of orientation and a subsequent intercultural experience. With this new skill, people are then able to progress from a rather narrow and self-absorbed ethnocentric orientation to one that is more ethnorelative, open, inclusive, empathic, and interculturally sensitive and aware.

But predeparture orientation really only begins to only scratch the surface of what is necessary to become interculturally skilled. Individuals must ultimately embark upon a sojourn that fully engages their cognitive, affective, and behavioral domains. It is the kinds of experiences that students have while in a country that become critical to achieving the desired goals of meaningful international travel. And, it is the teacher who is the significant force in the design of this plan.

Everything people perceive in their environment is filtered through a set of lenses that function to bring meaning to the stimuli in their world. Ethnocentrism refers to the tendency people have to interpret phenomenon and judge others according to their own culture's lens or standards. Although a certain degree of ethnocentrism is essential in that it serves to bind a group of people together, it can become a serious obstacle when those who have internalized different ideas and behaviors begin to interact with one another.

A statement Thomas Jefferson made in the mid-1800s comparing "sophisticated and cultured" Europeans to the native people of the Americas demonstrates how such an orientation and perspective enters our collective mindset and then is applied across entire groups of people. Jefferson wrote (cited in Pearce, 1965):

Let a philosophic observer commence a journey from the savages of the Rocky Mountains, eastwardly towards the seacoast. These he would observe in the earliest stages of association, living under no law but that of nature, subsisting and covering themselves with the flesh and skins of wild beasts. He would next find those on the frontiers in the pastoral stage, raising domestic animals to supply the advances of civilization, and so on in his progress he would meet the gradual shades of improving man until he would reach his, as yet, most improved state in our seaport towns. This, in fact, is equivalent to a survey, in time, of the progress of man from the infancy of creation to the present day.

Such a statement helps us to understand how hierarchical terminology such as First World versus Third World or developed nation versus underdeveloped nation easily finds its way into people's thinking and vocabulary. It is then perpetuated throughout a society and becomes quite difficult to reduce or eliminate.

One of the major consequences of ethnocentrism is the tendency people have to resist change. If people believe that their way of doing things is best and they have the power to choose to continue in familiar ways, why should they change? Consider the case of the United States and the adoption of metrics. At this time, all other countries of the world except for three, the United States, Myanmar, and Liberia, have adopted the metric system as their primary means of measurement.

Although many attempts have been made in the United States to adopt the metric system, significant resistance remains despite the difficulties it causes travelers, manufacturers, scientists, and others who must interact in a variety of ways with people from other nations. Failure to convert English measures to metric values by NASA scientists was the cause of the September 1999 loss of the Orbiter spacecraft as it approached Mars. This oversight resulted in the destruction of a $125 million spacecraft and jeopardized the entire Mars programs until the successful landing of Spirit in 2004.

Intercultural educators strive to help people reduce their tendency to respond from an ethnocentric perspective and to grow in terms of their understanding, openness, and skill in interacting with others who may be different. This is no simple task given what we know about how people learn about culture and the inherent obstacles and resistance to change most people exhibit.

We are thus left with many questions. Just what does it mean to be interculturally sensitive? How do we know when we have achieved it? What are the attitudes and behaviors of people who are comfortable and effective working across cultures? How would you recognize such an orientation in teachers, students, or yourself? How can teachers best assist others along this path?

Until relatively recently, little was understood about the development of intercultural sensitivity, and few benchmarks existed to guide our understanding of how people can become more interculturally competent. Different from such terms as *multicultural* or *international*, the term *intercultural* refers to a penetration at the interpersonal level where there exists an exchange between individuals of different groups. The focus here is on building trust, understanding, and thus interpersonal relationships so people can begin to collaborate across cultural boundaries and address common concerns.

The more comprehensive conceptualizations of intercultural effectiveness and sensitivity consider the interaction between the cognitive, affective, and behavioral domains, and teachers must understand this interplay. People with an intercultural mindset, for instance, move from avoidance or a tolerance of difference to a respect and appreciation of difference. They move from an unconscious ethnocentrism to a more ethnorelative orientation, becoming increasingly aware of their own as well as others' culture and behavior. Instead of trying to avoid racism, sexism, and other prejudices, such individuals seek out ways to create respectful, productive intercultural relationships.

Intercultural competence, a behaviorally focused notion, comprises an open-mindedness and genuine interest in other cultures, being observant and knowledgeable about cultural differences and similarities, an ability to resist stereotypes and anticipate complexity, and being able and willing to modify behavior so people can interact and communicate effectively with those different from themselves (Deardorff, 2009). In essence, this reflects a balance of a mindset, a heart set, and a skill set.

Interculturally competent individuals are thus able to shift their frame of reference as required, recognize and respond appropriately to cultural differences, listen empathically, perceive others accurately, maintain a non-judgmental approach to communication, and gather appropriate information about another culture. In real life outside the classroom, such skills are critical when people engage in decision making, negotiation, or problem solving across cultures; when subordinates and authority figures from different backgrounds interact extensively; when individuals or families make major transitions; or when nations and people come together to resolve major differences.

Intercultural education and training, however, are delicate and difficult endeavors that must be approached with the greatest of sensitivity. Milton Bennett (1993) points out that intercultural interactions among human populations have typically been accompanied by violence and aggression when he states:

Intercultural sensitivity is not natural. It is not part of our primate past, nor has it characterized most of human history. Cross-cultural contact usually has been accompanied by bloodshed, oppression, or genocide. Education and training in intercultural communication is an approach to changing our "natural" behavior. With the concepts and skills developed in this field, we ask learners to transcend traditional ethnocentrism and to explore new relationships across cultural boundaries. This attempt at change must be approached with the greatest possible care. (p. 21)

Bennett's Developmental Model of Intercultural Sensitivity, referred to as the DMIS, is one of the most widely referenced conceptions of intercultural development (Bennett, 1993). The DMIS provides a framework for understanding intercultural development and awareness along a continuum from a highly ethnocentric or monocultural orientation at one end to a more ethnorelative or intercultural mindset on the other end. In explaining the DMIS, Bennett notes that an increase in cultural awareness is accompanied by improved cognitive sophistication. Specifically, as people's ability to understand difference increases so does their ability to negotiate a variety of worldviews.

According to the DMIS, three stages lie on the ethnocentric side of the continuum—Denial, Defense, and Minimization—and three stages reflect increasingly ethnorelative perspectives and skills—Acceptance, Adaptability, and Integration. The Intercultural Development Inventory (IDI), the most widely used assessment tool designed to determine where on the DMIS continuum an individual or organization falls, places people along five of these stages—Denial, Polarization (referred to as Defense in the DMIS), Minimization, Acceptance, and Adaptation (Hammer & Bennett, 2003).

ETHNOCENTRIC STAGE OF DENIAL

Denial refers to the inability to see cultural differences and is evident when individuals separate themselves into homogeneous groups. Individuals at this stage tend to ignore the reality of difference and often are characterized by well-meant, but ignorant, stereotypic and superficial statements of tolerance. At this stage, an individual's understanding of cultural difference is minimal and if considered, is typically attributed to a deficiency in intelligence or personality. There may also be a tendency to dehumanize outsiders, thus making them easy targets for discrimination or exploitation.

When traveling, if they do, people in this stage emphasize familiar categories—just not seeing differences. If they are Americans in Tokyo, for instance, they have an "American" experience and may say things like "Tokyo is like the United States—lots of cars, tall buildings, and McDonalds."

Bennett calls this stage the "stupid questions syndrome," suggesting that those in this stage tend to have a few simple ideas or pieces of stereotypic knowledge about a country or culture. The stereotypic knowledge many European Americans have of Africa, for instance, might include wild animals, poverty, disease, and jungle. Everything about Africa then is thought of in terms of these four ideas. Upon meeting an African, all these images come to the forefront. Such a person may think or ask, "So when you leave your hut in the morning, aren't you afraid the wild animals from the jungle will attack you or that you will get sick from everything?"

Stop for a moment and ask yourself about the categories many around the world might have of Americans (or whatever your nationality)? Do they tend to see Americans as overweight (lovers of fast food), lazy, rich, and driving big cars? If so, upon meeting an American, such a person might ask, "So when you leave your big house in the morning, do you get in your big car and drive to McDonalds for your big breakfast?" They are bringing forth all of their stereotypic information in their judgment of you.

Stereotyping is one of the ways the human mind operates in an attempt to simplify the world, and their use is quite common in this stage. People cannot respond to each individual stimulus received on their senses and thus have a tendency to categorize information. That is, people put similar pieces of information into common groups, or categories, merely as an attempt to bring some order to the complex world in which they live. Stereotypes are merely categories of people that are socially constructed by a given group to simplify the identification of individuals who are in some way "other."

The term *stereotype* refers to any sort of summary statement or prototypic image that obscures the differences within a group. People, in this stage especially, have a tendency to view others' behavior as negative and then to use this information as trait labels. These negative trait labels then become associated with groups of people, thus becoming stereotypes of that group. And because it is oftentimes easier for people to think categorically, the use of negative stereotypes becomes more common than we would like.

The distinction between stereotypes and generalizations is important to consider at this point. A generalization refers to the tendency of a majority of people in a group to exhibit a certain trait or characteristic. Thus, when applying a generalization, we could safely say that most people of a particular group hold certain values or share certain nonverbal communication patterns. The Japanese, for instance, have a tendency to be more collectively oriented than their individually oriented Northern European counterparts. Such information can be supported by research and safely applied to a large proportion of a group.

Stereotypes, on the other hand, refer to the application of one piece of information, whether accurate or not, to every member of that group. Thus, unsupported information blurs specific knowledge about other individuals, and people operate under the assumption that all people in a particular group act in the same way. For instance, although the majority of Japanese people exhibit collective behavior, there will always be times when people exhibit individualistic behavior—people do have individual preferences. The same can be said of the more individualistic Northern Europeans, who will at times exhibit a collective orientation. Because people sometimes have limited and occasionally negative stereotypic knowledge, people may interact with others with inaccurate and dangerous information.

Individuals in the stage of Denial are generally not capable of thinking about differences and must discover commonalties among people before they can move on. Moving from this stage to the next involves helping individuals to develop better skills of discrimination and to create other categories, thus becoming more sophisticated in their thinking and more complex in their cognitive processing. When traveling, it becomes the teachers' responsibility to help their students see beyond that which is immediately visible and to point out the underlying differences, motivations, and practices that may not be evident on the surface, or objective level.

ETHNOCENTRIC STAGE OF DEFENSE/POLARIZATION

Movement into Defense or Polarization is driven by the inadequacies of the existing rather simplistic categories. This stage is characterized by the recognition of cultural difference, with one's own group seen as the only real and viable one. People operating at this stage tend to focus on objective, or surface-level, cultural differences (e.g., eating habits, clothing) while coupling this with negative evaluation of others. Strong dualistic us–them thinking seems to be common in this stage. The greater the cultural difference, the more negative the accompanying evaluation.

The strong dualistic us–them thinking that is common in this stage is often accompanied by overt negative stereotyping. When forced into contact with others, individuals in this stage often become defensive, exhibiting a "hardening of the categories" so to speak; focus on a small, typically elite sample of a society; and tend to defend their own way as the one best way.

It is not uncommon for people to be in the Defense stage, but they must be encouraged to move on. The developmental tasks to move out of this stage require supporting people affectively while stressing the commonalities among people. When traveling, teachers may need to spend considerable time in one-on-one discussions or small-group debriefings with students to gently nudge them on toward the next level.

TRANSITION STAGE OF MINIMIZATION

Bennett asserts that a paradigmatic shift in thinking must occur for an individual to move from the ethnocentric stages of the continuum, where difference is viewed as something to be avoided, to the ethnorelative side, where difference is something that is seen as an asset and sought out. Minimization, recently considered to be a transition stage between an ethnocentric and an ethnorelative orientation (Hammer, 2011), is entered into with the discovery of commonality.

Movement from Defense to Minimization comes with the discovery of commonality. People in this stage tend to recognize and accept superficial, objective cultural differences, such as eating customs, money, and so forth, while holding the belief that all human beings are essentially the same. The emphasis at this stage is on the similarity of people and the assumed commonality of basic values, with the tendency to define the basis of commonality in ethnocentric terms. A person in this stage, for instance, might think that "because everyone is essentially the same, they're really pretty much like me."

This perceived commonality could exist around physical universalism (saying such things as, "We are all the same—we all eat, sleep, breathe, bleed red, and die" or "We are all people of color after all") or around spiritual universalism (saying such things as "Deep down we are all children of the same God, whether we know it or not").

This is a very profound stage, and there is evidence to suggest that most teachers are at this stage. People in this stage see others as basically the same with little recognition of the differences that do in fact exist. People may make reference to physical characteristics—race for instance—believing that it is not important as long as all people are treated the same. In Minimization, people tend to ignore the influence of culture and lived experience that may be quite different between people, tending to believe that all people have the same needs—when in reality they do not.

Minimization is a comfortable place for people to be as they make positive-sounding statements to themselves and others such as "I don't see difference—I treat all children alike" or "When you really get down to it, we're all the same. I don't discriminate." This in reality is a color-blind notion that ignores the very real experiences of some children and families that may impact learning in significant ways. It thus becomes difficult to move people from this stage because they think they are doing okay.

Yet it is exactly the ability to discriminate that Mahon (2006) suggests is essential if teachers are to fully understand the influence that such factors as culture, race, ethnicity, gender, and socioeconomic status may have on the experiences that students and their families as well as teachers bring to the school context. Teachers must understand how their own rather narrow perspective and experience may influence their ability to accurately perceive and understand the children in their charge. It is also essential that they under-stand their own resistance to difference—a characteristic of individuals in the ethnocentric stages of this model.

The developmental task to move people out of Minimization is cultural self-awareness. Aspects of one's own culture should be pointed out and shown how it might differ relative to another's. However, this does not mean that people must like and accept everything—people can maintain a moral compass by contextualizing another's behavior and beliefs. Take nudity for example. Is it appropriate to take off your clothes? Well, it matters—the con-text here is critical. In certain circumstances it is appropriate to take off your clothes, as in the shower, but in other circumstance, as out in public, perhaps not. The context explains the behavior.

Culture thus becomes the context from which to explore another's values. When the context is set (i.e., greeting behavior in Japan), then people decide whether they will behave according to that context and bow or shake hands. Once this is accepted, the person can move from Minimization to Acceptance. When traveling with students, pointing out subtle differences in people's experiences, for instance, are important. Having discussions with host nationals about how Americans or others are perceived locally will help to point out the significant differences that do make a difference.

ETHNORELATIVE STAGE OF ACCEPTANCE

Acceptance of difference is the first stage on the ethnorelative side of the continuum. Individuals at this stage have the ability to recognize and appre-ciate cultural difference in terms of both people's values and their behavior, understanding that there are viable alternative solutions to the ways people organize their existence and experience. At this stage, individuals demon-strate the ability to interpret phenomena within a cultural context and to ana-lyze complex interactions in culture-contrast terms.

Teachers at this stage, for instance, might understand that family or other collective influences may be greater for a Latino or Asian child than for an Anglo counterpart. They might then temper their expectation that students make their own independent choices on major life decisions and seek out more culturally appropriate ways to work more closely with a student and his or her family. Or student travelers staying with host families in Mexico might understand that family or other collective influences may be greater in a Latin culture and thus better understand why they are expected to be in with the family on most evenings instead of being free to roam the community as they might be back home.

But acceptance alone is not sufficient to drive effectiveness with another culture. The development of new skills in communication and behavior becomes essential.

ETHNORELATIVE STAGE OF ADAPTATION

In Adaptation, the individual begins to see cultural categories as more flexible and becomes more competent in her or his ability to communicate across cultures. Individuals thus are able to use empathy effectively, to communicate cross-culturally, and to shift frames of reference and are better able to understand others and be understood across cultural boundaries.

Two forms of Adaptation exist. Cultural adaptation refers to the ability to consciously shift perspective into an alternative cultural worldview and to use multiple cultural frames of reference in evaluating phenomena. Behavioral adaptation enables people to shift into different frames without much conscious effort and then to act in culturally appropriate ways.

Movement into Adaptation is driven by a need for action—improving communication skills to build better relations, for instance, and cognitive empathy—the ability to change frames of reference. It is at this stage that we say that people are becoming bicultural or multicultural. A teacher at this stage, for instance, would understand that the needs of refugee students are quite distinct from those of international exchange students—even though they may both be from abroad—and will in turn respond differently to them.

A significant amount of groundwork must be laid before people are ready to learn new skills and such a shift can occur. The greater the cultural gap, the more difficult it will be to make such a shift. One begins to experience reality in a more "other" way and can understand and feel about the world as the other might. At this stage, people are not simply acquiring skills nor are they simply regurgitating lists of do's and don'ts. Knowledge and behavior here are linked by conscious intention, with category boundaries becoming more flexible and permeable, and intentional perspective taking and empathy.

STAGE-APPROPRIATE INTERCULTURAL
LEARNING FOR TODAY'S TEACHERS

Acquiring intercultural competence is developmental and comprehensive and takes time (Bennett, 1993; Cushner, 2014). That is, it is a process that is more evolutionary than it is revolutionary, and it cannot be achieved quickly or with a cognitive-only approach. Significant firsthand experience or encounters with difference over a sustained period of time that integrate the affective and behavioral domains seem to be essential if people are to advance to more complex intercultural thinking and behavior.

In many respects, culture learning is no different from the way people learn anything new, following a predictable progression from unconscious incompetence, where people are initially not aware that they lack a skill; advancing toward conscious incompetence, when they become aware of what they do not know; to conscious competence, where they work hard to accomplish certain skills; and finally to unconscious competence, where exhibiting the skill takes little conscious effort.

Not only is the acquisition of intercultural competence developmental and comprehensive; it also requires a combination of cognitive, affective, and behavioral interventions and experiences. The DMIS can be instructive here as well. If we know where an individual lies on the continuum, we can be mindful of the particular strategies and experiences that can be utilized to move people from one stage to another.

When considering how to enhance the knowledge and skills of teachers, we must consider the prior experiences, or lack thereof, that most bring to the profession as well as where most fall on the intercultural continuum. And the particular needs and approaches we might use when moving someone from Denial to Polarization can be significantly different than those that we would use when moving someone from Minimization to Acceptance.

Recent research using the IDI provides us with some evidence that the majority of today's teachers and teacher education students encounter others from an ethnocentric orientation or, at best, are on the cusp of Minimization. Mahon's (2002) study of 155 teachers from the American Midwest placed all of them at Minimization or below. Her follow-up study (Mahon, 2009) found that of eighty-eight teachers in the American West, 84 percent were at Minimization or below. Bayles (2009) reports that 91 percent of 233 teachers in a US urban, Southern school district were at Minimization or below.

Such findings are not limited to the United States. Grossman and Yuen (2006) found that of 107 teachers in schools in Hong Kong, 55 percent were in Denial or Defense and 43 percent in Minimization, with only 2 percent fully on the ethnorelative side of the continuum. And Yuen's (2009) survey of 386 teachers in nine schools in Hong Kong revealed the majority to be in Denial/Defense, emphasizing cultural similarities with minimal recognition given to cultural differences.

Understanding that intercultural development is an evolutionary and not a revolutionary process should greatly influence the manner in which we educate not only our students but ourselves as well. Intercultural competence is not achieved in one course or one single experience. Rather, it comes about after recognizing where one is on the developmental continuum and then, while providing both support and challenge, engaging students in systematic, oftentimes repetitious, and well-planned exposure to intercultural interactions that nudge one to increasingly complex levels.

Moving too quickly along the continuum is akin to the scuba diver plunging immediately to a depth of a hundred feet without taking the requisite time to equalize pressure and accommodate to the new environment—the shock can just be too great for the body to accept. Alternatively, gradual movement or immersion enables the diver to adjust to the changing circumstances and thus to function more effectively in the new environment. So too should it be with intercultural development. Understanding and integrating what we know about intercultural development and sensitivity into the education of young people will result in a more culturally effective and culturally competent citizenry.

Chapter 6

Change Your Latitude, Change Your Attitude: Facilitating Adolescent Adjustment

No one who has lived through the second half of the twentieth century could possibly be blind to the enormous impact of exchange programs on the future of countries.

—Bill Clinton, 1993

It is within the formal educational context where many adolescents participate in international travel and exchange programs. This travel experience can operate and have an impact in two directions—sometimes, it is we or our students who are the ones traveling, and at other times, we play host to international students who come to our schools and live in our communities. Such experiences can take place in a variety of ways, including structured semester- or year-abroad exchange programs where students live with a host family and attend a local school; through formal travel experiences undertaken by a foreign language class or musical group that spends one to two weeks traveling and/or performing abroad; or through a focused summer experience.

Approximately 73,000 international students were in attendance in US schools in the 2013–2014 school year. This number includes not only those on the traditional year-abroad exchange program but also a surprising surge in the number of international students pursuing their entire secondary school degree in both private and public schools in the United States. All can grow in significant ways as a result of the experience. This chapter will explore various phases of intercultural adjustment with particular reference to the adolescent student exchange experience in the school context.

The adolescent exchange experience allows participants to learn about a new culture in the same way they learned their original one—by living with a family. As the students struggle to accommodate the differences they encounter and make sense out of their new home and school, they slowly begin to trust others and ultimately gain a feeling of being at home in a new context.

Intercultural adjustment refers to the processes people experience as they begin to understand and adapt to the very real differences encountered while making a transition to new surroundings. There are, not surprisingly, a number of things at both the objective and subjective levels to which people must adapt to as they encounter a new culture. Early in an experience, one must make numerous adjustments to physical differences in the environment—new foods or differing systems of work or study that are encountered; the ways people use transportation, local weather, or climate conditions; and so forth.

People must also adjust to differences in the ways people interact with one another, sometimes confronting significant differences in the more deeply held value and belief systems. Here, the individual may begin to wrestle with her or his own commitment and willingness to make changes in her or his manner of thinking and acting. Later on, one may begin to experience significant internal change in terms of intercultural identity and development—just the steps needed to advance toward more ethnorelative stages of intercultural sensitivity.

Studies by early researchers into cross-cultural transitions suggested that people experience a predictable pattern of adjustment when they undergo significant, long-term encounters in new cultural settings (Lysgaard, 1955; Oberg, 1960; Trifonovitch, 1977). These early models, although brought into question more recently (Ward, Okura, Kennedy, & Kojima, 1998), presented a visual representation that plots people's experiences on a graph, with emotional experiences along the vertical axis and time across the horizontal axis. The resulting image appearing in the shape of the letter *U* and conveniently referred to as the U-curve hypothesis was meant to characterize the experience of what is commonly referred to as culture shock.

Early adjustment models suggested that people experience four phases throughout their adjustment, and they have been given some rather clever names. Imagine the letter *U* with four spots identified along the letter.

The "honeymoon" phase occurs early in the experience at the top left of the *U*. Here, everything is new and exciting—there are new foods to eat, new people to meet, and new sights to see. There can also be new ways of getting around town, with people looking forward to giving up their dependence upon their own automobile perhaps and using public transportation so they might "mingle with the locals."

Typically characterized by exhilaration, discovery, and anticipation, this rather euphoric stage usually does not last long. Additionally, people may encounter an array of emotions, from anxiety, uncertainty, and ambiguity, to excitement and enthusiasm—in other words, stress. The demands of setting up a new home and learning how to function in the new setting can have tremendous emotional demands. One's body can't differentiate good stress from bad stress—it just reacts to the sudden flow of adrenalin and other hormones that are flushed into the system. People thus cannot remain in this state, whether positive or negative, for long.

The next phase, sometimes referred to as "hostility," is then experienced as one moves down the left side toward the bottom of the *U*. After some time, one's behavior may not bring about the expected results, or it becomes challenging to find one's comforts, from favorite foods and toiletries to "a good cup of coffee." And although it may have been initially exciting to get around town as the locals do, the fact that the public transportation system may not run on time, thus causing people to be late for appointments, begins to be bothersome.

At this point the individual must make a critical choice: remain and learn how to function effectively within the new setting or allow the frustrations to build and eventually retreat from the unpleasant situation. Those individuals most likely to succeed in their new setting begin to confront their new cultural environment. They learn to cope with embarrassment, disappointment, frustration, ambiguity, anxiety, and identity problems at first, and then they begin the process of culture learning by focusing on the subjective culture of the new environment.

Here, the fact that people may be late is not taken as being inconsiderate or insensitive but rather understood that an emphasis on time may not be the same for all people. In some contexts, people may come to a meeting any time after their set appointment and not be considered late, the important thing being that the meeting occurred.

If people stay and begin to learn effectively, they emerge from the bottom of the *U* and enter a state often referred to as "humor." This stage suggests that as people learn more culturally appropriate behavior they can begin to laugh at how they might have looked to locals when they first arrived. It is a good sign and suggests that one is well on the way to adjustment.

Finally, as people reach the top of the *U*, they can now see the world from two equally valid perspectives. It is in this state, sometimes referred to as "home," where people are thought to be when they are well adjusted and bicultural. It can take a considerable amount of time—up to two years—for people to make a full and complete cultural adjustment and to arrive at the top of the *U*, this being full immersion.

Building upon this idea, other researchers proposed the W-Hypothesis, extending the initial U-curve of adjustment to include the return to one's home culture (Gullahorn & Gullahorn, 1963). People find that when they return home after an extended time away, there is often an unexpected readjustment, or reentry shock, to being home (LaBrack, 2015). It can be quite difficult to integrate one's new learning and perspectives into their lives when others around them have not had similar experiences and similar growth.

These are easy and convenient models for people to adopt, and it is not uncommon for a student to approach a teacher saying something like "I think I need to talk to you. I feel like I'm at the bottom of my *U*." Such a model makes intuitive sense; is easy for people to remember; and although not supported any longer in the research literature, can still be a useful pedagogical tool to help people anticipate the changes they are likely to experience.

Let's look a little deeper into this phenomenon. A term that is perhaps more accurate and useful than culture shock—*transition stress*—captures the variety of ways that individuals may experience the challenges that accompany major transitions. Within the course of a day, a week, or a month, for instance, an individual in a new setting may experience transition stress as a result of many things: changes that occur in his or her identity and/or role, confusing or misunderstood communication styles and interactions, the energy required to learn new ways, coping with the fact that one's normal behavior does not produce the expected results, the perception of being judged or stereotyped by others, and the need to build new relationships as well as managing the sheer emotional complexity of going through many of these simultaneously (Berardo, 2012).

Since these initial hypotheses were proposed, more comprehensive analyses of the adjustment process has been explored by a number of researchers (Pedersen, 1995; Ward, Bochner, & Furnham, 2001). Regardless of the model used to describe the process of adjustment, something impactful does go on during a sojourn—it just may not be as easy to document and explain in a neat little image as was suggested by these early models. Adjustment, however, can be thought of as an ongoing process that is generally experienced in five phases, including predeparture preparation, arrival and settling in, culture shock, culture learning where relationships are built, and reentry.

PREDEPARTURE

Predeparture and trip preparation, at least for the overseas exchange experience, includes the period of time that begins when individuals complete an application to when they have been accepted and ultimately placed with a host family. For the class preparing to travel overseas, it begins from the moment students, teachers, and families hear about the possibility that they may travel overseas, as when my students began preparing for the Belizean adventure months before their actual sojourn.

The predeparture stage is typically characterized by excitement, anticipation, new discovery, and positive perceptions. As departure time nears, the students are busy saying their goodbyes to family and friends, shopping for last-minute items, and perhaps sending a letter of introduction off to a prospective host family. The host family too is usually busy preparing to welcome a new member to their family.

This is also a time when students should begin preparation for the intercultural exchange and interaction that are certain to occur, but this is seldom the case. It seems to be difficult for most prospective sojourners to anticipate the kinds of communication problems, intercultural misunderstandings, and other potential pitfalls they will encounter, and many just do not pay much attention at this time to issues related to culture and adjustment.

This is one of the ironies of cross-cultural orientation and one of the counterintuitive findings in the research. Few people, especially those who have not traveled before, tend to pay much attention to cross-cultural issues during predeparture orientation sessions. It is generally not until they arrive at their destination and begin to have some concrete experiences that may not make sense that people begin to question the reality of their new environment and express an interest in cross-cultural issues. Most tend to be too caught up in the excitement of leaving to attend to such "academic" issues.

After returning to Ohio after four years living and studying in Hawai'i, our family decided to host a visiting high school exchange student. Already quite involved with AFS Intercultural Programs through my dissertation study in New Zealand as well as knowing that our local AFS community group was quite active and supportive, we applied to host a student. We reviewed papers of a few potential female applicants who were interested in living for a year in the United States. Yuzuki's application stood out among the rest for our family. Coming from the island of Kyushu in Japan, Yuzuki described herself as interested in being a "big sister," eager to become active with a variety of things during her stay in America, a musician playing classical piano, quiet and reserved.

That she was—when she arrived. After a year with us, Yuzuki returned home to play drums in an Irish rock and roll band and subsequently married an Irishman (although they have since divorced). We continue to remain in close contact with Yuzuki and have visited one another a few times since she returned home, and Hyla has provided advice and guidance to her throughout her pregnancy and the birth of her first child via phone and e-mail. To say that the experience had an impact on her life would be an understatement. The same could be said for us as a family.

Our first personal contact with Yuzuki came during her predeparture stage the preceding summer. We wanted to initiate some correspondence with her before her arrival. Still homesick for Hawai'i, I had arranged to teach summer school classes at the University of Hawai'i, planning to spend the best part of a summer there with my family. We wrote a letter to Yuzuki introducing ourselves and letting her know how much we were looking forward to having her stay with us. If she wished to write us back, we would be at a given address in Honolulu through mid-August.

A few weeks into our stay in Hawai'i, we received a response from Japan, addressed to where we were staying—in "Honoruru, Hawaii!" And to top things off, Yuzuki informed us in the letter that her mother ran an English language school and that she had spent quite a number of years studying English. This was our first introduction to the kinds of learning and growth experiences that were to occur for all of us as the year progressed. This was also our first taste of the reality of disconfirmed expectations—especially from one who was actively learning English. Oh, what else might we expect?

It wasn't long after Yuzuki arrived in our home that we all began to realize there were problems in adjustment. But this was not only happening to Yuzuki; it was happening to others as well—our entire family, other exchange students and families, and local kids in the school as well as the teachers.

Good exchange programs are characterized by supportive networks of community volunteers, host families, and schools that come together to ease the adjustment shock the student is certain to experience. It is not uncommon for these school and community support groups to host regular gatherings designed to allow international students and their host families as well as teachers to discuss their experiences—both the joys and the frustrations. It can be quite enlightening for all as they began to learn more and more about each other's cultures and the cross-cultural adjustment experience.

ARRIVAL AND SETTLING IN

Arrival and settling in can span a rather lengthy period of time as students initially integrate into a new family and community and ultimately become included in a new school. Although students may feel comfortable and at home in some settings, they are constantly being introduced to others where they may be exposed to countless new stimuli. When the novelty of the experience begins to wear off, it may feel like the host culture is beginning to intrude on the visitor's life. This stage is often characterized by confusion, self-blame, tension, frustration, loss, depression, and withdrawal. One's emotions can become quite engaged, and physical manifestations of these psychological challenges, such as headaches and stomach pains, may occur.

In many ways, the exchange student experience is similar to that of many other sojourners' experiences. However, there are some significant differences. For one, the student is generally on her or his own. That is, although the exchange students may travel to their host country with a group of fellow nationals, usually within a few days of arriving they are matched up with their host family and off they go.

After the initial arrival into a new country, the process of settling in begins with the sojourner experiencing many new and unexpected things. It is not uncommon for new sojourners to have the sense that things, or people for that matter, all seem to look alike. Because so much is new and different and the stimuli are in most cases not what one has been accustomed to, it may be difficult to distinguish the details, and things pretty much blend together.

Developing an insider's perspective and an ability to differentiate the finer differences between individuals takes some time and familiarity. Outsiders just don't see most of the detail and thus miss out on much until they have been around for a longer period of time. Extended immersion in a new context provides the time one needs to learn to focus on the new details and begin to make sense of the new environment.

When entering a new country and/or interacting within a new cultural setting for the first time, the sojourners confront another surprise—how powerfully their emotions are aroused (Cushner & Brislin, 1996). Although people may expect there to be objective, or physical, differences across cultures, they are often surprised at the degree to which their own emotions will be engaged and how this will impact their initial adjustment.

Exchange students as well as their host families eagerly anticipate the arrival and initial meeting that will take place, each having some expectation of how those awkward "getting-to-know-you" moments will unfold. It is from this first moment when people greet one another that emotions are high, and the ambiguity of the cross-cultural encounter and the reality of cultural differences become increasingly evident. A number of emotional experiences occur in the early stages of a sojourn as a result of confronting disconfirmed expectation and experiencing a certain degree of anxiety and ambiguity as well as having a need to belong and "fit in."

Rosa's host mother shared her first encounter at the airport when Rosa first arrived from the Dominican Republic.

We all waited in anticipation for the plane to taxi from the runway. All of us, that is, except my husband, as he couldn't get off work to come to the airport. But I was there with my kids, Roger, our twelve-year-old son, and Lisa, our fourteen-year-old daughter. We all ran over toward the entranceway holding our "Welcome Rosa" sign as well as a few balloons and streamers we had brought as people were arriving at the airport. You know, kind of what you'd expect when you welcome someone new. We had our photo of Rosa with us so we would recognize her when she got off the plane.

We recognized Rosa right away. She had this big grin on her face as she walked toward us. I introduced myself to her and then introduced the kids.

She smiled, let out a big "Hola," and proceeded to kiss each of us on the cheek. I didn't quite know what to do and was at a loss when she offered her face to me. We all kind of stood there, quite astonished! And the kids! Well, they didn't stop talking about that for a week. They never expected to kiss anyone they really didn't know, especially the first time they met. I warned my husband that this might happen before he got home so he wouldn't be as shocked as we were. But it didn't happen. I guess Rosa learned pretty quickly that we don't kiss one another when we first meet.

That is the essence of the cross-cultural encounter; people go about their business behaving as they would under their normal circumstances but may unintentionally offend or shock the other. As you can imagine, Rosa saw the same situation somewhat differently. Rosa shared her perception of the same experience with the other students, and she felt as if her host family really didn't want her.

When I arrived, I was all excited and happy to meet my new family. I had been up half the night unable to sleep, I was so excited. When we finally arrived, I gathered my stuff, walked off the plane, saw that wonderful welcome sign the family had made, and ran up to give my new family a kiss. That's how we greet at home; it's only natural to kiss people when you meet, especially among women. And you expect a kiss in return.

Well, when that didn't happen, I thought the family really didn't want me. I could sense that something was wrong. Perhaps they had been forced to take an exchange student; I didn't know. I was really uncomfortable at first and didn't quite know what to do. It took a day or two until we could talk about this as a family. Now, I understand that Americans just don't kiss like we do; they are much more formal in their interactions with others. I guess shaking hands helps to keep people at a comfortable distance; I don't know.

Good cross-cultural training strives to have both people in the interaction make the same judgment about the other or at least be able to understand and explain an encounter in the same way. The technical term used by psychologists is isomorphic attributions, or making similar judgments about the other person that they would make about themselves. In Rosa's case, both she and her host family would have understood the greeting behavior of the other and made similar judgments about one another.

Greeting behaviors can occur for quite some time and in a variety of contexts for exchange students, even after the initial welcome is long past. Mrs. James, one of the high school counselors, is the faculty advisor to the international student group. In this capacity, she interacts with students in a number of ways, helping them get settled into school, linking them up with American students who serve as mentors, and just being there as a general support for students in need. She related an incident that happened a year earlier on one of the first days of school as she welcomed two new immigrant students from Vietnam.

These kids had been in the country only a short time and were new to our school. I needed to administer a placement test to them so I would know which math class to put them in. They were sitting in the office waiting area when I came out ready to take them to the library, where they could take their test in some quiet space. I gestured to them with my arm as I said something like, "Come with me to the library so you can take the placement test." As I called to them, I felt a sudden panic—they weren't coming with me. I waved harder, smiled bigger, and spoke louder and slower. Still nothing.

In retrospect, I understand how my words said one thing, but my body language communicated something totally different to these students. You see, in their culture, as with many from Southeast Asia, having the palm upward with the fingers moving toward you is an insult. This is a gesture one would use to call a dog or someone in a lower status than you. At that moment, I was belittling and downgrading them. No wonder they weren't following me—I had inadvertently insulted them.

If I was to be more culturally appropriate, I would have gestured with my palm toward the ground with my fingers moving toward me. This may have been a simple error, and I certainly did not mean to offend anyone. But it sure carried a strong, negative message. I wonder how often that happens, especially early in relationships between people?

Another common occurrence in the cross-cultural exchange is that people's expectations are often not met. And again, it is not that people are ill-mannered or inconsiderate—some things are just not anticipated. The Anderson family shared their experience when Seiko came to live with them from Japan.

A few weeks after Seiko arrived, we were able to discuss with her how she felt when she first settled into our home. It certainly was not as we had expected! We thought that from the very beginning we went to all extremes to make her feel a part of our home and family.

Our family life was rather busy at the time. Although we thought of ourselves otherwise, we probably weren't much different from many other American families with young children. We seemed to constantly be on the run between both of our work schedules that included some evening meetings or teaching, getting our children off to school in the morning, making sure they got home afterwards to go to soccer practice, music and dance lessons, and visiting parents an hour away on a weekly basis. And, to top it off, we had just bought our first house and were preparing to move within six weeks of Seiko's arrival.

Yet, through all this, we wanted Seiko to just feel comfortable, be as one of the family, and fit right into our schedule. In fact, we expected that our approach would help, so we did as most American families would do. In the first days, we showed Seiko where everything was in the house, taught her how to operate various appliances so she could cook herself a meal if she was hungry before we all got home, and told her to make herself at home and to do whatever she wanted.

Well, in talking to Seiko a few weeks into her stay, we quickly found out how awkward all of this made her feel. She was quite uncomfortable helping herself to food in the cupboard or refrigerator and doing things like operating the washing machine or sitting down to watch television alone. We prided ourselves on treating Seiko as one of the family. She, on the other hand, thought of us as unfriendly and felt rejected, expecting us to treat her as a special guest, especially in the first weeks after her arrival.

Here, we have a classic case of disconfirmed expectations experienced by both Seiko and her host family. People tend to have certain expectations of how a new place or situation will be as well as how they will function in the process. The reality of the situation, however, can often be quite different from that which one expected. What one expects to find may not, in fact, materialize. Reconciling the difference between the dream and the reality is necessary if people are to make good cross-cultural adjustments. Sojourners must come to grips with the reality of where they find themselves, or they will emerge deeper into a culture shock that can color their subsequent experience.

CULTURE SHOCK

The next phase, oftentimes referred to as culture shock, occurs when the individual becomes quite confused, often disregarding both the similarities and the differences between the host culture and the home culture. This stage too can be highly emotional and is often characterized by hostility, defensive behavior, a feeling of vulnerability, rebellion, blame, and rejection of much that the host culture represents. Many of the reasons for this culture shock are related to some of the emotional issues discussed earlier. However, once the initial settling-in has occurred, more significant cultural differences become evident and can be the cause of more complex problems. It is here that real culture learning occurs.

One aspect that new students must attend to early in their experience is that of language. Once the jet lag has diminished and the student has learned his or her way around a new home and neighborhood, it is essential to begin tuning one's ear to the local language. Where the languages spoken are different and one is building competence in the new tongue, one is simultaneously building trust and understanding between student and other significant people.

Even when the local language is the same that is spoken by the student back home, which is the case for those moving within English-speaking countries, a considerable amount of new vocabulary may not translate, may be used in a very different manner, can be spoken with a new accent, or is accompanied by nonverbal expressions that are either poorly understood or misinterpreted. When the same language is spoken, it is also possible that people may feel comfortable and familiar with one another before a deep and trusting relationship has actually been established, thus bringing student, family, and teachers into potentially difficult situations.

Jean, an American student who had spent the previous year in a school in Queensland, Australia, was serving as a local peer-counselor to new exchange students. She had a very important role, especially early in the school year. During one of the orientation sessions that took place about a month after the new students arrived, she related the following story. It was her attempt to help these new students feel more comfortable by sharing an experience she had early in her sojourn. As she puts it,

Australians are much more aware of the subtle language differences that exist between Australian English and American English than I was, especially during my first months in the country. I knew about some pronunciation differences that existed between Australian and American English—such words as "tomato" and "aluminum" are pronounced differently, for instance.

There are certain "Australianisms" that one comes across as well that are fairly common, like "fair-dinkum," meaning honest or legitimate, and "ta" instead of thanks. Likewise, I was aware that different vocabulary existed for many words—"bonnet" for the hood of a car, "boot" for its trunk, or "jumper" for what I generally refer to as a sweater. Then, there are some terms that one had better not use. You don't "root" for a team down under like we do at home; you "barrack" for the team. To root means to have sexual intercourse, and accidentally asking someone who they root for can get you some pretty strange looks.

There were also different terms used for some common school supplies. At the beginning of the semester, the teacher would read a list of required school supplies, pencils; byro, which is their term for a pen; paper; notepads; and so forth. I eagerly wrote this list down in each class on my first day, feeling somewhat like a kindergarten child on their first day of school. In biology class I had this young, rather cute teacher who seemed to kind of flirt with me when my host sister introduced us at the beginning of class. I was looking forward to being in his class. He proceeded to do the same as the other teachers and read his list: pencils, byros, paper, and rubbers. Rubbers? I had no idea what he could have been talking about? The only rubbers I knew of my grandfather put over his shoes during the winter, and the other, well, I didn't even want to consider it at the moment. I was really thrown by that one.

I finally had to ask my host sister what it meant, but I waited until we got home that night—I was too embarrassed to ask anyone in school—even

her. Boy did we have a laugh when I learned that "rubbers" refers to pencil erasers! I then could go on and enjoy the rest of the semester with this teacher.

So my message to all relatively new exchange students is to ask questions early when confused or when something is not understood. It oftentimes is a rather innocent difference that can be explained quite simply. Language plays a critical role in adjustment, and the sooner one becomes competent in it, the easier the transition will be.

One of my own experiences also relates to language and occurred in Australia. This incident points out the difficulty people can have communicating across accents.

Throughout much of the 1970s, Australia was recruiting planeloads of American teachers to fill badly needed vacancies in many of their schools. Not able to let an opportunity go by, Hyla and I went through the interview process, and two days later, we were offered a contract. We were married six weeks later and one week after that, departed for a two-year teaching stint "Down Under."

We met many other young American teachers at the time and became quite close to Barb and Terry, another young couple from Seattle. We shared many things together over the course of the two years, an interest in photography and travel during the school holidays, and we both gave birth to our first child while there.

Few of us had telephones in our homes, especially early in our experience, so we often left messages for each other at our respective schools. One day, Terry received a message at his school that was rather ambiguous, causing him some embarrassment as well as some confusion. The secretary left a note in his mailbox one day that he was to return a call to "Hare Krishna." The word quickly got out among the other teachers, and many were talking behind his back about "this new Yankee teacher who was a member of the Krishna Consciousness movement."

Terry was totally confused by this message and bothered by the reaction of his peers as he began getting the cold shoulder from many on staff. It wasn't until the next weekend when we inquired from Terry why he hadn't returned our phone call that he figured out the problem. You see, my wife, "Hyla Cushner," telephoned the school and left a message for Terry to return her call. The secretary, unaccustomed to an American accent, heard the voice say "Hare Krishna." Mystery solved.

But spoken language is not the only aspect of communication that sojourners must work to understand. A significant amount of our communication takes place at a nonverbal level. In this instance, Ibrahim, from Turkey, was quite offended and on guard the first days in his art class, the result of a misinterpretation of a nonverbal message.

I was in my art class on the first day when our teacher asked us to make a collage about our experiences during the summer. It wasn't much, just to take a few photos from various magazines that kind of captured what we had done or how we felt. We were to try to communicate our experience to others and to see how they might interpret what we created. I wasn't quite sure how to begin or really what to do for that matter.

The teacher saw me, and I must have looked rather confused. She came over and handed me a pair of scissors, telling me that I should begin cutting from the magazine. Well, I was quite shocked, and I'm afraid I might have offended my teacher. You see, in Turkey, we never hand someone a knife or scissors. I guess it goes back to times when not everybody could be trusted. We always place knives or scissors on a table or somewhere in full view and let the other person pick them up themselves. When the teacher handed me the scissors, I had an immediate gut reaction and pulled away in horror. I think I may have startled the teacher as much as she startled me.

CULTURE LEARNING

It is in this stage that relationships have begun to crystallize and more meaningful culture learning can take place. Although the time required to reach this phase varies depending on any number of factors (family support, individual coping strategies, linguistic competence, degree of cultural gap, etc.), it is here that significant culture learning begins to occur. Likened to the "bottom of the U-curve," this is the point where people begin to understand another's perspective and more accurate attributions about behaviors begin to occur.

The key to success at this phase is the interpersonal relationships that develop. It is when safe, supportive, and trusting relationships have formed, be they among host families, local friends, or teachers, that people begin to open up, expose their inner feelings and thoughts, and more freely inquire about many of the questions and concerns they may have. This was evident in Yuzuki's interactions with our daughter Shannon who was thirteen years old at the time. Yuzuki explained it as follows:

I am the youngest daughter in my family and with that comes certain expectations. My older sister too has certain things that are expected of her. I was quite excited when I learned that I would be staying with a family that had two daughters—both younger than me. I always wanted to be a big sister and have younger sisters look up to me. I think I have quite a bit I can offer them. But now, in retrospect, I don't think that's what Shannon had in mind. And it took a few weeks until this was clear to all of us.

When I first arrived, we shared a bedroom. I was on my best behavior—my mother told me to pick up after myself, help out around the house, and be a good role model for my new sisters. Well, I think I may have overdone it a bit. I tried to give all kinds of advice to Shannon—about who she should spend her time with, to make sure to do her homework, how she should speak to her parents—all the things my sister talked to me about back home in Japan. Well, this didn't go over too well with Shannon, and she got quite angry with me. I was in tears and didn't know what to do. I thought about going home or changing families; it was so awkward.

When we finally talked about it as a family, it became clear to me that young Americans Shannon's age are just beginning to step out on their own and want their own independence. And here I was, trying to be a mother to her, exactly the opposite of what she wanted. No wonder she got so mad at me. It also became clear that while I assumed I was to be a big sister, Shannon had always been the big sister in the family and resented me trying to take her role. We can laugh about it now, but I really learned a lot about American teenagers and families through that experience.

REENTRY

Regardless of the length of time one has been overseas, returning home can be a mix of excitement and joy and reluctance and dismay. On the one hand, the students are anxious to return to family and friends they have missed and to share with others all that they have encountered and learned. On the other hand, they may not want to give up the fun, excitement, and new learning that an overseas experience inevitably brings and return to the "normalcy" of their home culture. This ambivalence is to be expected and will differ depending upon the individuals and the kind of experiences in which the students participated.

For those who spent most of their overseas time with fellow nationals or on a brief study tour, the return home may be easy because they really did not enter the host culture to any degree of depth. For some, if the experience is followed up and built upon after the return home, or for those who have fully entered another culture for a significant length of time, reentry into one's home culture can be a more severe adjustment than the initial culture shock experience primarily because one has not anticipated the changes one has gone through—and it is so unexpected.

The travelers have usually had such an incredibly enriching experience, have changed in so many ways, and are eager to share the new understandings with family and friends once they return home. Most of those who remain at home, however, have not had similar experiences and thus may have a difficult time relating to the changed returnees. Although the sojourners have changed dramatically, family and friends typically have not. It is not uncommon for returnees to find that others lose interest rather quickly in hearing about their overseas encounters and in seeing photographs of their new friends. Although the return travelers may be welcomed home with open arms, they are often met with closed eyes and ears.

Many find it is more difficult to return home than it was to make the initial adjustment to the new culture. Although the individuals who went overseas expect to come home changed people, those who remained at home do not expect to see them any differently. Entering a phase that can be very similar to the initial culture shock, home may feel as if it were new and different. The returnees may feel as if they are strangers in their own homes, feeling out of place, alienated, alone, unable to fit in, and having significant difficulty communicating with friends. Some of the social difficulties encountered include having to deal with stereotypes, uncertainty over cultural identity, and social withdrawal (Ward et al., 2001). Such is the nature of reentry shock and why it is so important to be prepared for this unexpected inevitability.

Reentry, or reverse culture shock, can be attributed to a number of possible causes (Austin, 1986; LaBrack, 2015; Martin & Harrell, 2004; Wang, 1997). For one, there can be a challenge to one's self-concept. Even before individuals return to their home culture, they may have become aware that they are not the same as they were before they left home and that significant changes may have occurred. Their sense of identity with a particular country may have changed, or they may have acquired new nonverbal as well as verbal communication behaviors. The returnees may not identify with the same groups they did prior to their experience, or they may not agree with the values of a given group any longer, including, perhaps, their own family. Until they find their new niche back home, and often a new peer group, they may feel quite out of sorts.

Second, returnees must often reconcile any number of disconfirmed expectations, beginning with the realization that they may feel as a foreigner in their own home. If people have been away for a significant period of time, they may have difficulty readjusting to traditional foods or keeping abreast of conversations because local knowledge and attitudes may have changed. While away, the travelers often build an idealized vision of home—of spending time at favorite places, eating missed foods, visiting with special friends, and so forth. The stage is then set for an enormous letdown when things they return to do not live up to what they expected. Returnees quickly find that relationships have changed and people do not need to hear about the overseas experiences, seeming to be more interested in local gossip.

Others too may have equally unrealistic expectations of the returnees, thus confronting their own disconfirmed expectations. Family and friends may become upset that the returnees seem critical of home or that they do not seem happy. People at home often become confused or upset that the returnees do not seem as interested in local happenings and sometimes may not be able to fully understand what people are talking about. And loved ones may become impatient with the returnees who want to continually share their international experience, feeling that they are unwilling to "get back to normal."

Third, there is often a sense of loss. When people return home, they are oftentimes leaving people and a way of life that they have grown to love, having to say goodbye to people they may never see again. And students on exchange programs may have enjoyed a special status or identity while abroad, being the focus of people's curiosity and interest. Many may miss certain day-to-day amenities they have come to appreciate, such as efficient mass transportation systems or low-cost public health services.

Finally, perhaps the greatest challenge facing returnees, especially those who have been away for a significant period of time, is that of finding an appropriate way to integrate their international experiences into the day-to-day realities of their home culture. Successful returnees work to identify those changes in their own values and attitudes that are most worth integrating into their life now that they are at home. At the same time, a fine line must often be drawn between what the returnees wish to try to change in others and that which they are willing to keep to themselves.

Understanding and addressing issues of reentry may be the most critical phase in integrating the goals of the international experience and should really begin from the moment of initial trip planning. After all, it is really the postexperience impact and change on the individual that is the ultimate purpose of engaging in an international sojourn. An expected outcome thus is to see growth along the Developmental Model of Intercultural Sensitivity, with individuals becoming less ethnocentric in the way they interact with others in the world and moving toward more complex levels of ethnorelativity.

The ultimate goal is to have had such a significant impact on the individuals that upon their return home, they have greater understanding of the world and subsequently do things differently in their everyday personal or work life. Considering this from the outset helps to remind us that although the actual experience is exciting, it is what we do with the new attitudes, knowledge, and skills that is of most importance. It also helps teachers to extend the learning beyond the orientation and actual trip.

Chapter 7

Learning to Live Together: Bridging Intercultural Boundaries with Youth Dialogue

One of the higher callings for young people in the coming century will be working to increase intercultural understanding. Such people will be the missionaries of the new age, spreading light among groups ... by giving them a modern vision of the new global community.

—Carl Coon

Neither war nor intergroup violence, unfortunately, are new in modern society. The scale of such events against civilian populations, along with the complexity of the impact on young people and thus the future of multiple societies, however, is unprecedented. During major conflicts, masses of people are regularly displaced and their communities destroyed, resulting in an increasing number of refugees and internally displaced persons (IDPs). Not only are youth often targeted during conflict, either as victims or child soldiers, but also their schooling is often disrupted, which can leave them as ideal targets for recruitment by terrorist organizations.

Traditional mechanisms at conflict management and resolution have often proven ineffective at addressing both the root causes of conflict and the immediate needs of the next generation of leaders—the youth. Greater attention needs to be given to strategies that create opportunities for young people in regions of conflict to develop greater trust and understanding of those on both sides of the issue if they are ever to gain the skills needed to live in harmony with their neighbors. This chapter considers one such program that brings young Israeli Jews and Palestinians in collaborative interaction while introducing concepts of intergroup interaction.

"We've been struggling in our region with misperception, miscommunication, hate, violence, and war for decades," Mohammed began, speaking to a group of American young people at a summer program in California. "Each

73

time one person is attacked in Israel or Palestine, there is retribution from the other side. Violence in each case leads to more violence—and a vicious cycle is established that never seems to end. Aren't we sick of this already?"

Then, he poses the most profound question to his young students. "How many of you are willing to put aside your preconceived ideas and listen to the other? I mean really take the time to listen to one another. Can you listen to their pain—because it's there on both sides of this conflict? We're all hurting, and for some reason people think that retribution will reduce their pain. Unfortunately, that only leads to more violence, and we all lose."

Mohammed sits back to let his words sink in for a while. The young people in this particular group are quiet and contemplative, as the heat of the day, as well as of the moment, simmers through the group. It is, after all, relatively early in the summer experience, only the second week of the camp. These young people are just beginning to get to know one another. After a long pause, Stephan finally speaks.

"I know when I was growing up in California," he offered, "I had very limited understanding of the conflict in the Middle East. I was raised in a Jewish community where I was taught that we were the good guys and we wore the white hats, and everyone else, meaning the Arabs, were the bad guys, and they wore the black hats. I'm sorry to say that I didn't even know who the Palestinians were. I was told that I could not trust people in the Arab community. I'm really glad to have the opportunity to learn firsthand from all of you what the reality of your lives is like."

"I feel really ignorant about your situation and rather guilty because I know so little," added Sarah, a sixteen-year-old camper who lived outside Washington, DC. "In the United States, we're somewhat protected from the pains and struggles of many of the world's people and don't have much of a clue about what's going on. I know many people stereotype others quite a lot. This camp experience is helping me to understand that all Arabs are not this way and all Jews are not that way. There's quite a bit of ignorance, but I do believe interest among Americans is changing."

"I am told that I cannot trust Jews anywhere in the world," Rema interjected. "I grew up in East Jerusalem, and my family, and entire community for that matter, filled me with stories of the atrocities that were directed toward our people simply because we were Palestinian. Some members of my family were shot during a recent confrontation in Jerusalem. Now, I'm considered a traitor by some in my community for wanting to spend time with this mixed group of Arabs, Jews, and Americans in the United States. They tell me that I cannot trust the motivations of most of you. That's what I'm struggling with right now. I want things to be different, but it's so hard."

Ibrahim, a young student from the West Bank town of Hebron, spoke next. "My major concern and reason for coming to the United States was to be a spokesman for my people. You are the future leaders of this country," he said, as he focused his gaze upon the Americans in the group. *"Some of you will be judging my future or my people's future some day. I want you to be informed so you are able to see all sides of a problem or situation."*

There was a lull in the conversation as Mohammed scanned the group. Looking around at one another, many were fidgeting and obviously uncomfortable.

"I heard the same things from my parents that Rema heard in her home," added Schmuel, an Israeli Jewish student from Rishon le Zion, a suburb of Tel Aviv. *"It wasn't until I was in high school and we spent a week at Neve Shalom that I began to seriously question what I was hearing at home and in my community. Until recently, I wanted all Arabs out of Israel. I thought that there was no way possible that we would ever be able to live side by side. I now think that it may be possible, although I don't quite know how! It's very frustrating and scary, especially at the moment."*

"What's Neve Shalom?" asked Natalie, a young Quaker participant from Chicago. *"And why did it give you such hope?"*

"Neve Shalom is a joint Arab–Jewish community composed of equal numbers of Arab families and Jewish families who are devoted to living together and learning one another's language, religion, and culture," replied Schmuel. *"There are about 30 families who live in the community, midway between Tel Aviv and Jerusalem. They also offer workshops and opportunities for outsiders to learn about their efforts and to explore the possibility of coexistence. I found it an extremely valuable and worthwhile experiment. Me and some friends from my high school spent a week there last year. That experience really inspired us and left me with a lot to think about."*

"Why do you think people are so afraid of trying and of trusting one another?" asked Mohammed. *"And what do you think can be done to change things?"*

Again, there was silence, the questions seemingly as profound and troubling as the situation itself.

"Again," Stephan offered, *"I may be rather naïve, but it seems to me that just doing what we're doing here today is a beginning. I know in my school when there is conflict between, say Blacks and Whites, teachers try to get both parties to sit down and talk about their differences. It doesn't always work, but at least it's an effort."*

"But it doesn't work like that in the region," Rema interjected, obviously becoming upset. *"It seems rather simplistic from your point of view, I suppose, why people don't just begin to talk to one another. But you don't understand the stress that we live under, the histories of our people, and their experiences with one another. Back home, we don't go to school with one*

another—we have separate schools for Jews and Arabs. And we don't live in the same communities like you do in the United States.

"I realize that here in the United States you have your tensions too, but they are different. Maybe young people in America worry about their parents getting divorced, they live among others who use drugs, they worry about what to study in college or who to date. I understand these are all stressors. Young people all over the world live under stress, but they are stressors of a different kind. I don't think you can truly understand the tensions we live under without experiencing it yourself. And I also understand, I think, the stress that Schmuel lives with. As an Israeli, both he and I know that when he returns home he will join the military and will probably be dispatched to the West Bank and have his weapons aimed at my people. How should I feel when I am here with him?"

She paused. "Schmuel, what will you do? I wish things were different. It is all very confusing." Rema sighed, as if she had been waiting to say something like this for a long time.

Schmuel was speechless, and a silence once again fell over the group.

And so begins the exploration, introspection, shift in perspective and bridge building that unfolds, layer by layer, as these young Americans struggle to gain a deeper understanding of the range of issues that face their peers in other countries while trying to develop trust in one another. Over time in such an environment, these young people grow in their understanding and appreciation of the tensions that exist among people, in their understanding of the role of culture on people's lives, and in their own knowledge and comfort in working across cultures as well as of their role as agents of change. New friendships develop over the summer weeks that, for many, evolve into continued relationships and new opportunities when they return home. It is a powerful and life-changing experience.

How can people learn to mediate among those who experience conflict in the world today? What role can young people play in bringing about peace in the world? How might people learn to reach out and touch those from communities that are in conflict? What is the potential for altering one's perception of the enemy? These are critical questions that in many ways underlie a significant amount of intercultural activity today, and adolescents may hold a critical key.

Perhaps more impactful than school-based international experiences are those that young people have during their summer holidays. The Legacy International Youth Program (recently renamed the Global Youth Village) is one such program that provides intensive international and intercultural learning experiences for young people from a variety of backgrounds. Nestled in the foothills of the Blue Ridge Mountains in southern Virginia and founded by educator, scholar, and humanitarian, J. E. Rash, Legacy is a living-learning center devoted to establishing an environment that provides young people with the opportunity to experience life in a global village.

Each summer, up to 200 young people from more than twenty countries leave their homes, some coming from homelands where they endure considerable hostility, to live with peers and learn firsthand about global problems and opportunities, conflict and communication across cultures, and leadership in a global context as well as social action. Legacy's special talent lies in creating an atmosphere where young people from regions in conflict, such as the Middle East, can come together in a safe space and learn how to see beyond the stereotypes and anxieties they are exposed to at home, ultimately building bonds of friendship and trust that are rather unique among their peers from their region. These young people actively build bridges where walls typically stand, a sign of hope that things can change and that adversaries from home may be able to shed some of their misunderstandings and begin to trust the "enemy."

It is not easy to establish such a setting, nor is it easy for some of the young people to be in such close contact with one another while they struggle to unlearn many of the hatreds that have become so ingrained at home. It can be equally difficult for others, even young Americans who may come from relatively privileged, peaceful, and secure environments, to witness and participate in the heated dialogues and conversations that take place between conflicting parties. But this is real life, and all become intimately connected with one another throughout the summer as the comfort level and sense of trust grow.

All participants must reach beyond their traditional zone of comfort as they learn about others' experiences, develop insight into the global condition, and struggle to understand how each can work to improve upon people's circumstances. One of the long-term goals of Legacy is for young people to become reflective, interculturally sensitive change agents in their communities when they return home—wherever home may be. Thus, in many respects, the entire Legacy experience is an exercise designed to broaden one's means of perception and thus prepare young people to function more effectively as global citizens.

Mohammed Darawshe is an Israeli Arab who was affiliated with Legacy from the mid-1980s through the mid-1990s. He was born, and still lives, in the north of Israel—in Iksal, a village that has such a long history that it is mentioned in the New Testament. About 60 percent of the residents of Iksal are related to one another. Iksal is located close to Kibbutz Mizra, a Jewish community founded in 1923 by a group of pioneers from Russia and known worldwide, ironically, for its exceptional sausage products. The city of Afula, an important development town founded in 1925 that serves as the market center of the Jezreel Valley, is nearby. Like most of Israel, this is an extremely culturally diverse region.

Mohammed is an activist, who still today, remains committed to establishing linkages between Arabs and Jews, believing that it is by developing mutual understanding and reconciliation that peace will ever come to this troubled region. He has made this his career, working tirelessly with young people as well as professionals from both sides of the conflict, encouraging them to set aside their differences and learn to listen intently to the pain, struggles, and experiences of the other.

During his time with the summer program, Mohammed could often be found sitting with mixed groups, encouraging them to rethink their present orientation, showing them how their present behavior and way of thinking serves to perpetuate problems and the status quo. He did this almost daily— the dialogue at the start of this chapter taking place with a group of young people who were preparing to attend a conference in the Mediterranean region later in the summer.

After years of evaluating the summer program in Virginia, Legacy had established a formula that proved quite successful at bringing opposing groups together. Believing they were now ready to try their program in the real-world setting of the Middle East, Legacy sponsored a unique project, the goal of which was to provide a context that would facilitate dialogue and the building of trust among young Israeli Jews, Israeli Arabs, and West Bank Palestinians. The context of an international setting was proposed that would demonstrate to others that it was possible for these parties to come together over a period of time; learn to trust and understand one another; and ultimately, collaborate in important and very real ways. It was during this particular summer that preparation was under way for this event.

Research on efforts to improve intergroup relations has steadily evolved over the past half century (Allport, 1954; Amir, 1969; Sherif, 1958; Stephan, 1999; Stephan & Vogt, 2004). Central to this research are a number of criteria that appear to be critical when attempting to bring opposing groups together, be they international adversaries or domestic groups in segregated settings. Legacy had, coincidentally, stumbled upon these criteria on their own, and it was reinforcing to find that what they were doing was supported in the research literature on intergroup relations. The criteria are collectively referred to as the Contact Hypothesis (Allport, 1954).

Four dimensions of the Contact Hypothesis have been identified that facilitate success in improving social contact and intergroup relations and thus reducing prejudice: (1) People should come together to achieve some superordinate goal or common task that could not be achieved without the collaborative efforts of all parties. (2) Individuals who come together should have equal status, meaning they have equal access to any rewards available.

(3) Administrative support should encourage collaborative efforts. (4) A high acquaintance potential should exist that encourages rather intimate contact between individuals in a given situation. Coincidentally, in addition to being addressed in the summer or other special programs, all of these factors have curricular implications for schools. They can also be integrated and applied in well-developed travel programs.

SUPERORDINATE GOALS

Individuals who come together and work toward achieving some superordinate goal or common task that could not be satisfied without the participation of all involved are more likely to learn to get along. This concept stems from the work of Sherif (1958), who worked, like Legacy, among children in summer camps.

Sherif found it relatively easy to create hostility and aggression between two groups of boys at summer camp, to the point that name-calling, food fights, and cabin raids at night were common. He found it quite difficult, however, to bring these groups of children back together again as one larger, cooperative group. After much trial and error, camp staff staged an incident in which a bus got stuck in the mud while on the way to an outing. For the bus to continue on its way, all of the campers had to work together to push the bus back onto the road. This superordinate goal, which could not have been achieved without everyone's participation, provided the means to bring the two opposing groups together.

Teachers can apply this in the school context in any number of ways. Superordinate goals are readily available in the form of team sports, drama productions, and music performances as well as through cooperative learning activities that can be easily integrated in the classroom setting. In the Legacy summer camp experience, numerous opportunities are present that encourage groups of young people, many who originate in countries in conflict, to come together to achieve some superordinate task.

In addition to the everyday needs of maintaining a certain degree of cleanliness and orderliness at camp, programming required these young people to collaborate in the preparation and presentation of a number of cultural programs depicting the people from their region of the world. Thus, Irish Catholics and Protestants would come together to make a presentation on Ireland and Irish culture, or Israeli Jews and Arabs would come together with the task of presenting a balanced view of their part of the world.

Although never easy, over the weeks these young people inevitably worked through their differences as well as their apprehensions and developed a level of trust and friendship among one another that could not have been achieved in their homeland. In the process, they also learned a significant amount about each other's culture, their particular circumstances, and the chance for peace and reconciliation.

EQUAL STATUS CONTACT

Working in integrated school settings in Israel, Amir (1969) found that if individuals coming together perceive that they have equal status, or equal access to any rewards available, conditions are set for improved relations. Travelers who look closely at the social fabric in many countries find that although given equal status on paper, many citizens of a particular country may not, in reality, have all the benefits afforded others in that particular nation. This was certainly evident under segregation in the American South until the Civil Rights Movement took hold in the 1960s, under Apartheid in South Africa until the early 1990s, or in some countries of the Middle East.

Visitors to Switzerland, on the other hand, quickly learn that French, German, and Italian are all recognized as official languages of the country, with official documents and most communication to the public made available in all three languages. Similarly, in Canada, French and English are both recognized as official languages. In these nations, speakers of diverse languages, and thus cultural backgrounds, are all valued, kept informed, and encouraged to participate in the society at large. Such a practice seems quite different in the United States, where the movement in many states has been to make English the official language—even though the United States boasts the fourth or fifth largest Spanish-speaking population in the world.

In the summer camp setting of Legacy, young people share cabins as well as daily chores with others from around the world. Legacy works hard to bring an equalizing force to all of the participants, believing that not only should the young people from overseas experience culture shock, but the American participants should as well. Thus, all participants are provided a vegetarian, natural foods diet—something to which all have to stretch and adjust. It is a leveling experience, providing all with something to learn and experience together. And by reducing the sugars and dyes from many foods, young people's energy levels change dramatically, and they are better able to engage in long dialogue with one another about some very sensitive topics.

On a global scale, the environment is perhaps the most visible or tangible evidence we have that demonstrates how all forms of life are interconnected. It was with this in mind that Legacy, very wisely, chose the environmental condition of the Mediterranean Sea as a common theme to explore for a summer conference, a superordinate task, so to speak, something that could bring Arabs and Jews as well as others in the region together.

But bringing Arabs and Jews together for such a program had never before been successfully achieved. Here is where the subtlety and power of the summer program came into play and how it served as an orientation and preparation for something greater. Legacy invited four youth leaders between the ages of sixteen and twenty-one from most of the nations that border the Mediterranean to an environmental conference in Cartagena, Spain, to learn about the broader region and consider long-term, joint activities. So it was that a number of young people from such countries as France, Spain, Italy, Greece, Turkey, Lebanon, Israel, Morocco, Egypt, the United States, and Jordan joined together for a week to learn and live together.

A frequent message often promoted by Legacy was "What appears to be primary may actually be secondary, and what appears to be secondary may actually be primary." Thus, although on the surface this conference would appear to be of environmental concern, and in fact that was its emphasis, the primary purpose of the effort that was at work behind the scenes was to create a venue that brought Arabs and Jews together in a collaborative, equal-status project. Thus, what appeared to be primary, the environmental conference, actually was secondary, and what appeared to be secondary, the bringing together of people from different backgrounds, actually was the primary purpose of the event.

In the school context, equal access to rewards can mean that all students have equal access to knowledge as well as extracurricular offerings. Teachers who are sensitive to this are more inclined to employ culturally relevant curricula and instructional strategies in the classroom, thus assuring that more students achieve. Of equal importance is the necessity to encourage all students to participate in extracurricular activities in school—of which travel may be included. But because of the inequities in the socioeconomic status among many children in schools, those from lower social groups may never have the opportunity to participate in after-school activities, let alone travel programs. They thus do not gain the benefits these offerings provide.

Administrative support must exist. To be effective, efforts to reduce prejudice and improve intergroup relations must be seen as important at all levels of an organization. Such efforts cannot be seen entirely as the whim or "cause" of a particular group or individual. In the context of the Legacy summer program, counselors and administrators always focused their attention on dialogue and making evident to all how people should come together to discuss their differences. In the school context, teachers and school administrators must actively encourage and show support for such efforts.

HIGH ACQUAINTANCE POTENTIAL

A fourth tenet from the Contact Hypothesis is that people should come together in such a way that they have intimate, close contact with one another. In this way, people get to know one another beyond the stereotypes that may prevail.

It was obvious how this was attained during the summer program because participants shared common living quarters, meals, recreational time, and so forth. To guarantee success at the conference in Spain, Legacy planned to seed the project by introducing a significant number of participants to one another before the larger gathering took place. Thus, ten American alumni from the summer program traveled to both Egypt and Israel prior to the conference to serve as bridge builders.

In Egypt, the American participants joined a group of ten Egyptian young people, where they spent a week in Cairo and the Sinai studying Egyptian culture and learning about the local environment while simultaneously bonding as a group. From Egypt, the group of Americans traveled to Israel and joined a group of ten Israeli Jewish and ten Palestinian young people from various communities in Israel and the West Bank. Together, this group studied one another's cultures and learned about the environment of the region. It was then that representatives from these groups who had already developed a comfort level would travel to the conference site in Spain, where representatives from the other nations would join them.

It was in Israel a few weeks before the conference that the American team from Legacy, a group that included Stephan and Sarah, was reunited with Rema, Ibrahim, and Schmuel along with a few others who had attended Legacy in previous summers. This group was warm and welcoming from the outset, and the new Jewish and Arab participants who joined them from the region found it easy to fit in. The group in Israel now numbered about thirty.

In Israel, while actively studying the local environment of the Negev, the young people were also engaged in a number of cultural encounters designed to enhance everyone's understanding of Arab and Jewish culture as well as the conflicts inherent in the region. The program was to include visits to Arab villages and Jewish communities as well as an experience in Jerusalem.

An underlying objective was for the American participants to serve as a bridge and assist these Jewish and Arab young people to get to know one another beyond the stereotypes that were rampant in their lives. For the most part, as Rema had hinted back at Legacy, Arab villages and Jewish communities remain rather isolated from one another, with interaction restricted to brief encounters in the marketplace or perhaps in a work setting. Children in both communities, even though in close proximity, grow up having limited if any contact with one another. As a result of having little substantial firsthand information about the other, stereotypes and anxieties that are learned in their respective communities are perpetuated.

After the first week of environmental education in Israel and once a certain level of trust and friendship had been established, the program turned its focus to that of culture and the cross-cultural experience. The goal of this effort was to get to a point where the young people could spend a couple of nights with families in one another's communities. That is, Jewish young people would spend a few nights in an Arab village, and Arab youth would spend the same amount of time with Jewish families.

Very quickly those enjoyable and friendly times spent outdoors and in various activities with the "other" became extremely stressful as each began thinking about what it would be like to live in the other's home. Some had visions of being kidnapped in the night or beaten and robbed by others in the community; that's how strong the stereotypes and fear of the other had become. Anxiety aside, they all went off to their respective host families with their characteristic openness and trust.

After the homestay, the group came together to share their experiences. Schmuel was among the first to discuss his feelings about the homestay during a debriefing session.

"I really wasn't too concerned about staying in the village when we had planned this portion of the trip," he said. "After all, during the summer I had become rather close to Rema and a few of the other participants. I trusted her and truly believed she was a friend. But when we got to the village, I suddenly realized that this was not Rema's home. No one there knew anything about me, and I would have to begin at step one in establishing a relationship.

"The family was welcoming, and the food was fabulous. I was surprised that I found quite a few similarities between our two cultures. What shocked me, though, was how anxious and nervous I became, and to be honest, I had trouble sleeping the first night. The sounds outside my window were different, some of the smells in the house were not familiar, and I was not quite sure what would happen in the morning.

"I was pleasantly surprised when I woke up. Many from the extended family were coming in and out of the house all morning long, I think, in part to interact with me because I was somewhat of an oddity. I was a bit nervous and unsure throughout most of the morning. And to be honest, I was really looking forward to when we would all get together that afternoon. But it all went well. And I really enjoyed the wedding celebration we were able to observe the final night in the village."

J. E. Rash, founder of Legacy and program director for much of the Israel experience, spoke next. "What kinds of conversations did you have with members of the families or others in the communities? And what did you learn from them?"

Ibrahim reflected calmly, "It was awkward at first. We talked about lots of surface things—similarities in food and language, for instance, just like Schmuel said."

"We typically refer to that as surface-level, or objective, culture," offered Rash, listening intently. "Objective culture refers to those aspects of a people that are visible or tangible, things that are on the surface and easy to see and discuss. The more powerful aspects of culture, though, are its hidden, more subjective elements, sometimes referred to as deep culture. Here, we are talking about such things as people's values, their attitudes, and the way they interact with one another. These are much more difficult to get out on the table and discuss. But they are a critical dimension of all people and their interactions."

"Well," Ibrahim continued, "we eventually began to talk about the current conflict, but I had to bring it up. Up until that time, we were all being polite to one another. I asked the father what he felt about the current situation."

"And what did he say?" asked Rash.

"He felt that we are all suffering under the current circumstances, and he blamed the leaders on both sides. He believed that most of the people really want peace and that they were willing to negotiate a just settlement. He was very concerned about the recent increase in what he called terrorist attacks. I tried to help him see that my people consider what the Israeli's are doing as terrorist activities. He couldn't see that, however. But he was obviously interested and willing to talk with us. He truly wanted to learn about my family and how we are coping with the situation. I felt good about that. I guess it was a beginning."

Schmuel spoke up again.

"I learned quite a lot from my host family. I have never really spent much time with an Arab family. They too were very hospitable. I'd say everything I'd ever heard about Arab hospitality was true, and after a while I felt quite comfortable. I was uncomfortable bringing up the topic of the conflict, but the father and his brothers were not. They didn't seem angry at me, but they did speak quite heatedly about the situation.

"This is really the first time I had ever spoken face-to-face with Palestinian families that were affected by the situation. They told me that their family village was destroyed after the war in 1948. Some of their family had moved to Jordan, some were killed in the conflict, and others remained in Israel. It's been very difficult for them to remain together and keep in touch, and they really feel displaced by all the problems."

Schmuel continued. "They did say that they understood the need for a Jewish state, especially after the Holocaust. But they also insisted that all the people in Israel could live together, side by side, and that perhaps we all had an obligation to learn to do this as a model for the rest of the world. I was quite taken by that thought. I'd never really thought Arabs could feel that way."

Then, Rema spoke. "I had similar feelings when we stayed with the Jewish families. It took a while, but I was finally able to relax and feel comfortable. The kids in the family were nice enough, but you could tell that they too were unsure of things and how the few days would be. I'm glad I had the opportunity to stay with them.

"We talked a bit about the conflict. The younger kids in the family, once they spoke up, began to blame me for the current situation. I guess I can understand that from the perspective of a young child; if there was any blame to give, it would be targeted at me because I was a Palestinian in their community and seen as the enemy. The parents, however, quickly jumped into the conversation and helped their children see things from another point of view."

J. E. Rash posed one final question, this one particularly for the Americans to consider: "I want you all to think about your role in perpetuating or resolving this conflict—especially the Americans. What will you do once you return home?"

It was on Thursday, around lunchtime, when the group traveled on toward Jerusalem. It was here that they would spend the last three days in Israel before departing for the conference in Spain. There was a sense of anticipation among all. For both the Jewish and Arab participants, Jerusalem represents one of the most important sites for both Judaism and Islam. For the Americans, both Jewish and Gentile, it was their first experience in this city that reflects so much controversy.

Jerusalem may be the holiest city in the world, considering the number and diversity of people who refer to it as their sacred place. For Jews, it is the site of Solomon's Temple, the City of David, and the capital of the Israelite nation. For Christians, it is where Jesus spent the last days of his ministry and where the Last Supper, the Crucifixion, and the Resurrection took place. And for Muslims, Jerusalem is where the prophet Mohammed ascended to heaven.

Although visited by thousands of pilgrims and sages each year from all three of these major religions, it has experienced thirty centuries of struggle and strife. Although it is a place of beauty and divinity, it is also a place of mystery and paradox—and a city of contradictions. Referred to by many, ironically, as the City of Peace, Jerusalem has a history of conflict that rivals most anyplace in the world, crying out during its troubled history.

I had visited Jerusalem a few times prior to this visit but not with all the tensions and concerns of the moment, there having been a major confrontation in the West Bank just two days earlier. And never had I been in the city with a mixed group of Arabs and Jews. There was a silence on the bus as we drove along the highway from Tel Aviv. There are repeated reminders of the struggles and the Jewish lives that have been lost while passing, on both sides of the road, the remains of military vehicles and monuments to fallen soldiers. I wondered how our Arab participants felt as we made our way toward the city. One passes no such reminders of Arab losses, and there are no memorials along the road when one enters Jerusalem from other directions.

Looking out over the city from the Mount of Olives is an awe-inspiring sight because from this vantage point, one can see directly to the Old City with the Dome of the Rock glistening brightly in the sunlight. After posing for a number of photos with Jerusalem at our backs, the group drove down toward the Old City. Upon entering the Old City, one can immediately sense the tensions as well as the possibilities that permeate the entire region.

Old Jerusalem is divided into four quarters—an Armenian sector, a Christian sector, a Muslim sector, and a Jewish sector. One can find almost anything, from the freshest of foods and spices, to leather goods, musical instruments, fine clothes, and jewelry, amidst the hundreds of shops that line the narrow streets. Shopkeepers and shoppers alike banter back and forth as they seek to agree upon a fair price for the goods and services available. Meandering among these close quarters, one is just as likely to rub elbows with an Orthodox Jewish seminary student, a devout Muslim cleric, a religious Christian on a pilgrimage, or young students from all walks of life wearing their uniform T-shirt and jeans.

The Dung gate, one of the seven entry points to the Old City, so-called because it is from here that garbage was removed from the city in earlier times, opens to the Jewish Quarter. Entering amidst tight security, one can't help but take notice of the Western Wall. Located in the midst of the Jewish Quarter, this is the section of the Western supporting wall of the Temple Mount that has remained intact since the destruction of the Second Temple in 70 CE. Since about 1520, all literary sources describe it as a place of assembly and prayer for Jews. Thus, it has become the most sacred spot in Jewish consciousness and tradition, being a center of mourning over the destruction of the Temple. Since then it has been known as the Wailing Wall.

From 1948 until 1967, Jews had no access to this area. After regaining control of the Old City, the area in front of the Western Wall was cleared and converted into a large, paved, open space. The lower square near the Wall is an area set aside for prayer where one finds Jews praying or studying, either singly or in groups, both day and night. Hands that have touched the wall in prayer throughout the centuries seem to have polished the surface of the stone. Today, it is even possible to fax or e-mail your prayer to individuals and groups who will insert them in the wall. Thus, prayers from around the world find their way to the Wall each and every day in a kind of technology-to-theology connection.

Just over the Western Wall lies the Dome of the Rock with its golden dome that can be seen lighting up the Old City from most anywhere. The tenth Caliph, Abd al-Malik ibn Marwan, built the great Dome of the Rock between 687 and 691 as a shrine for pilgrims. Perhaps the greatest monumental building in early Islamic history, it stands twenty meters high and ten meters in diameter. This reportedly is the spot from which Mohammed ascended to heaven. Originally covered in pure gold, today its anodized aluminum skin is seen from miles around. Adjacent to the Dome is the Al-Aqsa Mosque.

As we arrived at the Wailing Wall, both men and women, separated from one another, were worshipping. A few of our participants, Stephan among them, approached the Wall to offer prayers. A few tourists could be seen having their Bar Mitzvah at this sacred site. We could hear the afternoon call to prayer coming from over the wall, and a few of the Muslim members of our group went to pray. At the time of this visit, one could still move freely between the sites. It is, unfortunately, forbidden today.

The spiritual energy of this region has been enriched by the many different groups that have laid claim to the city over the centuries as well as by the many individuals who continue to be drawn to it. This is, by all means, a sacred site, with an infectious power that seems to radiate such force that no modern spiritual seeker should fail to miss.

All the young participants were moved by the experience of the afternoon, and this served as a backdrop for the last two days in Israel. The spiritual underpinnings, although discussed only briefly, seemed to permeate the group as they prepared for travel to the conference site in Spain. There was much discussion among the Israelis and Palestinians in the group about what they would do when they returned from the conference.

Rema began. "When I stayed with the Jewish family, we talked about the possibility of meeting once we returned from the conference. I think my parents would even be interested in the possibility of meeting with the family. And the children and I talked about the possibility of getting our schools to do some joint activity."

"And Ibrahim and I talked about doing something similar when we get back," added Schmuel. "Once he gets his driver's license and saves some money from working, we're going to visit one another. I'm excited about that possibility. In our own reality at home, this would never seem possible. Now that we've had these summer experiences, I think other things might be promising."

Sarah finally spoke up. "I guess this has been a real dose of reality for me. I continually have to challenge the stereotypes I grew up with, and I guess that's a good thing. But it sure is difficult, not really having much of a background in these affairs. This experience has opened my eyes up to so much, and I'm glad I had a chance to participate in it. I feel emotionally exhausted but refreshed and enriched nonetheless. I hope I have the energy to sustain myself during the conference in Spain."

Although not naïve to the tensions that continue to exist in the years since these early meetings occurred, there still are signs of hope. It is very satisfying to turn on CNN, for instance, and see some of these former participants being interviewed, still expressing optimism and hope that things can improve. Many of these young people, now young adults, continue to work toward reconciliation and understanding. This alone is an important lesson for us all.

Chapter 8 ✯

Global Learning: How International Student Teachers Grow into World Class Educators

Martha Lash and Justine DeFrancesco

Travel—leaves you speechless and then turns you into a storyteller.

—Ibn Battuta (1304–1369)

In spite of significant effort in recent decades to diversify the US teaching force, American teachers, teacher educators, and teacher education students continue to be relatively homogeneous and interculturally inexperienced, and this trend is likely to continue well into the future (Cushner, McClelland, & Safford, 2018; Zimpher, 1989). Approximately 85 percent of the US teaching force is European American and middle class, and almost two-thirds, female. These demographics are similar in many other countries of the world as well, with the majority of teachers in such countries as Australia, Canada, Great Britain, New Zealand, and the Netherlands reflecting the majority culture of the nation—even with the increasing cultural diversity that is found in all of these nations.

Teachers, as well as those who are studying to be teachers, at least in the United States, continue to be relatively cross-culturally inexperienced, having limited knowledge and experience living or working with other cultures. Close to 70 percent of White teacher education students reportedly spend all or most of their free time with people of their own racial or ethnic background. Particularly alarming is the fact that the majority of teachers have limited expectations for the success of all of their students, believing that low-income and minority students are not capable of learning the higher-level concepts in the subjects they are preparing to teach.

Teachers also tend to be linguistically limited, with fewer than 10 percent claiming fluency in any second language and fully three-fifths being monolingual—and that with the United States being the fourth or fifth largest

Spanish-speaking country in the world! The majority of teacher candidates live within 100 miles of where they were born, with most wishing to teach where they grew up or in areas very similar to where they are from. And of all college majors, teacher education students tend to have the least knowledge and interest in international affairs.

Although there may not be much optimism in this information, there are increasing efforts to internationalize teacher education. This chapter explores the experience of those who embark on an international student teaching venture through COST, the Consortium for Overseas Student Teaching, an organization directed by Ken Cushner from 1995–2000 and again from 2011–2014. These future teachers are taking the first steps toward becoming more interculturally sensitive and are fast becoming world-class educators as they immerse themselves into a new culture, learning to adjust not only interpersonally but professionally and then working when they return home to integrate an international perspective to the students in their charge.

COST is one small group working hard to give US student teachers a meaningful, professional overseas experience. Since its inception in 1972, hundreds of American students have had the opportunity to teach in national schools in such countries as England, Scotland, Ireland, Wales, Australia, New Zealand, South Africa, Canada, the Netherlands, and the Bahamas as well as in international English-speaking schools in such countries as Switzerland, Greece, Italy, China, Mexico, Ecuador, Spain, and Costa Rica. For most of these students, teaching abroad for eight to fifteen weeks is a life-changing and career-altering experience (Cushner, 2009; Cushner, 2014; Cushner & Brennan, 2007; Cushner & Mahon, 2002; Cushner & Mahon, 2009).

The focus of this chapter will be on the experiences of six US overseas student teachers: Jacob and Emily teaching in South Africa, Chris teaching in the Netherlands, Carolyn teaching in Mexico, Morgan teaching in Australia, and Justine teaching in New Zealand (and a coauthor of this chapter). We follow a number of their blog posts in response to questions posed by their university coordinator and other coauthor of this chapter, Dr. Lash. As their journeys unfold, students are challenged to dig deeper into their experience, sharing their cultural observations, new educational understandings, and overall reflections on their individual sojourns with one another through this shared blog.

TO: All Overseas Student Teachers

FROM: Dr. Lash

RE: Why student teach nearby when you can Student Teach Overseas?

DATE: September 2

Congratulations, you have safely arrived in your countries, met your homestay families or settled into an apartment, checked in at your schools, met your students, and are starting to answer (or question) the subject line of this group e-mail. You most likely have had initial waves of culture or adjustment shock and are beginning to acclimate. How do these real experiences compare to your preconceptions of your host country and its people?

Although I know you are excited and recovering from jet lag, I do want to check in and remind you that occasional feelings of loneliness or anxiety are not unusual as you travel and immerse yourself within another cultural context. Although we had talked about this before you departed, it can be quite different once you find yourself immersed in the experience. Please know that international travelers frequently experience loneliness, some anxiety, and a range of adjustment challenges. Those feelings don't last throughout the experience, but it is normal to have occasional pangs that you'll need to push through. Working through these struggles can help you clarify your priorities as well as your understanding of the greater world in which we live.

Have you had any similar feelings or struggles? Have you had times of feeling sorry for yourself? What may have brought this on? What did you do to overcome this? I say this to reassure you that if you are having these feelings, they are normal. It might help to blog about these, and of course you can send me a private e-mail or reach out to your fellow student teachers.

Sharing a group overseas student teaching blog will have the advantage of multiple voices from other student teachers worldwide who are having a shared, yet individual, international experience. It will be interesting to share commonalities and differences and to see what different ways of learning, understanding, and knowing we each encounter, struggle to understand, and ultimately practice. It is important to reflect on our experiences because reflection "seals" the learning by challenging us to examine our experiences and conclusions into a higher order of metacognition. By examining our experiences collectively, we can use this reflective process to consolidate and solidify our cultural and teaching experiences.

I'm posing the first blog query as a series of questions to act as provocations for reflection of your new and varied experiences. Don't worry about reflecting on all of these—choose one or two ideas or questions that resonate with you.

What and how are you learning about your new country, culture, school and/or students? How are you acclimating to the local terrain? What sources of information are most helpful and reliable in helping you to make sense of your new surroundings? What sources do you trust and why? How did the advance review of websites, readings, speaking with others, and films help to prepare you? Did you find these strategies accurate or useful? What stereotypes have you dispelled, and which ones might be taking their place? What cross-cultural and travel advice do you wish you knew before you arrived? Basically, what are your real experiences, and how do they compare to your preconceptions of your host country, people, and schools?

BLOG RESPONSES

Student: Chris
Placement: Amsterdam, the Netherlands
Date: September 4
RE: I made it … and some half-asleep airplane thoughts

I'm not in the classroom yet, but I am sitting at my desk in my new room at my host family's house in the Netherlands! Now, on to my first experience with a person with a very different culture than that of my own … someone I met in the airport. Before I arrived at JFK, I promised my mother that I would find a glass of wine, some food, and make a friend … his name ended up being Alfred (he was my waiter), and he was originally from the Philippines.

Before I even had the chance to ask him something, he said with a full smile, "This year has really been my year!" I asked him why, and he replied something like this, "Well, working this job you get to talk to a lot of people. Some are great and have wonderful things to say and others not so much … but I've realized this year, I've just matured. I know everyone likes to talk but also everyone really likes to listen, and if you let go of worry and just hear what's around you, you can find yourself—at least that's what happened to me this year. Anyways, wanna be Instagram friends?"

As I write now from memory, I think about all of the expectations I have for this student teaching experience. Before leaving the States, my professors and COST coordinator advised me to let go of all expectations, and yet as Alfred searched for my profile on Instagram, I couldn't help but feel all of my expectations flooding back into my mind. This person who I had just met moments ago had the ability to say something so incredible and moving that his words forced one small expectation to resurface. As he walked back to the kitchen, I thought to myself, I hope my mentor teacher is as open minded and thoughtful as he is.

With that, I realized I had never really let go of all expectations but just prepared myself for this trip by saying, don't expect the absolute best from every person you encounter but expect the absolute best from yourself and somehow, someway, happiness and learning will follow. I always try my best to adhere to the advice I receive from mentors and friends, but even with this consideration, I find myself sitting here in my new room in the Netherlands, waiting for my alarm to go off for my first day teaching at my field placement, and all I can think about is what I expect tomorrow to be like.

I expect the school community within my placement to work collaboratively on common goals for our students while also creating various avenues for each child to take to achieve them. I'm imagining my students enthralled in the work that I plan for them and to be just as inspired by this experience as I am. Finally, I expect my overseas coordinator, professors back home, and colleagues working on finishing their last semester of student teaching to "have my back" and support my endeavors to the best of their abilities.

Writing out my expectations for this trip feels quite odd to me, especially when I consider the expectations I have for myself. My main goal is to make a consistent effort to consciously consider what I expect from myself and then attempt to reach a little bit further, challenging my personal and professional knowledge every day at my field placement. This goal makes me certain that this trip will be all that everyone has told me it will be. No matter the situation or experience I have in this school and in this country, I know I'll be changed by the learning that happens here. And when I'm in my own classroom thinking back to this experience, I will remember the moments of frustration, loneliness, confusion, happiness, understanding, and contentment, and every success tied to these emotions will inspire me to keep going, keep motivating, and continue learning.

All in all, I guess I have to let go of some expectations. I'm not sure what will happen tomorrow when I walk through the doors of my new field placement in this country that is entirely new to me, but I do know one thing for certain. I expect to grow, somehow and in some way, and I will become better because of this experience teaching abroad. I guess I'll have to wait and see, and so will you!

Until next time,
Chris

Student: Carolyn
Placement: Guadalajara, Mexico
Date: September 10
RE: I'm adjusting

Because I'm still in North America, I wasn't quite sure how international my experience would be. I can already say—it is very international. Signs, street conversation, food, music, and transportation might all be considered the surface-level parts of the culture, but it feels like full immersion to me. I can easily spend the day in Guadalajara without seeing anyone from the

States or hearing English. When I go to the school, it is a relief to hear English and to speak easily with others. I'm thankful that this school uses English as the language of instruction; otherwise I couldn't participate!

I'm at a disadvantage though because everyone else also speaks Spanish fluently. Whenever coteachers take me into the community, they immediately become my link—my translators for language and culture. I'm dependent on them—at least for now. I'm hoping to meet someone to hang out with outside of school; it would be nice to make a friend who might know a little English or is bilingual in Spanish and English.

Before leaving, I was worried I might not make any friends and might not have much to do outside of school-related activities. Everyone here seems very helpful and friendly so far, especially with the language barrier, so I feel less worried about this right now. I haven't really had a moment to feel lonely yet because I'm so busy getting to know my new community and the staff and students at my school.

I think of all the host countries, and Mexico was probably the one that I was most familiar with because it borders the States, we hear about it in the news a lot—trade, resorts, walls, drugs—in other words, I had information but a number of misconceptions as well. First, I feel really safe in the parts of the city where I live and shop, and certainly the school and the children seem relaxed and safe. This doesn't live up to the stereotypic image I or many other Americans have of Mexico—people are busy working and taking care of their families, barbecuing, and going to the park, just like back home.

I wonder if others are experiencing something like this, that once "here," it really is different from what was expected. I think you referred to this once as disconfirmed expectations! One thing I have discovered is the availability of fresh fruit and vegetables that are really juicy, delicious, and affordable at the markets. And I almost forgot to say, the open-air markets are fabulous and fun—I'm even learning to enjoy bartering. My first weeks here are positive, my stereotypes have been challenged, and I'm excited to teach in a beautiful school where the children wear uniforms and eat lunch outside at picnic tables EVERY DAY—that's their cafeteria! I'm adjusting—and loving it!

Adios, Carolyn

Student: Jacob
Placement: Port Elizabeth, South Africa
Date: September 12
RE: From student to US representative

I've often had to defend American policies and actions since I've arrived in South Africa. There is considerable criticism of how the United States seems to impose itself in many countries overseas and, especially now, on how the United States seems to be pulling its support away from many parts of the world. There is a lot of controversy over the price of prescriptive medications to fight AIDS here, for instance. The whole world says it's concerned about the high incidence of AIDS in Southern Africa, but the drug companies seem to be fighting really hard to keep the prices so high that few Africans can afford them. I don't necessarily agree with these practices, but I've had to explain them more than once.

America's poor record of involvement in the Palestinian–Israeli conflict seems to be a special concern here, especially given the US response to Apartheid a few decades ago. And to many people here, our actions in Iraq, Afghanistan, and elsewhere are suspect, and I've had to explain our policies and actions even though I don't always agree with them. It's hard at times, and now that I'm living here and experiencing this, I'm realizing nothing really prepared me for this responsibility. It's like whenever anything big happens in the world, people come right over to me and ask for my insights, and oftentimes I can't give them an answer that satisfies them. I never expected to experience something like this, and I wish was better prepared for this before leaving.

I'm going to reiterate what Dr. Lash suggested in our orientation—that others planning to live overseas become more knowledgeable about world affairs as well as what's going on within our own country before leaving for their journey. Read the *New York Times* or *Time* magazine, download news apps on your phone and check these or at least the headlines daily, or watch the news and listen to it on the radio. Do this for weeks before you leave so you can speak, rather intelligently, about things going on in the world.

A representative with a bit of social and political culture shock,

Jacob

TO: All Overseas Student Teachers
FROM: Dr. Lash
RE: He Said, She Said … I Said, They Said …
DATE: September 15

I appreciate the optimism, open-mindedness, and willingness to sift through the ambiguity that is emanating from your blogs and e-mails. This mindset is a good one to anchor yourself to as you continue to acclimate, learn, and process things as you settle in to your new country and culture. It is fairly common to be misunderstood in words, and that is one of the major tasks in learning to communicate in any setting and especially now that you are doing this in international schools, homes, and community settings.

There are a variety of expectations put on each of you by the citizens in your host countries. It sounds as if some of you may have also become more knowledgeable about US policies and practices, or at least the perception of them, from another perspective. Keeping up to date with US policies and political happenings cannot only help you to be more knowledgeable but also can help to facilitate conversation and dialogue with others.

Jacob reminded us about what we talked about in orientation—that many others in the world are much more conversant in global affairs and that if you wanted to be considered one of the ingroup, it was in your best interest to keep abreast of current events. It sounds as if Jacob has been called on to be a US representative on the most emotional, controversial, and current issues of US world involvement in global conflicts as well as HIV/AIDS. Remember, it isn't too late to download an app for various news agencies and to read the headline stories daily—just like the citizens in your host country are doing.

While we are on this topic, let's remember that knowing about your host country's cultural, social, and legal rules can further your relationships and ensure your safety. Remember the university student from our own state of Ohio that we discussed? Otto Warmbier, a University of Virginia under-graduate student, was enrolled in a study abroad program when he opted to take a side trip to North Korea for five days. As Otto was boarding his flight to leave that country, he was detained by the North Korean government who claimed Otto went to a restricted area of his hotel and stole a poster with a photo of North Korea's leader, Kim Jong-un. In North Korea, it is a serious offense to harm or steal items with the name or image of the leader, and Otto was subsequently sentenced to fifteen years of hard labor.

Taken into custody as a healthy and bright twenty-one-year-old, he was released seventeen months later and returned to his home in Ohio as a weakened twenty-two-year-old man, in a coma and state of unresponsive wakefulness. He died a few days later on home soil. Although this may be an extreme example, it is a current example of the possible perils of not understanding the cultural rules in oppressive regimes. In our country, an apology and return of the poster might be an appropriate response, and the issue would never appear in a courtroom. Otto, in Korean court, made a tearful apology to the Korean government (possibly coerced) but no doubt heartfelt in some sense, then to receive a sentence of fifteen years of hard labor. Again, this is thankfully an extreme case and not common, but it can serve to remind us of the importance of understanding and abiding by cultural norms and legal expectations.

Has anyone had their actions or intentions misunderstood? Intentions are particularly harder concepts to share and explain. What are your experiences with language, actions, and/or intentions? Have you been understood, misunderstood, or perhaps misconstrued? How did you initially respond, and how else might you have responded? Have you had to interpret your own culture to others? In retrospect, what might you do differently in the future?

BLOG RESPONSES

Student: Justine
Placement: Auckland, New Zealand
Date: September 17
RE: My first day on the job

Before I get into my first experiences of teaching in a year three classroom (equivalent to that of a second grade classroom in the United States), I need you all to know some important facts I've learned that are in tune with the posed questions. The following list is made up of words, phrases, and general details about the area that I have discovered since my arrival in New Zealand a few weeks ago.

1. The way US citizens pronounce the word *water* is utterly hilarious to my year threes, my teacher, and basically the entire faculty at my school.
2. The pharmacy is referred to as the chemist.
3. The wind is so fierce here I woke up at three in the morning because I was afraid I was experiencing an actual tornado. The entire house shook.
4. Sandals are jandals.
5. Students like huggies, not hugs.
6. Cross country is morning gym class.
7. Peppers are capsicums.
8. Children and adults walk around the city and school barefoot.
9. I have yet to see one shred of litter on the ground.
10. And my personal favorite, snack time is teatime. Teatime is a twenty-minute morning break the entire school takes between arrival and lunch—about 10:20. The teachers come together in the kitchen (lounge) and drink tea or coffee and sometimes eat some biscuits (cookies) or fruit. While we eat, we discuss our plans for the day or week and collaborate on ideas. During this time, students have a snack and play on the school grounds with two teachers supervising the entire school of students. This is one thing I already think US schools should adopt!

Like any first day of student teaching, my morning started with my introduction. Unlike any of my past introductions, today's greeting started out in a very special way. I sat down entirely prepared and believing I would say my name, where I'm from, tell them how excited I was to be learning with them in the next few months, and so on. I sat down, and almost immediately the entire room fell silent. As educators, we know that a room full of twenty-eight students falling silent simultaneously without any warning or suggestion is not the norm.

Luckily within seconds, a boy broke the silence. First, we made eye contact … I smiled … he smiled … he turned red and blurted, "Say water!" Following this, the entire class started buzzing, laughing, and turning to me for a response. With my brows furrowed and squinted, I scanned the students, leaned forward, and said, "Wader." The entire classroom burst into laughter, and after my hello ended, we were on with our day.

As my students started on their morning work, I experienced the following two conversations:

Student A: "Did you know that water in Sweden you say with a v?"

Me: "No, I didn't! So vader?"

Student A: (laughing) "No, like this, vatah. I know because I was born there."

Student B: "I spell color like you!"

Me: "Oh really, how do you spell it?"

Student B: "C-O-L-O-R."

Me: "And how do your classmates spell it?"

Student B: "C-O-L-O-U-R. It's because I'm from China and we spell it like the USA."

Soon enough, the students gathered on the carpet in front of my mentor teacher, and she grabbed a book from behind her whiteboard easel. She took it out and said, "Time for 'The BFG.'" I recognized the novel instantly. "The BFG" is an amazing story that my mother reads every year in her third grade classroom back in the United States. As I listened to my mentor teacher read, I kept an eye on our students' faces. Most were engaged and mesmerized by one of the main characters—Mrs. Clonker and her footsteps through the hall—and a few students were poking at one another and making silly faces, both but moments away from being pulled back into the story.

I took in this moment and felt a sigh of relief. All of these amazing differences and experiences were occurring that I was so enchanted by and enthralled in that I hadn't even realized that I might miss home. So for those fifteen minutes of reading, I completely immersed myself into the moment, and it was incredible. One-half of my heart was in Ohio in my mother's classroom, and the other half, here in my new home in Auckland, New Zealand, learning alongside my new students. It was a nice reminder of home and a great connection to make in this new place with my very new family. Even here on the other side of the world, you can find people, places, and things that are not only entirely new to you but simultaneously remind you of the amazing people, places, and things that you have known all your life.

Eager to continue learning tomorrow,
Justine

Student: Chris
Placement: Amsterdam, the Netherlands
Date: September 28
RE: Aboard a ferry

I made a long weekend trip to Britain via the ferry from Holland. As I settled into my seat on the boat, I looked around at my fellow passengers. I sat people watching; some couples were laughing, other adventurers were sleeping, and then I noticed the family seated in front of me. Through the small opening between the back of two older women's heads, I spotted a mother and her two sons. They were sitting in a booth, and after overhearing some of their conversation, I found that the older son was four and the younger son had just turned three.

After a few minutes into our journey, the boys began to explore their new environment. The older boy started playing with his mother, pulling her hat off and putting the oversized play toy on his own head. Through all their laughter, the younger son stood up on his seat, pulling himself up using the windowsill, and stared out into the water.

Suddenly, we hit a wave at just the right angle and splat! The water started hitting the window and continued to do so for a few minutes. The boy's eyes widened, and his jaw dropped and quickly formed into a smile. He turned to face his mother and shouted, "Mama, it's raining! It's raining, look mama!" His mother turned to him with her other son on her lap and said, "No, sweetie, it's the waves." Her son's eyebrows lowered and his nose pinched. "No, mama. It's raining outside, look!" he said as he pointed out the circular window. His mother went on to explain that the water from the North Sea was simply hitting the window in a way that made it look just like rain. It took a few minutes of back-and-forth discussion, but soon the son accepted his mother's words, and he returned to his original position watching as the sea "rained" down onto his window.

As I watched the son debate with his mother about what he was certain was rain outside his window, I started thinking about the various perceptions my students hold as a result of their own experiences and then how they may change as they further develop. I began thinking about how a child's use of their five senses can affect the way in which that particular child interacts with the world around them. I considered the incredibly varied outcomes and the way in which a child would experience this particular moment differently based on the sense(s) the child chose to focus on.

While imagining the possible outcomes a child could draw from this encounter, either rain or ocean spatter, I began to think about the different ways in which we all perceive the world. This moment reminded me of how I used to understand the concept of culture. I used to focus only on the objective culture. That is, I scratched the surface, knew of some traditions a group of people celebrated, the foods they ate, and some of the music that accompanied their dances. But I never thought to dig deeper into the subjective or deeper culture that belonged to other people. Why did these traditions exist in the first place? What brought these people to celebrate this event, and what did their ancestors learn from this moment in time? What was that particular food tied to, and how and why was the recipe passed on through the generations of their people? Lastly, why were they dancing? What was their motivation, what drove them and inspired this unity—this togetherness?

As I reflected on this idea, I thought back to the little boy. I imagined how he would perceive this world, how my students perceive the world in different ways because of who they are and the experiences they've had. In this moment, I considered a sixth sense. Of course, there's sight, hearing, smell, taste, and touch ... but what about human and cultural connections? We use our senses to help us with everyday interactions; who's to say that we don't apply our culture—something that we carry with us always to assist us in our journey as learners? Our perceptions of the world are based on who we are and how we came to be that person. Who's to say that one sense is more important than another or that a sixth sense can't be accounted for in moments such as these?

Feeling changed and challenged.
Chris

TO: All Overseas Student Teachers
FROM: Dr. Lash
RE: You're nearly halfway through your experience!
Date: October 9

I've loved keeping up to date with you through your blogs. It seems like you're having an incredible experience in your placements and countries. It's fun to play with language, daily living patterns, and expectations and consider how the newly experienced cultural habits can begin to show you the benefits and limitations of your own as well as your host country's. It's revealing how many of you are experiencing language differences, even in English-speaking countries—clearly, a great way to learn about yourself and the world.

Your blog reflections discussing various perspectives on language and culture especially stood out to me this time and reminded me of one part of the International Baccalaureate (IB) Organizations' mission statement that may resonate with you—that these programs are designed to encourage students across the world to become active, compassionate, and lifelong learners who understand that other people, with their differences, can also be right.

Perhaps emanating from those feelings, but more broadly now that you've been living and teaching abroad for half a semester, I have a question I'd like you to consider. Many travelers often share how being an outsider (perhaps a man or woman, a citizen of a particular country, a person of different ethnicity than the majority, etc.) has shaded their experiences. What has the separation from family, friends, school, and a familiar way of life revealed to you about yourself? What do you know about the process of culture learning in view of all you have experienced in student teaching, living, and traveling overseas?

BLOG RESPONSES

Student: Carolyn
Placement: Guadalajara, Mexico
Date: October 11
RE: What is culture learning?

Before leaving for this sojourn, I was unsure of what culture learning actually meant. I considered Inhelder and Piaget, two scholars I'd studied in class, as I tried to wrap my brain around this new experience. I considered their ideas and considered culture learning from the perspective of an individual traveler and how I would come to new understandings about culture, life, and myself. These new understandings would lead to personal maturation and change, which would be possible only if I submitted myself to moments of discontinuity, disjunction, and disequilibrium amidst moments of continuity.

In their 1958 book, *The Growth of Logical Thinking from Childhood to Adolescence*, they discussed the notion that when individuals are traveling, changes in their environment will cause them to gain new understandings about life, specifically in reference to culture and self-identify. As I peered over the seats in front of me and saw the bobbing heads, I had a physical representation of these theorists' ideas about culture learning as experienced by many. The numerous "students of the world" who I was coinhabiting this bus with represented a potentially different perspective on culture based on their unique life experiences and cultural influences.

With my future classrooms of children in mind, I began considering that our planet and its people continue to evolve and learn as our world progresses. Moments of discontinuity and disjunction, or disequilibrium, occur when a problem arises, but equilibrium takes over when a solution is found internally or a partnership with others is formed. It is our responsibility to move forward once this solution or merger is created. After it takes place, we are able to share what we are learning and then teach those among us who are willing to open their eyes and ears. And as this sharing of knowledge takes place, new thoughts and discoveries are made, and with that a new journey into learning commences. This new disequilibrium marks the beginning of a new discontinuity and disjunction within the minds and lives of people—and thus the process continues in a never-ending manner.

We are all students,
Carolyn

Student: Justine
Placement: Auckland, New Zealand
Date: October 12
RE: Dinner with a Kiwi Asian

I've recently become great friends with Rose, a teacher at my field site. Rose is in her second year of teaching and working in one of the new experience classrooms (equivalent to that of the kindergarten in the United States). She's this bright, bubbly, and confident person, and after meeting her I began to wonder how she grew into this incredible and inspiring human being at only twenty-four years of age.

A few days ago during a track and field meet, Rose asked if I'd like to get dinner after school, and I happily agreed. Over tea and appetizers, our dinner quickly turned into an interview ... I couldn't help it.

J (me): "Living in the United States, I kind of grew up unaware of the struggles you might have faced. I, for example, never moved to a new home more than two hours away from my previous home. Your being someone who moved from Taiwan to New Zealand at such a young age, I was wondering, what were some of the struggles you faced? Was prejudice or racism ever something that you and your family had to deal with?

R: "Well, it's kind of always been a challenge for me as a Kiwi Asian."

J: "What exactly is a Kiwi Asian?"

R: "Well, that's kind of hard to explain. When we first arrived in New Zealand, I was four years old, and my mom always said to me and my little sister, Jo-Jo, don't forget to make a range of friends, which really meant, go make non-Asian friends. This was hard at first, but as soon as I picked up some of the Kiwi lingo, it became easier.

"Even with friends, we kind of always faced subtle racism; I especially remember it happening at school. Jo-Jo didn't like to take rice or sushi to school because that was really Asian and kids would say stuff like, 'What is that? That's not a sandwich' or 'Why can't your mom make normal food for you; yours is so funny.' Our parents would just tell us not to worry about it, and so we tried our best to not let it bother us. Jo-Jo still ate next to me whenever mom packed us sushi. After a few years at school, Jo-Jo and I made a lot of friends from different backgrounds, and my mother and father were happy knowing we sort of found ourselves in this new country. But then Jo-Jo and I started to feel like we weren't full Asians anymore."

J: "What's a full Asian?"

R: "Knowing the language and the history of our people, like really knowing it."

J: "When did you guys start feeling like that?"

R: "We didn't realize we were losing our Chinese until we joined a Taiwanese dance group. That's when we realized how Kiwi we really were. We had been isolated from our relatives back in Taiwan for thirteen years, and entering this room full of Asians who were all speaking Chinese, made us really happy at first. But once we realized how much we had forgotten, we started to become really confused about who we were."

J: "So what did you do after that?"

R: "We made a range of friends again, but this time within our dance group. I met two girls, Jenny and Amy, who were both Asian—one originally from Cambodia and the other from Hong Kong. I quickly realized how you can feel a lot more Kiwi when you're hanging out with real Asians."

J: "So what about now? Do you consider yourself Asian, Kiwi, Kiwi Asian ... or what?"

R: "I'm a Kiwi Asian. But that kind of means I'm always stuck in the middle—you're not really Kiwi but you're not really Asian either. The Kiwis look at you like you're foreign, and the full Asians look at you like you're not really Asian … but for the most part, I hang out with Kiwi Asians like me. We share the same language whether that be Mandarin with a hint of Kiwi or Kiwi with a hint of Mandarin, we eat like Asians, and we do things Kiwis like to do, like playing rugby. I'm still kind of trying to figure out what I am."

Our dinner ended up lasting much longer than either of us had planned, but through it I came to a new understanding. The process of culture learning has a lot to do with the popular saying "walk a mile in another person's shoes." I left this dinner with new knowledge of Rose's past. She faced struggles as an immigrant to a new country that I would have never predicted or understood if she hadn't opened up to me. If not for this dinner and my experience living, student teaching, and traveling overseas, I would have never met this incredible educator, who helped me to understand the perspectives and feelings of another student of this world.

This is especially important to understand in this day and age with so many people all over the world who are in transition—as immigrants or refugees, for instance. Culture learning is a living, breathing thing. And without this trying on of one another's shoes, shirts, pants, languages, foods, and histories, a great deal of knowledge and potential for growth among people and cultures is lost.

Feeling inspired,
Justine

TO: All Overseas Student Teachers
FROM: Dr. Lash
RE: Intercultural Competence, your new thoughts
DATE: November 2

My extrapolation from your blogs this time shows me how your international student teaching experiences challenge Steven Covey's (1989) quote, "Most people do not listen with the intent to understand; they listen with the intent to reply." Your experiences are begging you to understand the people, teachers, families, and culture in which you are currently immersed. This is hard work—you might be feeling drained and eventually exhilarated during your forages into authentic understandings and connections. Because you are so immersed and working hard, it is now time to reflect on two of the most difficult questions for one of your final blogs.

How do you define international mindedness or a mindset for global learning? And then, how do you attain intercultural competence?

BLOG RESPONSES

Student: Chris
Placement: Amsterdam, the Netherlands
Date: November 4
RE: A worldly student with little knowledge about the world

Now that I've been living and teaching in Amsterdam, I'm slowly realizing how very little I actually know about the world. I've formed a lot of relationships with colleagues at my school as well as with people within my community. A lot of our initial conversations these first few weeks focused on similarities and differences I had noticed since I arrived. I was rather embarrassed at first during these interactions, especially about how little I seemed to know, both about the Dutch as well as about most of the rest of the world. Because of these conversations, I've been trying to consciously consider the differences I observe around me.

Since then, I have picked up on issues related to language that I never experienced back in the States. It's really helped me to see just how linguistically limited we are back home. Since I've arrived here, I've been able to travel a bit around the continent. In the United States, you can travel thousands of miles and rarely hear another language. In Holland, it's much different. I guess in the Netherlands, and many other places in the world for that matter, one would be surrounded with different languages growing up as a child. I think we in the United States are at a disadvantage when it comes to this.

This realization helped me to gain a new perspective on the interactions I was initially having with my colleagues and peers. Whenever I'm left not knowing the answer to a question or even not understanding the basis for a topic we were discussing, the Dutch seem to take it in stride after they've poked a bit of fun at me. It was almost as if they expect me to be this way. I often wonder why it is that the people of Holland expect me to be somewhat naïve about the rest of the world. Now that I have traveled a bit around the continent, I understand this better. Americans in general, and many of the teachers I have had past experiences teaching with, know relatively little about the rest of the world. I think that's a shame.

Wondering and searching,
Chris

Student: Justine
Placement: Auckland, New Zealand
Date: November 8
RE: A run in with a Maori legend

Near the beginning of my journey in New Zealand, a few days after I had
unpacked and was feeling settled, I decided to go for a run in the native bush.
Why do I blog about this two months later? Because the experience has stuck
with me, and as I look back, it still remains the best answer to this question—
it was a big growth step on international mindedness.

As I ran that day, I listened to the sounds of the forest—birds singing,
water dripping from plants nearby, and the occasional scattered footsteps of
small forest animals, all alongside my hurried breathing. I was alone. I could
see that my path veered to the right up ahead, and as I made my way to this
corner, my heart skipped a beat. I thought I saw a face in the woods, a human
face, hiding low on the ground behind a tree. I ran. I was still running full
speed when I looked up and saw an opening, a man-made door opening to
what seemed like more dense forest. As I ran through the doorway, my pace
slowed, and soon I was standing completely still, surveying my surroundings.

I was in a wooden room, with no ceiling, that the forest had taken over.
There were bushes, vines, a few daunting unfamiliar insects, and finally—
The Tree. It was the largest tree in the wooden room, and right dead in the
center of its trunk, eye level with me, was an iron sun with piercing eyes and
its tongue sticking out. I have come to know this decoration as a symbol rep-
resentational of the New Zealand legend "How Maui Slowed the Sun." The
children at my field school study and create artwork in honor of the story
connected to it. But at this moment in time, I was unaware of such a legend,
and so Maui and his sun only fueled the fire under my feet.

I took off running. Have you ever tried to run away while in an enclosed
room with only one doorway? You don't get very far. I took the only available
path, the one leading back to the area where the human face resided and my
escape journey initially began. As I ran, I began slowing my pace. I thought to
myself, Justine, are you really doing this right now? You're twenty-two years
old, you traveled to New Zealand on your own, you are about to graduate
from university and then get a real job where you are responsible for keeping
all of your students safe and unafraid, and you are frantically running in
circles to avoid a metal sunshine nailed to a tree and what was most likely a
weirdly shaped formation of leaves and sticks on the ground.

I quickly calmed myself and decided to continue my exploration of the
native bush. I made it back to a fork in the woods, and I had a choice to make,
turn left and return home or move forward and explore the track I hadn't
taken before. I felt this jolt of energy, and before my mind knew what my

body was doing, I was hopping over some vines and bumps in the path directly in front of me, onward on my adventure into the unknown.

As I ran, skipped, hopped, tripped, stopped to smile, and continued walking, I began thinking. This is just like the journey my students are taking. They walk into the classroom every day, and they make choices. They decide to read on their own or work with a partner, they choose one book over the other, they decide the answer is six rather than seven, they dribble left with the basketball and pass it to one of their teammates rather than shoot from the three-point line. They make such decisions every day and all because they are inspired and choose to do so.

As I chose to continue down the unknown path rather than go back home, I felt this surge of energy, of excitement, of inquiry and passion. That's the kind of environment I want to create for my students—one in which we take their interests and what they wonder, choose their own path to learning, and discover more about themselves while on this journey. I'll help them in any way that I can, but in the end, it's their adventure into learning and it's what they make of it. Sure, they may encounter a few scary tree face-like moments along the way, but those moments, when you are scared or unsure or even alone, are the moments in which you find your true character, your sense of responsibility, and your dedication to every passion that you hold.

While on this run, I found out how one attains intercultural competence—by making yourself uncomfortable or even afraid. These moments when you are challenged to stand up on your own two feet, to use what your family and professors have taught you and apply what you have learned within past fieldwork experiences, are the moments in which you grow. These are the moments in which you find the passion and strength to become the brave educator you've always dreamed of being for your current and future students.

After realizing this, I thought of a new question for myself. How would this experience help my students grow? How can I help them grow into internationally minded human beings? Now, I knew for certain! It's my turn to make them uncomfortable.

An experienced traveler … a changed educator,
Justine

Student: Emily
Placement: Port Elizabeth, South Africa
Date: November 17
RE: We were here

How do I define international mindedness? As I started to consider this question, I began an exploration into the intricately developed tunnels and avenues within my mind, and I came across a moment in time that I had experienced a few weeks ago. A perfect picture appeared in my mind. I saw a pile of pearl white rocks that I noticed down by the entrance to a beach at Table Mountain National Park outside of Cape Town—a park I visited during a two-week bus tour I went on during school break. I remembered how I had walked up to this pile of seemingly regular looking rocks and how in just seconds the purpose of my entire experience in South Africa was made evident to me for the first time through the means of pebbles and dirt.

As I approached the rock pile, I bent down to better focus on bright rock that caught my eye, and as I picked it up, I noticed it had writing on it. As soon as my eyes adjusted to the tiny letters on the rock, I stood up, and as my view broadened, I found that nearly every rock had some form of writing on its surface. Some were in English, others Chinese, and a few in languages I didn't recognize. Other rocks were marked with a date, a few with two names and a heart, and I even saw one with the South African flag drawn on the entirety of one flat side. Soon, I happened upon my most favorite memory rock. On it was a list of names followed by a date and after that was the ever-popular statement "We were here."

Later that week, I attended a middle childhood education conference in Cape Town, and while listening to various presentations, I started to recall that "we were here" feeling. As I reminisced, I considered just how many people had left their mark on that place, and I felt this overwhelming feeling of change tickling the backside of my heart. I felt one way to perceive the world around me dwindling downward and becoming the foundation that now lay way for my newly formed international mindedness—supported by pillars made up of new experiences, new people, and memories of the emotions I had felt while on this sojourn.

Shortly after the conference ended, I began to reflect on my journey. I was able to listen to educators from around the world come together to talk about what matters most to them. Some of these people spent their lives working toward bettering education and improving the quality of their students' learning. And now, today, each and every presenter from various parts of this world took the role of student. We sat together in large rooms with attentive eyes, tuned ears, and open minds and listened as the presenters expressed their findings, feelings, and possible solutions. We concluded each speech with a time for discussion and questions because as educators we know our learning never ceases. We learned, we laughed, we were challenged to think outside of our ever-evolving ethnorelative orientations, and we all became better for it.

We live in a very vast world, one in which you can take a plane, hop on a bus, or even walk a few minutes outside of your own neighborhood and find new and engaging people awaiting you with open arms and open minds. So how do I define international mindedness? I choose to believe that this world is full of young people who are becoming more caring human beings each and every day as they walk among the footsteps of their own as well as their ancestors' past. We learn from the journeys that have already been taken and from the ones we all wish to embark upon. We grow as individuals while on these journeys, but I have found that this personal growth is worthless if not shared with those who are willing to listen and understand. We may grow to become greater human beings and more knowledgeable educators as we partake in experiences such as these, but we can become one greater being, one greater world of people, only if we share with others what we have learned and discovered while chasing our passions.

A new thinker—a new learner,
Emily

Student: Morgan
Placement: Perth, Australia
Date: November 23
RE: Penguin Island

Yesterday I explored Penguin Island with four friends, and the adventure was spectacular! Around 10:00 in the morning, a fellow teacher, her sister, a friend of hers from college (which is what Aussie's call high school), another friend of a friend, and I met on the ferry and departed for our journey. After our hellos and nice to meet yous, we got to talking. Two of my new adventure partners lived their entire lives in Australia, another one was born in Saudi Arabia but raised in England, and the fourth one grew up in South Africa before making her way here. As we climbed over hills and rocks, we talked about our experiences and how these experiences led us to this exploration amid new friends.

As the day progressed, we proceeded on our trek to the top of the summit while continuing to get to know one another. We discussed the different cultural aspects of our hometowns and how they varied in comparison to that of Australia's. We talked about the different forms of respect for women as well as prayer in Saudi Arabia. We discussed vegetarianism as well as veganism and how these personal choices make changes to our economy, to the lives of many animals across the world, and to the planet in general. We talked about the varying education systems we were all a part of as children and are now implementing and making changes to as educators.

All of these conversations happened throughout the day. We'd partner off and share about ourselves, what brought us to this moment in time and what experiences have shaped us into the human beings we are in this moment. Then, near the harbor where our ferry that was to take us back was waiting, we got back together as a group to move as one being over roots and rocks, and as we ventured toward our destination, our heated debates about vegetarianism and current political events came to a close.

We laughed, we smiled, we tripped, we debated, we held one another's hands when our trek took a turn or became bumpy, and all the while, we made new friends and added a new adventure to our personal histories. I think that's what international mindedness is—placing yourself in situations where you will share a new experience with people who have cultural backgrounds unlike your own and sharing an experience together that leads to discovering more about the people you walk beside and how their personal journey led them here, to this particular moment, learning alongside you.

I believe the act of purposefully placing yourself in situations like this, your own approach to being an internationally minded person, leads to the attainment of intercultural competence, although this attainment occurs only if you take the time to reflect on your shared experience and what you've come to understand about your fellow travelers while walking side by side.

A spectacular day—an inspired educator,
Morgan

TO: All Overseas Student Teachers
FROM: Dr. Lash
RE: Welcome Home—time to acclimate … again!
DATE: December 6

Amazing intercultural growth and furthering of your international mindedness worldview are evident in your blogs. I challenge each of you to bring parts of your newly found perspectives and experiences into your relationships, classrooms, and teaching back in the United States or internationally. And, of course, on the practical side, consider how you weave these new learnings from your overseas student teaching experience into your upcoming job interviews—how lucky a principal will feel to know you have all the skills and knowledge of your stateside classmates and worldly experience too.

And, as I officially welcome everyone back to the States, it's time to warn you that you will need to allow some time for readjusting to home. Although you'll be welcomed back home, others have not had your experiences, and you may find that their interest cannot be sustained at the level you need in order to talk and process your travel.

Please consider this blog, your overseas student teaching friends, and me as additional outlets for processing your experiences. And, as we know, those experiences go well beyond your schools and homestays—congratulations, you have become world-class learners and educators. You have met students, citizens, and immigrants as well as world travelers to your host countries; you are pulling those people and experiences as well as your classroom teaching and school philosophies into your worldview. I've so enjoyed your blogs while you student taught and traveled abroad and hope that you'll continue reflecting on your experiences and perceptions as you personally and professionally continue to grow.

I also think that you have seen the value in reflection and writing as a way of solidifying experiences, emotions, and ideas as well as to move yourself forward as educators and human beings. Remember, John Dewey's (1938) philosophy: We do not learn from experience … we learn from reflecting on experience. Please consider the following questions as your final blog.

A significant amount of research suggests that people who participate in international experiences not only develop on a personal level by increasing their self-confidence and independence but also their tolerance for ambiguity and adaptability to life in general is altered. Would you agree with these ideas? Why or why not? What experiences support or question these assertions?

BLOG RESPONSES

Student: Chris
Placement: Amsterdam, the Netherlands
Date: December 8
RE: Me … a representative?

I faced many challenges while abroad in Amsterdam. Most of them were more or less connected to the adjustment period early in my trip when I was getting used to the area, the bus system, and the language barriers and coming to understand some of the commonly used sayings or slang that I had never heard of before. In retrospect, these seem like relatively easy and surface-level differences to which I had to adapt. But the biggest challenge I faced while abroad was the fact that I was from the United States. I hadn't expected to feel this way, and I was slightly unprepared when I realized I was the "outsider" for the first time in my life. I acquired a new responsibility that I did not anticipate. Unknowingly, I became the representative of the United States in the eyes of the people in my community.

We were overseas during the 2016 presidential election. Everyone I met asked about the cultural norms back home, what I thought about the current state of political affairs, and how I was going to combat any negativity that was going on when I returned. I would walk into a classroom and be met with questions like "Did you know he's trying to build a wall?" And "What are you going to do if he wins?" But it wasn't these types of questions that challenged me; it was finding a way to give hope to those friends, parents, and students who shared their worries with me.

On the day the election results were broadcast, five of my students offered for me to move in with their families. I was asked nearly every hour if I was now making my move permanent. And during class, one of my students, Omar, calmly brushed my hand and asked me if I was scared to go home. Later on during the day, my mentor teacher's daughter, an eleven-year-old girl with the wit and intelligence of a much older student, found me during lunch. "I'm worried about Trump's son," she said. "Why's that?" I responded. "Well, during the speech, he just didn't look happy. I feel like kids won't want to be friends with him at school anymore because his dad is mean, and then he'll just be sad and alone. Nobody likes that feeling."

Nearing the end of the day, one of Omar's parents approached me and said, "This morning Omar asked me, 'Mom, will we ever be able to go to the United States to see where my student teacher lives?' And I had to respond to him, 'I don't know.' We're Muslim, and trying to explain this situation to him was very difficult—he just couldn't wrap his head around it."

This particular day was quite odd and challenged me in a way I had never predicted. At that moment in time, I was overwhelmed by the responsibilities I had attained as the "outsider" and "US representative" in this country. It was as if I was responsible for all that was going on in my home country and my students and their families were looking to me for answers and solutions.

But as I reflect on this moment, I now realize how courageous it was of my students, their families, and me to be hopeful, optimistic, supportive of one another, and brave enough to discuss the political events that were going on during this time. I felt as if the cross-cultural connections I had made over these past few months were undervalued by some of the people currently representing our country, and the possibility that these types of intercultural experiences could be restricted in the future scared me.

But everyone I was with helped to give me hope. The fact that we were able to confide in one another about these political and social issues and our overall trust in each other allowed for these moments that on some levels were characterized by hate, segregation, and disconnect to become an opportunity for us to come together.

As I continue to look back on this day, I realize that in moments when parents, teachers, and most people were going slightly crazy, my students reminded me of what was important. Nobody likes that feeling of being sad, alone, or scared. Now that I have traveled abroad and had this experience alongside the people of Amsterdam, I can confidently say that our best approach in dealing with major changes occurring around the world that affect us all is to take a moment to think about such events from the perspective of a child. It may just help us to open our eyes and remind us of what really matters. This shift in perspective may help us to see how to respectfully fight for those things we hold dear to our hearts in a way the children of our world would be proud of.

Changed,
Chris

Student: Morgan
Placement: Perth, Australia
Date: December 10
RE: Reflecting

Many people asked me why, as an African American, I wanted to go to Australia in the first place. I had read about the struggles of the Aborigines, and I was interested in their experience and in learning about their culture. At the same time, however, I was a bit nervous that I might suffer some of the same discrimination they had encountered.

When I arrived in Australia, I quickly noted that I was the only Black person in my school and community, and at first, I was scared and a bit nervous about traveling around Australia as an outsider. But soon I found I felt more welcomed as an African American in Australia than I typically did back home. Most people were really welcoming and interested in me as a person as well as in my African American heritage. Many doors opened up for me, both in the school and in the community, especially through my host family. Although it may have been stressful at the beginning, I found I was able to adapt in this environment.

From this experience, I have been able to look back upon the United States and view it from a different perspective. I learned that other countries are not as openly racist as people are in the United States and that other cultures seem to be more open to minorities. Now, I know that, as a result of this experience, I can do just about anything I put my mind to. I've become much more independent and self-sufficient than I ever thought I could become. And I've learned to take chances in my life, something that I really never did before. I've also learned a lot about a couple of other cultures, both Australian Aborigines and White Australians, and for that I'm really grateful.

From outsider to community member,
Morgan

Student: Emily
Placement: Port Elizabeth, South Africa
Date: December 16
RE: Discomfort leads to new understandings

Now that I have returned to the States, I've started to reflect on my experience abroad. I like to believe that because of my experiences teaching and living in Port Elizabeth, South Africa, that I have become an educator who is now more attuned to my students' community influences and their family histories. I have learned how to empathize with others and to be sensitive to the needs of children at a much higher level. Being in a new and different situation has given me the opportunity to experience what it feels like to be away from one's familiar surroundings and to be the odd person out. This feeling of being the outsider for once in my life helped me come to realize that I didn't understand what others around me take for granted, cherish, and value.

I think I understand privilege better now as well as the responsibilities I have for all learners. I'm also beginning to understand how these concerns may be completely different from my own and something that I wouldn't understand if I didn't make a conscious effort to get to know the histories tied to my students. I also learned to be much less suspicious of people and to trust people much more than I ever had before. I met some incredibly nice, giving people. Most of the time, people are good and can be much more helpful and kind than I had ever thought.

This is extremely helpful to me as I think about teaching children from different backgrounds back home. I learned how to be accepting of differences. Even people completely different from you have something in common. I learned to listen to what others are interested in and in what they believe. It can be very scary and lonely at times, but you do get over it. This is one way I have become more sensitive. This will definitely help me if I ever get a student who is from another country, or even another state, in my classroom. I learned so much, especially about myself. I also learned that teaching is a passion of mine that I cannot wait to pursue.

I'm ready to teach,
Emily

Student: Justine
Placement: Auckland, New Zealand
Date: December 17
RE: Becoming independent

Being totally responsible for finding a place to live in a large foreign city was one of the most difficult things about my experience. Now that I'm back in the States, I realize this major challenge abroad actually allowed for me to become more independent. At first, I thought it strange that no one had arranged any housing for me. But my supervisor said that he couldn't predict the kind of living arrangement I would like, so he asked me to find my own housing. I guess it saves problems for him later if people are unhappy with a host family or an apartment he chose. It took me a few days, but eventually I found a room to rent that was close to the school in which I was teaching. And I met some pretty nice people as a result of this that I get together with now on a regular basis.

The experience made me more independent, and I feel that I can do anything now. In fact, I was offered a teaching position in maths, that's how they refer to math in New Zealand, at the school in which I student taught. Now that I'm back in the States, my plan is to attend graduation, visit family and friends as much as I can, and four weeks later, return to Auckland. What I first viewed as an obstacle quickly became an opportunity for new friendships to form, and my ability to function on my own in a foreign country was challenged. Now, as I decorate my cap for graduation and repack my bags for Auckland, I do so with a weight lifted off my shoulders. After this experience, I know that I can make it through anything no matter what it is.

Back to the airport and onto my next adventure,
Justine

Student: Jacob
Placement: Port Elizabeth, South Africa
Date: December 19
RE: My final thoughts

My experience in South Africa helped me to become more independent, that's for sure. I had a wonderful experience, but I was very lonely. And I had a difficult adjustment in the beginning. My host family was wonderful though. I stayed with one of the teachers from the school I taught at in Port

Elizabeth. He was very helpful and gracious to me. But when I went out into the community, now that was a different story. It's still a pretty stressful life in South Africa for most Blacks, even more than 20 years since the transition from Apartheid to a free and democratic society. But both Whites and Blacks have undergone a significant change, and it's not been easy for either side.

And the economic situation in the country is quite different from anything I have ever experienced. So many people are out of work and have little hope for their future. Yet many people are still optimistic that things will improve. After all, most of the world thought South Africa would explode in a civil war more than a few times after Apartheid, but that didn't happen. That was a positive sign for the rest of the world, I think. The people are hopeful, and they have so much to overcome. I was glad to be a small part of that effort.

Going into this I felt I was prepared for certain things. I knew to expect culture or adjustment shock, for instance, but I also remember thinking that it wouldn't happen to me. But it did—on many occasions. I naïvely thought that because I was Black my visit to the African continent would be easy, but there were many times when I just didn't understand what was going on. When that happened, I remembered some of the things that we had talked about in our orientation sessions, such as the adjustment cycle, so I knew I wasn't alone in my feelings.

But I wasn't prepared for the racial tensions that existed. And I'm not sure there is any way I could have been prepared for them because the way they are dealt with is much different from the way we approach these kinds of issues in the United States. I read a bit about the situation before I left, so I knew a few of the current issues. But until you really begin to meet people and learn about their experience firsthand, it is hard to understand the situation.

That is why I'm now a firm believer in the educational value of travel. Now, I can begin to understand the plight of others around the world because I have experienced it myself. This is so much better than reading about it in a book or in the newspaper. I think more teachers should have such experiences; it would make school a much more real and alive place. I hope to be able to offer similar experiences, although probably on a smaller scale, to my students once I begin teaching.

Transformed,
Jacob

Student: Carolyn
Placement: Guadalajara, Mexico
Date: December 20
RE: Go ahead and do it!

If you're considering student teaching abroad, go ahead and do it! I know it's scary … to think about living somewhere else for so long where you will be working alongside new people and in an unfamiliar environment. But isn't that what we ask of our students at the beginning of each new school year? If we expect our students to come into our classroom and form new relationships and build a community—like a family—how can we not take the leap and attempt to do so ourselves?

While abroad, I learned so much and grew into a different human being who has a new understanding of the world we share—a new understanding and respect for people, their culture, and the personal histories belonging to each new friend, student, and colleague. This change in me—this new acceptance and understanding of people—would never have taken place or at least not as quickly if I hadn't departed for this new learning experience.

When I first arrived in Guadalajara, I was overwhelmed by every experience. One of my first challenges was that I had to get over my fear of sounding stupid using the Spanish language. Although I'd studied Spanish in high school, I really couldn't speak it to anyone else. But using it daily with my host family and with the kids in the school, even though they all spoke English, was the only way that I was ever going to be able to speak the language. Because of this experience, I have a new respect for and understanding of people different from me who come to America and have to learn English. It is very difficult when you are older and can be a bit depressing and scary when you can't communicate what you want to be known.

Every day there was something new to discover, a new challenge to face. But with every challenge I grew, I became a little more confident and willing to step out of my comfort zone. I've always been a soft-spoken person and tried my best to avoid conflict. And when it did find me, I usually was the first to apologize, the first to conform, the first to give in, although I was never this way with my education—I always fought for what I wanted, needed, or thought was right for myself as well as my students. With this trip in mind, I was hoping that my confidence as an educator would expand and take root in the part of my brain that gave me the power and strength to be confident as a person.

Now that I'm back in the States, I can happily say that with each new challenge I faced in Mexico, that confidence factor within my mind traveled to whatever place inside me that used to say stop, be silent, be content. It now says grow, let your voice be heard, and be passionate! With this newfound confidence, I find I'm able to assist others in ways I never could before.

Remember at our "transition home" dinner meeting with Dr. Lash a week or so ago? It's amazing to think I was at this meeting one semester ago as I prepared to embark on student teaching. Now, one semester later, I serve as the "expert" or mentor to the next cohort of overseas student teachers who are about to leave.

While there, I sat next to two students who are planning to travel to Guadalajara to student teach. They asked me a few questions about the school, the city, what to pack, and how best to prepare. After the dinner, I gave them my e-mail address and phone number, and within a few days, general questions turned to more specific inquiries and conversations about culture shock, advice about homestays and teaching, learning stories from the classroom, and so much more. In my own small way, I was the expert, and I could confidently speak about travel and adjusting—my inner voice was becoming my spoken voice.

At the dinner, I also spoke with a student who knew of a position opening up in the spring at a private Muslim school in the area. I had never heard of it before, but I figured why not take a chance? I was able to get an interview and went into it with the general nervousness I think any new teacher would feel going into their first real interview. As I sat down in front of the principal and one teacher from the school, I felt this wave of contentment wash over me. I traveled, lived, and taught abroad in another country for an entire semester—I could do this and I could get this job. Soon enough, the interview began. All of my nervousness suddenly washed away. With every question, I had a story or insight from my experience in Mexico that helped to support my claims. I continued on about my growth, my students' growth, and soon we came to the final interview question.

The principal asked: Why do you want this job?

I responded: I just returned from this incredible experience where I grew so much as an educator and as a human being by fully immersing myself in the culture of different people in a different country. Now, I'm back in the States, and I can't help but want to learn more. I'm passionate about discovering more about people, their customs, and what they find important or special in this life.

My goal as an educator, especially now, is to reweave my perceptions of this world as well as inspire my students to do so, and I think I can do this best here, in your center for learning where I can work to enhance my understanding of your culture, your beliefs, and continue growing. I was offered the job two days later. I took the leap, I traveled abroad, and I became better for it. I accomplished more than the goals I set for myself. I am a more confident educator, learner, and communicator. If there is one thing I learned from teaching abroad, it's that one child's learning experience is not the same as another's.

The same goes for us as future teachers, so embark upon your own adventure into learning filled with endless opportunities to make new discoveries about teaching, learning, and living in this ever-changing and beautiful world. I can't tell you exactly what you'll learn, who you'll meet, or how those people and your students will change you, but I can say without a doubt that you will leave this experience feeling empowered and more confident as an educator and that feeling is something you can pass on to your future students.

It's your turn now,
Carolyn

TO: Overseas Student Teachers
FROM: Dr. Lash
RE: Final Reflection
DATE: December 21

Your final blogs show me that although student teaching is a capstone experience for your university education, being a learner in an international student teaching experience accelerated your global thinking, learning, and perspective taking as well as teaching abilities. As a full participant in experiential international learning, your lived experiences have proven invaluable to you in so many ways. I believe your experiences, questioning, and interest in exploring other countries and cultures will remain with you for many months and years.

You've also become more reflective and perhaps more critical in a constructive way of your own culture and what it means to be a US American. I wonder how this might impact your teaching in the future. How many of you will encourage your students to become more analytical, more reflective, more critical because now, you yourself, have these skills? Here are some final questions for you to consider as you all embark on this next sojourn as lifelong learners:

- What does it feel like to be an American in a foreign country? How does it feel to be perceived as the representative for 325 million Americans?
- Were you expecting to meet people/travelers from other parts of the world, not just your host country? Do you feel you are connected to a world of globetrotters that you may not have even known existed? How does that change you as a future teacher, as a lifelong learner, as a human being?
- How do you think your teaching will be changed in the short term? In the longer term? How do you think your perspective taking, analytic and problem-solving skills, questioning, risk taking, and world knowledge will

be realized in your future classrooms? Do you foresee that you will hold different expectations and standards for your future students?

And you know I enjoy quotes, so I'll leave you with one that surely captures your overseas student teaching experience. This quote comes from American storyteller and riverboat pilot, Mark Twain:

> Twenty years from now you will be more disappointed by the things that you didn't do than by the ones you did do. So throw off the bowlines. Sail away from the safe harbor. Catch the trade winds in your sails. Explore. Dream. Discover.

Chapter 9

I Came for the Animals—I Stayed for the People

> The sea is dangerous and its storms terrible, but these obstacles have never been sufficient reason to remain ashore.
>
> —Ferdinand Magellan

Reflect back in chapter 1 where I discussed my youthful desire to become a game warden, stimulated by Joy and George Adamson's devotion to educate the young of various animal species who had been orphaned or abandoned to survive in the wild on their own. Patiently gaining the trust of their "students," the Adamsons provided countless opportunities for them to practice and learn the survival skills necessary for them to gain independence and venture out safely on their own. This is not unlike what parents and teachers of our own species struggle to accomplish with their own children and students. If you recall, in addition to my interest in wildlife, I was a biology teacher early in my career. This chapter relates my return to the African continent—initially because of the lure of the wildlife but continuing still today because of the warm nature of the people.

The Swissair flight I was traveling on from Zurich landed in Nairobi's Jomo Kenyatta International Airport at 6:00 a.m. on a January morning early in 2001 when I otherwise would have been beginning a new semester. I was finally on my first sabbatical and on my way to fulfill a dream if even for a short time of volunteering on a wildlife research project in East Africa!

The capital city was already coming to life by the time I got out of the airport, the streets teeming with people on their way to school and work. Twelve Meribou storks perched atop large acacia trees greeted me as I entered the city limits. I know of few places in the world where one can be welcomed with fantastic wildlife right within the city limits. Even Nairobi National Park, located just eight miles from the city center, can provide the lucky visitor with a photograph of a rhinoceros with the Nairobi skyline as a backdrop.

The driver met me as planned and was to take me to the bus terminal in time for a 9:00 a.m. bus. From Nairobi, I was told to travel about six hours southeast toward Mombasa and request to be dropped off in the town of Maungu, about thirty kilometers past the regional center, Voi. Someone, I was assured, would pick me up.

The Taita Discovery Center, or TDC, located in a land corridor between Tsavo East and Tsavo West national parks, would be my home for four weeks, where I would volunteer and learn some of the skills of a wildlife researcher while assisting on an ongoing research project. Staff at TDC were most interested in understanding what might be done to improve the situation for the estimated 1,000 elephants and few hundred lions that use the area as a corridor as they migrate between the two parks.

TDC was a comprehensive conservation project that included study and collaboration with a number of communities directly impacted by the elephants. I would assist with some elephant research, work on a curriculum project, and explore possible linkages between American schools and universities and the local communities. It promised to be just the right blend of bush life, wildlife work, and community involvement.

I was dropped off earlier than expected at the bus station. There seemed to be tremendous pride in this station and its surroundings; when I arrived, they were sweeping the street clean—and it was a dirt road. The bus ride would take me past a number of small towns and marketplaces on its way to Mombasa, stopping only occasionally to pick up or drop off passengers. Nothing to eat or drink was available on the bus, and I was not told of this before I left. This didn't seem to be such a big deal because I'd been awake and eating all night on the flight from Europe. Anyway, being a vegetarian, I'm always prepared with a few protein bars handy if I grow hungry. There also was no toilet on the bus, and for this too I was not prepared.

Although we stopped at just about every town and village along the way as more and more people got on board, no rest stop seemed apparent. About two hours into the trip, which was now about four hours after I'd left the airport, I began to feel those lower twinges that remind me that I have a bladder—and at my age this was something to which I was beginning to pay attention. I really had no idea whether the bus had any planned stops where we could get off, but I sat patiently hoping my worst fears would not materialize.

But they were materializing—and fast! Another half hour into the trip and I had to pee—really bad! Fidgeting nervously in my seat, I tried all kinds of things—from loosening my belt and holding my waist to mind control—anything to relieve the pressure on my bladder. I even began to wonder whether it was possible to dribble a little urine down my leg every minute or so. I had read that this is something quite common in the region—at least among young male elephants when they are in the condition known as musth—constantly dribbling strong-smelling urine to mark and announce that they are in their sexual prime. Well, I certainly was long past my prime, and I wouldn't go out of my way to advertise what I was doing, but perhaps releasing a small amount of urine now and then would not be noticed—nor offensive—to my seatmate who joined me at the last stop. And given the heat of the day, evaporation would quickly take care of the evidence.

After a bit more time, the bus stopped, seemingly in the middle of nowhere. Two people got up, a man in the front and a woman sitting right behind me, and quickly ran off the bus, he running toward a bush. I glanced around, asked my seatmate if this was a toilet stop, and with a nod of reassurance, I quickly joined the other two in the bushes. It was awkward, to say the least, as I stood next to this man, trying to relax enough to pee into the bushes, with thirty or more of my fellow passengers looking on. And it was confusing as well because only ten minutes earlier I had read in my travel book that it was considered uncouth to urinate in public in Kenya. Later, I would learn that this was referred to as the "bush room" and was quite common where I would be spending my time.

The bus continued on, dropping me off in Maungu a short while later. I waited patiently in the searing sun and red dust that would soon become a part of every day, making friends and chitchatting with the cows and kids, both human and goat, that kept passing by to get a look at this new mzungu, or European, in their midst. Finally, after an hour and a half, someone from the TDC came to get me, he not knowing that I had been put on an earlier bus.

This was my welcome back to the African continent—and it can challenge the most seasoned of travelers. Not long after arrival on the continent, most people will confront their challenges. Whether it's the uncertain water, anxieties about the wildlife, fear of illness, the seemingly ever-present potential for thievery, working through bureaucratic red tape, or participating in the everyday frustrations of the people, Africa can try even the hardiest of souls. The traveler in Africa is truly on a safari—a journey as it translates from the Kiswahili—that can be as much an external adventure as it is can be an internal transformative venture. I had touched the continent a few times in the past and certainly many years earlier in my dreams, and it had touched me. I was glad to be back.

The Taita Discovery Center, in operation from the early 1990s through 2007, was located at the base of Mt. Kasigau in the corridor between Tsavo East and Tsavo West national parks, the largest of the national park systems in all of Kenya. There is a history of poaching, especially of the elephants, throughout the area. In 1973, Kenya boasted an elephant population estimated to be at 167,000. This number has been in perpetual decline primarily because of poaching and the illegal trade of ivory, reaching its current estimate in 2017 of just over 12,000.

With the ever-expanding human settlements, human–wildlife encounters are becoming increasingly frequent, oftentimes resulting in disastrous effects for both people and elephants. This area was being studied with the hope of reestablishing itself as an active, healthy, and safe region for wildlife, especially for the elephants that migrate within the corridor between the two parks and the various communities who live within this range.

Studying wildlife is not the same as the game viewing that brings most visitors to the African continent. Game viewing is like a game of BINGO in the bush. Small groups of camera-laden tourists typically go off in six-passenger minivans in search of the "big five"—lion, elephant, buffalo, rhinoceros, and leopard. The trip is generally not considered a success until all five have been seen and photographed. BINGO! Next in importance come such animals as cheetahs, baboons, hippopotamus, crocodile, wildebeest, giraffe, and zebra, among others. They are large, impressive, and photogenic, and I must admit to spending much of my time in search of the award-winning photo.

But game viewing in and of itself is not sufficient if we are to succeed in our efforts to conserve this magnificent resource. Although this activity may bring greater awareness of the splendor of these creatures to an increasing number of people around the world, the more hidden day-to-day struggles these creatures face is not as evident.

Such are the concerns of the wildlife researchers and many of the volunteers who were associated with TDC, of which I was to become one. Wildlife researchers at TDC, especially those studying the elephant, struggle to make themselves as inconspicuous as possible, sitting quietly for hours on end, waiting for the drama of life to unfold so that it can be documented and later analyzed.

When game viewing, if nothing is seen within a short period of time, one quickly moves on to another site, with drivers in constant radio communication with one another in search of the large game and the big tips from satisfied clients. It is not uncommon in the parks that within a few minutes of locating a lion or cheetah, van after van arrive, encircling the animal, making it nearly impossible for anyone to capture a photo without also snaring a bumper, a window, or other camera lens within your line of sight. So much for the isolation of nature.

It didn't take long to learn that research in support of wildlife is not always filled with the glamour of the Adamson's struggles with Elsa the lioness. I was invited to participate with a small team of researchers on my first full day to do animal counts at three dams that were originally constructed to provide water for the cattle grazing within the ranches. The dams were to be monitored for three hours each day for three days of every month over the next three years to determine the animal life that was dependent upon them. Because it is the little things that are important, patience and oftentimes loneliness become the researcher's constant companion. Without an unlimited supply, the work soon fails.

The difficulty of this work was evident from the start at our very first dam—it had no water! There we sat, for three hours at a time at three dams— one that had no water, one that was at less than 10 percent of its capacity, and one that although appearing full, was frequented by hundreds of cattle, sheep, goats, and people on a fairly regular basis, thus keeping wildlife at a distance. We sat patiently awaiting God's theater to begin, me expecting to see countless large animals.

In my first three days of monitoring waterholes, we saw a total of three wart hogs and three dik-diks, the smallest antelope to be found on the African savanna that are water independent, meaning they do not drink but instead obtain needed fluids from fruits, berries, and foliage! We logged countless birds, however, many of which I had never seen before. Rather useless in terms of my contribution to the project because I knew very little of the birdlife, I busied myself serving as secretary, primarily to keep from falling asleep, and in reading a book on elephant communication. And I slowly began to learn about the birds.

Hamisi Mutinda was head of conservation and animal research when I first ventured to TDC. A conservationist who had recently completed his doctoral studies on the social relationships of elephants, he is soft spoken, determined, and focused. Hamisi had been working with a group of young British volunteers in the weeks before I joined TDC. These young people, most of them between the ages of eighteen and nineteen, had come to Kenya in their gap year between secondary school and college to volunteer for four months in the local communities. They had recently completed their orientation at TDC and had begun spending their time in the local communities.

My real contribution to the work of TDC was in helping to build community and school relationships, of which, I was assured, was a critical dimension of this work. A combination of trust between the conservationists at TDC and local community members must be established and at the same time, provide people with the knowledge and skills that will enable and encourage them to be less dependent upon the land and more tolerant of elephants. It seems that I may have found the right combination of passion and profession to work for me—in such an arrangement I could bring my skills as an educator to the support of wildlife.

I was assured that there were many large animals in the region, some of them quite dangerous, but in the first week I had spotted only a few elephants. I was somewhat disappointed, to be honest, because this really is what I had come to see, as do many others who venture to the continent. Many are drawn to the drama of the chase, hoping to witness the life and death struggle that seems to be so much a part of the African experience. This also serves as a reminder of our evolutionary past, that we too are really an integral part of the natural cycle of things. But although we hope to witness this as a passive observer and not as an integral part of the chain of events, this is not always the case as I was to discover during my stay.

The morning of the seventh day, we were to go off elephant monitoring. That is, we were to travel across the property in search of elephants that can be spotted, identified, and recorded—again, to gain greater understanding of the range and population of these magnificent animals. It is easiest to locate elephants, or any of the animals for that matter, during the dry season because they tend to congregate at the waterholes to satisfy their thirst, which depending upon the species, can vary from once a day to once every three days or more. We depart, prepared with boxes of elephant ID cards that note unique ear notches and tears and tusk formations that are used to identify and thus differentiate one elephant from another. The elephants are also given names, such as Shiloh, Patty, and Hesse, and I have the chance to name quite a few over the weeks.

We arrive at Kongoni waterhole at about 8:30 in the morning. After circling the water, we notice recent elephant activity and decide to stay. Positioning ourselves with a view of the water and surrounding area, we turn off the engine and begin our long wait, something I had become accustomed to during the previous week's monitoring waterholes. Our presence has chased most everything away because there is hardly a sound or evidence of activity during the first half hour. Hamisi warns us not to take photos until the elephants, assuming there will be some, begin drinking and making their own sounds that drown out the noise of our cameras.

I sit atop our four-wheel drive Land Cruiser and wait in quiet meditation with Mt. Kasigau as the backdrop. The parched red earth, sparse vegetation, and dry heat are reminders of just how precious these waterholes are for all the living creatures. If animals are to survive in this environment, especially during the dry spells, they must eventually come here; these are not mirages. The air remains quiet, with only a few birds beginning to chirp and break the silence.

Although our main objective is to track elephants, it is the smaller life forms that keep us engaged. We busy ourselves observing the more than 160 species of birds found in Kenya, among them the colorful European roller, perhaps an unwelcomed seasonal migrant from Europe that we have observed in apparent competition for similar resources with the local drongo. There are also countless hornbills, a few extravagant secretary birds strutting around, and more than a dozen colorful bee-eaters that dart through the air. The sound of my pen on my notebook competes with the sounds of the birds as we continue to wait.

An hour passes, with the temperature increase causing the sweat to pour from my body. Although it is only 9:30 a.m., I am completely covered to protect my face and neck from the sun. Although this only makes me sweat more profusely, it is a necessary precaution for my sun-sensitive skin in this desert environment. Ever so slowly the scene changes, and I begin to lose all sense of time. A small group of Burchell's zebra warily emerge from the brush. Cautiously surveying the area for predators, they pay particular attention to our vehicle across the water. Pulling back both their upper and lower lips, they show their bottom and top teeth, a sign that they are investigating our presence. We are thus rewarded for our patience.

But there is more to come. It is obvious that this spot sees much elephant activity because there is evidence of dung piles, many a few weeks old to some that are more recent, perhaps left only yesterday. Footprints of all sizes seem frozen in the dried mud along the shore, and the air is full with a sweet odor characteristic of elephant.

Suddenly, and without any warning that we are able to detect, a large female emerges from the right. She hesitates briefly, raising her trunk high to sniff the air. Apparently satisfied, she continues to lumber toward us as eight others follow close behind. This is a cow and calf group, with four adults and subadults accompanying five calves that we estimate to be between one and four years of age. It is surprising how quiet such a large animal can be. If they are not breaking branches or pulling leaves, you would have no idea they were on the march.

The calves begin to move toward the water's edge until the matriarch, who typically brings up the rear, rushes forward, nudging the entire group to continue on. Perhaps she has spotted fresher water or wishes the young to enter from more stable ground. Regardless of the reason, it is obvious who is in charge. The group stops opposite our vehicle and like the zebra, stares closely at us until they are comfortable enough to continue. They work their way to their favored spot, which is luckily in better view for us. The group drinks from the water, we take our photos, and they begin playing and bathing nearby. The zebra have yet to step toward the water.

Vocalization plays a major part in communication among social creatures, and elephants are no exception. Having rather limited vocalization, however, elephants keep in touch with one another by making low growls, first thought to be tummy rumbles. Females are capable of making twenty-two different sounds, whereas males produce only seven; you are free to pose your own hypothesis as to why this might be. For years, it was thought by many that elephants had a sixth sense. That is, they appeared to communicate with one another over vast distances without making sounds, causing some scientists to suggest that elephants used ESP.

It is now known that in addition to the low sounds that are heard among elephants, they also produce a number of sounds that are inaudible to the human ear. Thus, a significant amount of communication by elephants is carried out through infrasound at a subsonic level that is more than an octave below the level humans can distinguish. Because of their low frequency, these sounds travel great distances in the bush and may be heard by other elephants up to six kilometers away. Elephants that are well out of sight of others in their family grouping can thus remain in contact using infrasound to coordinate their activities.

We should not be surprised then when from our left enters a rather large male and from just behind us, a young male. The young male is startled when he spots us. Somewhat threatened, he turns our way, throws his head and ears, trumpets a warning, and struts around a bit. This causes a slight adrenalin rush in me, but it soon subsides. Hamisi reminds us of the stressful experiences these elephants have had around humans and that in this early stage of the project, we are working to recognize the elephants while building trust among them. With time, they will become accustomed to human presence.

Backing away, our new arrival finds a spot between us and the cow–calf group, rarely taking his eyes from us. There is perhaps a larger message here that I have begun to understand—the slow building of trust seems as critical to the success of working with wildlife as it does to working with people of different communities.

At about the age of twelve, male elephants begin to mature and typically travel apart from the cow–calf groups. Although not yet socially mature for another eight to ten years, they enter a state called musth when they become sexually active. During musth, males seek out females in heat. The arrival of our two males is probably not a coincidence but perhaps the result of hearing through infrasound that the cow–calf group was to be at the waterhole. They are there to check out the females, and because there appears to be none in reproductive readiness, our male visitors depart shortly after completing their drink.

They do not appear to go too far, however, circling around our vehicle, perhaps to threaten us once again out of frustration because their sexual longings have not been satisfied. The air suddenly erupts with a frightening sound as one of the males has found a convenient way to scratch his side— and a nearby acacia tree begins swaying back and forth. Both males continue to hang out around the waterhole; perhaps they have sensed another group approaching and wish to see whether any of them are sexually receptive.

Then, almost as quickly as the elephants appear, they seem ready to depart. The cow–calf group leaves from the opposite side of the waterhole that they arrived. Like an adolescent boy teasing a girl in the school halls, one of the males follows the cow–calf group in hot pursuit—perhaps hoping that one of the females is in fact in heat. The entire group of females seems bothered by his persistence as they trot off in the distance. The zebras now feel confident enough to approach for their drink, and then they too are gone.

Our day ends with yet another treat. A lone giraffe slowly approaches as the sun begins to set, and we are rewarded with a scene many visitors rarely have a chance to witness. Like the zebras earlier in the day, this giraffe is cautious, taking most of an hour, slowly moving toward the water and checking from side to side each step of the way. Although its height is a marvelous adaptation for browsing among the tops of acacia trees and for sighting potential danger, it is a liability when it comes to drinking.

This dance to drink challenges the giraffe more than any other animal. Although all animals are vulnerable at the waterhole, the giraffe has the most concern, both in terms of its safety and for the effect that gravity plays on its blood pressure. For the giraffe, there is the potential danger of the brain being damaged each time it lowers its head, as when a person has a stroke. Although it has evolved various adaptations to prevent this from happening, it also explains why the giraffe is reluctant to lower its head too far.

We watch in awe as our giraffe begins, slowly and awkwardly, to splay its legs out, one at a time, gaining that sensitive balance that will allow it to lower its head to the water to drink. The water level at this particular spot, however, is about six inches lower than the edge of the waterhole, and it is just too far for our giraffe to manage. He catches his balance, almost falling forward into the water. Changing his strategy, he moves farther down the water's edge, peering in every direction as he saunters slowly toward our vehicle. He is successful at this next attempt. As he finishes drinking, he sways his head, pendulum-like, using the impetus generated by this motion to help lift the front of his body, bringing his front legs together, and thus regaining his upright posture. He slowly departs into the darkness.

The long rains begin within a week of my arrival. It's amazing how after a couple of days of good rain this semiarid region is dramatically altered. Along with the burst of greenery, flowers, and pollen—and hence my allergies—come the young of many of the animals and an onslaught of insects I have yet to see. Although we had been able to observe animals at nearby waterholes now that the rains have come and small basins of water collect almost everywhere, there is no need for them to converge at the few water sources available. It thus becomes increasingly difficult to locate animals for extensive study, presenting the perfect opportunity for me to shift my focus from the bush to the local communities. I welcome the opportunity to begin work in the schools.

Five communities make up the Nyangala cluster of schools at the base of Mt. Kasigau: Kiteghe, Rukanga, Jora, Bungule, and Makwasinyi. It is within these communities that a group of British gap-year students work, assisting in a variety of community projects. I plan to seek the assistance of these young people while working with the schools.

Among the volunteers is a young girl named Amy. It is easy to see why she is so well liked by the villagers in Bungule where she resides—she is vibrant, animated, open, and outgoing, just the attributes required of one who has to integrate into a culturally different community for just a brief period of time. Amy is among the easiest of the sixteen volunteers for me to get to know, reminding me somewhat of my own eighteen-year-old daughter. A parent would be quite proud of her, pleased with the experience she is having and the contributions she is making before moving on to her university studies. It is still hard to believe what happened to her.

Each of the five communities has one primary school serving children in standards (grades) one through eight. There is also one secondary school, Moi High School, a boarding school that serves about 180 children who can both pass the entrance exam and pay the $350 annual tuition. Each day I drive the one hour from TDC to the villages using four-wheel drive vehicles over roads that get worse with each rainfall.

It takes the better part of each day to move between two schools, meeting the school head and teachers to discuss a possible curriculum project and to interact with the many children who are as interested in being with this mzungu as I am to be with them. After three days, I have been introduced to key personnel at each school, and I am reminded of the time required to accomplish even the simplest of tasks—six meetings in three days. But spending this time is a critical element to the trust building that is essential if I expect to return with others to this vibrant region.

Although not in frequent use today, at the time I traveled with a small Polaroid camera that allowed me to snap photos of children and sometimes their parents and teachers, hand them the print, and watch them wait in amazement as their image slowly appeared on the paper. This worked magic at warming people up to me and allowed me to leave something with them. And for many, this was the first time they had seen an image of themselves. It also enabled me to enter their world, thus enabling me to photograph them later with my more sophisticated equipment. The children at the schools greet me on subsequent visits with huge smiles and repeated requests for "peek tours."

While here, I hope to begin a small curriculum project documenting the local culture and way of life. Change is slow as I've come to learn, and teachers here have never been part of a curriculum-writing effort, their own history, for instance, not written down. But the teachers are eager, and when

I return a few days after our first meeting, many have rough notes already in hand. Because I cannot be in each of the schools every day, I seek the assistance of the British volunteers, training them to interview teachers and other villagers to collect information on the culture of the region. This initiative becomes a major activity for many over the following two weeks, and we are able to provide the community with a written history of their own people.

Mornings in Africa are full of stories if one is able to read the signs left on the ground by the animals from the previous evening. The evening sounds also tell a story all their own. One particular evening, the story was not pleasant.

A small group of us, two volunteers and a staff of four, were having a quiet dinner together at TDC after returning late from the villages. The sixteen young British volunteers had spent the previous evening at the camp before taking off as a group for a weekend of camping at Lake Chala, about three hours south of TDC on the Kenya–Tanzania border. These young people were quite comfortable at TDC, having spent two weeks at the site during their orientation before moving into the communities. The night they were with us was much more active than most other nights with them playing guitar, singing, and generally having a good time. Amy was among the group and as always, an active participant.

Halfway through our dinner, one of the ground staff approached our table and in unfaltering Kiswahili began talking to the Kenyan staff around the table. He grabbed the immediate attention of all of us. Although three of us understood little of what was being said, the wide eyes and open mouths of others at the table told the story very well.

Two of the TDC staff had overheard a radio communication between the police in the town of Taveta, where the student volunteers had gone, and those in Voi, the town closest to TDC, about fifty kilometers away. The report said that one person in a group of British young people was missing in the waters of Lake Chala. This was all that was relayed—no name, no details, and no way to verify the message because the transmitter was broken and we had no way with which to join the conversation. The only real means of communication available with anyone more than twenty kilometers away was via satellite telephone that, throughout the evening, proved to be somewhat inefficient, occasionally losing its connection or delaying its message.

We were left only imagining what might have happened. Hamisi, who was familiar with the area, having grown up nearby, thought that perhaps some of the students may have gone out with a local fisherman in a dugout canoe, which then capsized. He quietly mentioned that there were crocodiles in the lake. After two hours of trying to obtain any information from local police headquarters and the Kenyan Tourist Commission in Nairobi, three vehicles left TDC to travel to Lake Chala. The time was 10:00 p.m.

The plan was to have two vehicles bring the young people back to TDC with one staying behind to work with the local authorities. I was initially invited to accompany the group, basically to serve as counselor to the young people on the ride back home, but this was changed at the last minute because of possible security threats and problems that might be encountered along the road, either by the common shiftas or bandits, who frequently attacked vehicles at night, or by local authorities questioning a convoy of Kenyans with an American among the group. I waited the night for the group, and their story, to return.

Two vehicles returned to camp about 10:00 a.m. the following morning, carrying fifteen exhausted and emotionally drained young people. Slowly climbing out of the vehicle, they dragged themselves and their gear ever so slowly into a large sitting area near the front gate. Not a word was spoken for some time until I cautiously began probing with a few questions. Not knowing how to begin such a painful conversation, I first asked whether they had found people willing to assist them. Very few, they said, disappointed with the lack of police response and assistance provided from locals as well as camp staff where they were staying.

I then invited anyone to relate the events that they had just experienced. Slowly and quietly, we began to understand the horror and trauma these young people had experienced. To be honest, it sounded like a script from a bad B horror movie—but it was very real.

It was late in the day when they all arrived. A few from the group asked some locals whether it was okay to swim in the lake. They were assured that it was, although they were told that the nearby hotel allowed swimming in their pool for thirty shillings a person (about forty cents). No warnings about potential danger were offered. After quickly setting up camp and gathering some firewood and water for cooking, half a dozen boys went swimming off a nearby rock. As the sun began to set and they began to feel a bit uncomfortable and nervous, they wisely got out of the water.

It was close to 7:00 p.m. when three girls, including Amy, decided they would go in for a swim. Amy, you should know, was an accomplished and confident swimmer, having worked as a lifeguard prior to coming to Kenya. The girls waded slowly along the shoreline, two of them up to their knees and Amy confidently moving out into chest-deep water. Suddenly, as the other two report, Amy was yanked underwater. The kids back at the camp all report hearing a scream, even those who were some distance from the water, they thinking it not much more than Amy seeing a snake along the shoreline. Amy remained under water for about ten seconds before she reappeared, her head breaking the surface of the water only momentarily before she screamed, "A crocodile has me." She was violently thrust back underwater, not to be seen again. One boy, Andrew, who had witnessed all the activity from the shore, waded out with a flashlight in search of Amy. He reported seeing a couple of large eyes along the surface of the water not long after Amy disappeared. This was witnessed by at least three others at the scene.

Crocodiles are one of the most feared animals in all of Africa. They, along with hippos and lions, account for more than a thousand deaths and disappearances a year. Several prey animals have been found wedged under submerged branches and stones, leading to reports that the crocodiles store unwanted prey until a later date. Some claim this is necessary for the prey to decompose before the crocodiles are able to tear portions of flesh. When feeding, a number of individuals will hold on to a carcass with their powerful jaws while twisting their bodies. The anchorage provided by the other individuals allows large chunks to be torn off for easier swallowing. These were the gruesome details we were reading about as we pondered Amy's tragedy.

The group apparently pulled themselves together long enough to begin a search and rescue mission, although they wisely did not reenter the water. Breaking into three smaller groups, one searched along the shore of the lake; one tried, unsuccessfully, to get help from the local fishermen and hotel staff; and one group went out to the road hoping to locate the police. This went on until 3:00 a.m. when the group stopped searching, took three rooms at the hotel, and tried to get some rest.

Because no telephone communication had been possible, they could only hope that staff at TDC would somehow find out about their plight and arrive. Knowing of the potential of meeting shiftas at night, they didn't expect that anyone from TDC would arrive until late the following morning, waiting until daybreak before taking to the roads. They were exhausted but nonetheless overjoyed when three TDC vehicles arrived at 4:00 a.m., thus relieving them of the pressures they were under to make decisions, attempt to take action, and deal with locals—all to no avail. Although happy to see staff from TDC, they were reluctant to leave without Amy.

The morning they returned was as somber as any that could be imagined. The group was given a decent meal and showered. Later, they would meet with the Kenyan director of their program, who along with the executive director from England, who happened to be in the country, had chartered a small plane and made a brief visit to the scene of the incident. The kids were encouraged not to make any rash decisions but to pack all their belongings and plan to leave for Nairobi the following morning. They would stay in Nairobi for a week to gain some perspective, telephone their families, and then decide their future course of action. After two emotionally charged days with little if any sleep, they welcomed a night of rest. The evening was spent with their directors sharing the experience as they remembered it before turning in for the night.

As a father of a daughter just one month older than Amy, I was moved by the actions of these young people. I was also encouraged by Amy's energy and eagerness to become active and involved in the lives of others. I cannot imagine the horror, however, of receiving a telephone call from overseas informing you that your daughter was missing and presumed dead—attacked by a crocodile of all things.

Amy's father flew to Kenya the morning following the tragedy and immediately went on to Lake Chala. The Kenya Wildlife Service was on hand, organizing a search party of divers hoping to locate the body. Three days later, after the father had returned to Nairobi, the body was discovered, missing most of an arm. At least the father had a body to take back home.

There is risk and danger in all we do, but we will never make this world a better place if we are not willing to take some risks, although guarded they must be. Most of the young people returned to their host communities and their volunteer work after a one-week stay in Nairobi. Their return to their villages demonstrated their commitment to the people with whom they had spent so much time. And although the most difficult of acts, Amy's parents donated the funds to build a community center in Bungule, Amy's village, in her memory.

Tragedy happens, but people must go on. Many years earlier, January 29, 1986, to be exact, I was sitting in an airport in Auckand, New Zealand, waiting to catch a flight to Melbourne, Australia, to visit friends I had not seen in over ten years. On a nearby television, a morning newscaster was broadcasting reports and images of the explosion of the Challenger spacecraft that had occurred just hours before on January 28, 1986, in the United States. To the horror of tens of thousands of schoolchildren and adults who were watching live that morning, seven US astronauts, including America's first teacher in space, Christa McAuliffe, perished in a tragedy just minutes after liftoff.

Later that evening, President Ronald Reagan, who had planned to speak on the state of the union, addressed the nation instead on the day's tragedy. In part of his message he addressed young people, saying, "I want to say something to the schoolchildren of America who were watching the live coverage of the shuttle's takeoff. I know it is hard to understand, but sometimes, painful things like this happen. It's all part of the process of exploration and discovery. It's all part of taking a chance and expanding man's horizons. The future doesn't belong to the fainthearted; it belongs to the brave. The Challenger crew was pulling us into the future, and we'll continue to follow them. ... We'll continue our quest in space. There will be more shuttle flights and more shuttle crews and, yes, more volunteers, more civilians, more teachers in space. Nothing ends here; our hopes and our journeys continue."

Our involvement with education in East Africa continues. Fast-forward about eighteen years after the tragedy that ended Amy's life. In 2015, Hyla and I retired from our full-time careers; our children were grown, married, well into their careers, and raising families of their own. We now have five beautiful grandchildren. To celebrate our retirement, we decided to take our then eleven-year-old twin grandsons on safari. We call this "global grandparenting," a responsibility we think all grandparents should assume with their grandchildren if they have the time, resources, and concern for the health of our planet.

Kenya, at the time, was not a place we wanted to risk taking young children—internal tensions and indiscriminate terror attacks were on the rise, challenging the country. Between December 27, 2007, and February 28, 2008, more than 1,000 people were killed in the postelection violence that occurred when allegations of voter fraud were raised by both sides in the hotly contested, ethnically based presidential election. In September 2013, the Westgate Mall attack in Nairobi kept the world on edge, leaving sixty-seven dead and 175 wounded. In two days in June 2014, more than sixty people were killed in attacks in and around the eastern coastal region in Lamu County. Then, on April 2, 2015, terrorist groups attacked a university in Garissa, killing 148 students, with Al-Shabab, a terrorist group based in Somalia, claiming responsibility.

We opted instead to travel to Tanzania, a safer alternative. Thanks to Facebook, I was able to locate a guide I had traveled with once before. It was our luck that Ernest had in the meantime established his own small safari company.

We wanted to track the Great Wildebeest Migration—the annual movement of millions of wildebeests and zebras that follow the rains and green pastures across northern Tanzania into southern Kenya. In preparation, we spent the year introducing Carter and Logan to the idea of international travel as well as to various aspects of pan-African culture, attending African cultural events at local universities; eating in one of the Ethiopian restaurants in our region; and watching countless videos depicting the people, cultures, and environment we were likely to encounter throughout our safari.

Wanting to ease the boys into international travel and being away from home with Grandma and Grandpa, we spent the first week in Europe. Our first few days were spent in Amsterdam shaking our jet lag, walking the canal-lined streets, and visiting sites we thought would interest the boys, including the Anne Frank House and Van Gogh Museum. Following this, we stayed with some Swiss friends in the quaint city of Lucerne and in their small vineyard in the Italian part of the country. The boys were great travelers—eager to explore new settings, open to new experiences, and engaging with the new people they met.

The safari itself was without a doubt the most engaging safari experience I'd ever had. Our adventures were many, and although I was interested and intrigued by the wildlife we encountered on safari as always, it is the inter-personal encounters with people that I truly value and strive to develop and maintain. On most trips I embark upon, as I've shared in earlier chapters, I seek out personal contacts whenever and wherever possible. This trip was no exception.

We remained in Arusha for a few days after our safari, intent on visiting a school I had learned about six months earlier while speaking at a confer-ence on the internationalization of agriculture education, a field of study that I never even knew existed before the invitation to speak. Ernest, our safari guide during the previous two weeks, drove us from Arusha, an hour west, passing the main city market, a few small coffee plantations, and the Arusha campus of the International School of Moshi, a school I'm sure I'd applied to early in my career, before heading toward the Monduli hills and the town of Monduli.

It was a good thing that we were in our four-wheel drive safari jeep because the road from the town to the school was not unlike many of the tracks we had encountered during the previous weeks on safari. And what a surprise it was when we pulled up to the school to find not only a sprawling school campus unlike any other we had seen along the Tanzania countryside but a full American-style basketball court to boot.

A tall, youthful young man greeted us upon our arrival and introduced him-self as Peter Luis, the founder and school director. Energetic, outgoing, and personable, Peter gave us a little background on the school before asking a couple of sixth form (twelfth grade) students to give us a tour of the campus. Enthusiastic and quite articulate, Lenge and Anna beamed with pride as they took us from classroom to classroom, introduced the twins to similar-aged students, and answered many of our questions. An unexpected treat was Peter's suggestion that Lenge take us to his family's boma (family homesite) for a brief visit. We had an engaging conversation with his mother and grand-mother, took a few photos, and exchanged a few small gifts.

The Orkeeswa School is a community-based secondary school founded in 2008. Located in an underserved Maasai community of Orkeeswa village about ten kilometers from Moduli, the school serves the secondary educa-tional needs of four villages covering an area of approximately thirty-two square kilometers that is home to a population of over 10,000 people, the majority of whom are Maasai. The school is supported by the Indigenous Education Foundation of Tanzania (www.ieftz.org), a US-based tax-exempt

501c3 that conducts fund-raising initiatives to provide scholarship support for the growing number of students.

The Maasai are among the most traditional of the hundreds of ethnic groups living in East Africa. Comprising a population of approximately one to one and a half million people, they live on semiarid and arid lands along the Great Rift Valley, spanning southern Kenya and northern Tanzania. Livestock, such as cattle, goats, and sheep, is the traditional and primary source of income and sustenance for the Maasai. Individuals, families, and clans establish close ties through the giving or exchange of cattle.

Traditionally a seminomadic people living under a communal land management system, the Maasai face an increasing array of challenges, from restrictions on where their cattle may graze (they have been forced off of many of their traditional lands that have come under the management of the various conservation authorities) to the effects of climate change increasing the frequency and severity of droughts. Family plots, generally no longer large enough to accommodate large herds of animals, force more and more people to farm—something traditionally frowned upon because cultivated land is no longer seen as suitable for grazing. More recently, the Maasai have grown dependent on food, such as maize meal, rice, potatoes, and cabbage, that is produced by others.

From its inception, the Orkeeswa School has collaborated with the local community leadership to develop a model of holistic education that responds to the specific needs and challenges of the students and their community while addressing the rather challenging Tanzanian National Curriculum. And unlike most secondary schools throughout East Africa where students live on campus, Orkeeswa students live and learn within their village, taking their education home every day and thus having an immediate impact in their homes and throughout their community. The school is grounded in a deep respect for the local culture, with students striving to develop the capacity to protect their values and prevent exploitation, all while learning to make long-term decisions that positively impact their community and preserve traditional practices.

Orkeeswa School lies within a traditional cultural community that has a long history of early marriage of girls via an intricate exchange of cattle and gender discrimination, thus severely limiting the educational opportunities for girls. The school, nonetheless, succeeds in offering a coeducational environment that allows girls and boys to learn and lead side by side while gaining respect and confidence in their abilities to become respected leaders in their community. The school has achieved remarkable success in this regard; in 2018, more than half of the school's 270 students were girls.

In addition to addressing the Tanzanian National Curriculum, the school curriculum is supplemented by an array of programs that are designed to nurture students' creativity, leadership, and capacity to think outside the box—educational elements that oftentimes remain outside the standard Tanzanian educational experience. Such programming includes a unique range of club activities (including such offerings as robotics, storytelling, yoga, art, and music) and multiple opportunities to engage in sports (including football/soccer, rugby, basketball, and netball) and community service (the 2018 fourth form, or tenth grade, contributed over 4,000 hours of community service by offering teacher assistance in five area primary schools) and provides a growing number of students the opportunity for exchange experiences in Great Britain, South Africa, Uganda, and the United States.

In just the first eight years of its existence, Orkeeswa School has exhibited multiple successes. Drawing students from four primary schools in the region that rank in the bottom 15 percent of schools nationwide, by 2018, 100 percent of the form four students had passed the national exams (compared to 70 percent nationwide), and 100 percent qualified for A levels (advanced levels) compared to 22 percent nationwide. What tremendous success!

When we returned to the school from our visit to Lenga's boma, the boys busied themselves playing basketball while Hyla and I met with Peter and a few others on his staff. We discussed the possibility of offering professional development for teachers over a period of time. We would consider returning twice a year at the start of each term to provide a few days of teacher training and then remain for three to four weeks to implement what we have taught. Hyla and I have been visiting the school twice a year since and now serve on its board of directors.

Not wanting the experience to fade into long-term memories for the boys was another of our hopes. Once we returned home, we approached their sixth grade teachers with an offer to assist in establishing a relationship between Orkeeswa and the middle school in Hudson, Ohio. The initial idea was to establish an international partnership story project, something I had been involved with many years earlier (Cushner, 1992). Through this initiative, children in Hudson, Ohio, would begin the writing of a number of stories about some global or social issue that would then be completed by children at Orkeeswa. One teacher in particular, Beth, embraced the idea and was willing to allow Hyla and me to enter her classroom periodically to work with her, others on her teaching team, and more importantly, her students.

Hyla and I helped Carter and Logan prepare an overview of their safari experience that they shared with all the sixth grade students. We introduced something about Maasai culture and the particular obstacles faced by families in the Orkeeswa community, such as the challenges girls face in pursuit of an education, practices of early marriage, and the impact of climate change on the local economy as a means of introducing the concept of global and social issues.

The students eagerly developed stories that focused on a range of topics with which they were familiar and were keen to explore, from hunger to bullying to school attendance. The initial effort had 100 Hudson sixth graders develop the first half of twenty-three partnership stories. I took these stories to Orkeeswa a few weeks later, and seventy-five Orkeeswa students finished the stories, translating them into Kiswahili. In mid-October I returned to Ohio with the finished stories, a variety of Maasai artifacts, and small handmade bracelets to give to each of the children. The result of this effort was twenty-three internationally collaborative partnership stories in Swahili and English that have been written by children in both countries.

This partnership story project has been repeated at least twice in addition to a number of other collaborative projects that currently link teachers, students, and both communities. The Hudson Middle School Student Council adopted Orkeeswa as a global fund-raising focus and has raised sufficient funds to sponsor at least one student at Orkeeswa with scholarship support. In December 2016, through the initiative of the student council, the Hudson City Council signed a resolution adopting Orkeeswa School, designating it as a "touchstone and point of contact for the commitment to supporting vulnerable populations … and a desire to focus efforts toward the solution of global problems. This adoption would serve as a focal point to allow the residents of Hudson, especially its youth, to learn more about global issues affecting children and to make a meaningful difference worldwide."

Building trusting and long-lasting relationships are key if we are to help people move beyond surface-level, or objective, cultural differences. Hyla and I continue to provide professional development support for the teachers at Orkeeswa through twice-yearly visits, and we have joined the board. Beth made her first visit to the school in July 2017.

Chapter 10

The Ultimate Global Education: A Semester at Sea

Ships can transport more than cargo—they can carry ideas. —C. Y. Tung, Semester at Sea founder

Four months, four continents, fourteen ports in eleven countries, multiple seasons, teaching, traveling, and touring. Biggest challenge? Two suitcases each! And we're off! So began my Facebook post on September 4, 2017, when Hyla and I departed for our around-the-world voyage during which we would be teaching on Semester at Sea. This chapter introduces a most unique and innovative global comparative educational experience, one that enables undergraduate students to travel the world onboard a ship redesigned as a floating classroom.

I had worked with Semester at Sea in the summers of 2010 and 2011 when I directed a small program for teachers who had the summers available and were interested in exploring ways to integrate an international component into their teaching. This rather unique Teachers at Sea program ended soon after that when the parent organization, the Institute for Shipboard Education (ISE), stopped offering graduate programs. When the credit-granting academic home for the program shifted from the University of Virginia to Colorado State University in 2016, an emphasis of the intercultural development of all participants was given higher priority, and I happily found a new niche where my talents and interests could be utilized.

I served as the Intercultural Specialist for the Fall 2017 voyage, which began in Hamburg, Germany, and sailed on to Spain, Ghana, South Africa, India, Myanmar, Vietnam, China, and Japan before returning via Hawai'i to San Diego four months later. My major responsibility in addition to teaching two classes in intercultural communication was to integrate an intercultural component into Global Studies, the one course that all students are required to take. Hyla would serve as an assistant in the Global Studies course while also working with students who required special learning accommodations. Who wouldn't pass up this opportunity? After close to a year of planning, we were about to set sail!

Semester at Sea is a comparative international study abroad program that takes place onboard the MV World Odyssey, a ship that sails for a semester, offering a variety of itineraries, the most popular being this around-the-world voyage. Students attend classes most days that the ship is at sea as they would on their home campus. Each course, however, is modified to take advantage of the ten to twelve international ports that are visited, giving students an opportunity to integrate the content of their courses with firsthand, practical experiences gaining a comparative, global perspective as they visit such places as schools, orphanages, religious and historical sites, natural wonders, local and international organizations, financial and business districts, and media outlets.

Some 550 students representing more than 200 US universities and thirty-five countries, twenty-seven faculty and twenty-seven staff (collectively referred to as staculty by ISE, the always inclusive organization), about fifteen young children accompanying their parents, and ten lifelong learners (adult passengers who enjoy traveling with young people while attending classes) along with a crew of more than 170 who themselves represented twenty-plus countries comprised our shipboard community.

The months of waiting for this day finally arrived, and we were off! Among the student participants, few knew anyone else who boarded the bus in Hamburg as they made their way to Bremerhaven, the port city where we would embark upon our new home, The World Odyssey. Questions, anxiety, and uncertainty abounded. What will my new roommate(s) be like? What about taking classes from professors I know nothing about? Even if they had mixed reviews on ratemyprofessors.com, there are no options to take the same course with another instructor! What is it like to live aboard a ship for four months? Will I get seasick, and if I do, how will I manage it? Are there seasickness days like snow days when classes are canceled? What about homesickness? What am I getting myself into?

Fast-forward a few weeks. We'd sailed for four and a half days from Germany to Spain, our first port of call. The first day at sea was spent in a variety of orientation sessions. Part of what I presented, six times in one day to groups of about eighty students per session, was designed to introduce basic concepts related to intercultural communication and interaction. We watched and discussed the often-viewed TED Talk, *The Danger of a Single Story*, where Chimamanda Ngozi Adichie challenges viewers to learn to see beyond the stereotypic single story they may have of others—a perfect way to ground our upcoming experience and begin to consider the various people and countries we would visit. Classes too had begun.

We arrived in Barcelona, our first destination, half a day late because of rough weather that led quite a few—perhaps as many as 15 percent of the shipboard community—to encounter their first days of seasickness. Our delay also presented the administrative team its first set of challenges because they had to reschedule more than half a dozen required field classes that we would miss. The ship stayed in Spain for four days—two in Barcelona and two in Valencia.

Eight days after departing Spain, we arrived in Ghana, where we would spend two days in its capital, Accra, followed by two days in the port city of Takoradi. Eight more days at sea found us in Cape Town, arriving a day late because of bad weather and rough seas, again having to cancel the first day's field classes and excursion. We were scheduled to depart Cape Town after five days but were delayed yet again, unable to leave the port because of local storms.

The entire shipboard community was called to meet that evening only to learn that because of our delayed departure from Cape Town, we would have to miss our one-day stop in Mauritius if we were to make our scheduled arrival time in Cochin, India. This meant that we would be on the ship for twelve straight days without a break. We had our first IPAD day—in port academic day—holding our regularly scheduled classes, all the while looking out at Table Mountain in the distance, unable to leave the ship. The frustration was beginning to build throughout the shipboard community before we'd even departed Cape Town.

But this was all a part of the experience—learning to accept the reality that we would be unable to control many factors on our voyage and that we would simply have to accept and adapt to the uncertainty that lay ahead. These are all, by the way, good intercultural attributes and skills to develop as we work to enhance our abilities to adapt to a rapidly changing uncertain and globally connected future.

My major responsibility was to integrate an intercultural perspective throughout the Global Studies course. I was to accomplish this by delivering a number of presentations designed to develop major concepts from the field of intercultural communication and education that were timed to coincide with the kinds of experiences the students were most likely to encounter on the voyage. One of the strands I focused on was to introduce the eighteen-theme culture general framework that I had coauthored early in my career (Cushner & Brislin, 1996; introduced briefly in chapters 3 and 4).

The first five themes devoted to emotional issues were especially relevant early in the voyage when students were undergoing the process of finding their place and space both within their new shipboard community and while engaging with their first real intercultural encounters in port. Later in the voyage, once students had become more comfortable moving in and out of various countries and cultures, the remaining themes designed to help them better understand some of the cultural difference and practices they were encountering would become more relevant.

Following most of my intercultural presentations, all 550 students would meet in twenty-five smaller groups scattered throughout the ship for reflective sessions designed to integrate the new concepts with the firsthand experiences they were having in port. Most students considered these staculty-led reflective sessions as the most beneficial component of their shipboard experience, allowing them to share their individual and group adventures, hear and learn from others' experiences, and begin to improve their understanding while connecting what they were learning to what they had encountered.

One of our reflection sessions captured in this chapter took place after our stay in Myanmar when students were asked to apply the culture general themes that reflect people's emotional responses—anxiety, ambiguity, belonging, prejudice, and disconfirmed expectations. Various conversations were going on throughout the ship among the twenty-five reflection groups. After the initial whole-group presentation, my role was to float among the various groups, facilitate if needed, and listen in on some of the discussions … as you can do now.

I came upon group twelve gathered on the port side of the dining hall on deck six, where Diane, one of the resident directors and group facilitators, had asked about any anxiety students may have encountered when in port. Sarah was the first to respond.

"Touch is an interesting sense that usually communicates intimacy, such as a hug shows support, a kiss communicates love, a handshake demonstrates a genuine greeting of hello and nice to meet you, and a bro shake or bro hug shows a certain welcome between males. I, for one, do not like human touch no matter how genuine it may be. I squirm when someone new extends his or her hand. I tend to shy away from hugs from my parents and cheek kisses from my grandparents. It is not that I'm germaphobic or that I do no not like people. Instead, I am simply uncomfortable with a new hand reaching for mine, an unanticipated hug with a stranger, or even a welcome-home kiss from my mother. So for me, I had various interactions in Ghana that caused me anxiety because everyone seemed to touch all the time simply as a sign of welcome, hello, and thank you.

"Back home in the United States," she went on, "people are much less welcoming, more often than not offering nothing but a glance, silence, or at best, mumbling little more than a hi. However, in Ghana I was greeted with the complete opposite. Hands reached for mine, arms wrapped around my side, and words were spoken so fast I could not keep up even though everyone was speaking English.

"As I stepped out of the bus once we left the port, I was really surprised to encounter a group of people who seemed so happy to see me before they ever even spoke with me! Some of this may be because I represented a potential source of income if I bought something from them. But I also found that many people welcomed me to their country; they wanted to call me by my name and help me out like helping me get a taxi when needed—all while holding onto my hand. I squirmed, but I couldn't get free; their hold was so tight. As friends dragged me away, I had to stop to breathe—I had not even looked at the city yet!

"As I walked around the art market and the surrounding streets, I was met with similar interactions. Women would grab my hand, and they would occasionally kiss it, while welcoming me into their shop. Children would run up to our group and seek high-fives. Men would hold onto my shoulders and tell me I was beautiful and ask if they could come visit me in the States. With each interaction, I became more and more uncomfortable and anxious. I dreaded returning to the bus and being bombarded by the locals I'd encounter along the way. I dreaded getting to the port and being bombarded with handshakes. I wanted my stern, unfriendly, yet comforting New Jersey neighbors back!

"And then I met my host mother for a home-hosted dinner. We had met only three seconds earlier, and she was already saying, 'Oh-oh! You are here, and you are welcomed.' Then, she greeted me with a hug and kiss.

"As we drove to her home, she did not let go of my hand. She kept shaking my arm and telling me how excited she was and asking if I could spend just one night so she could show me her village. I sat tense; I wanted my arm back, and I wanted a protective bubble around my body. The night went on, and with each introduction, a hug would follow. Although my body was still tense and uncomfortable, I became more understanding."

Obviously still shook up and breathing hard while relating the story, Sarah continued, "As I laid in bed journaling about my Ghanaian experience, I focused on the friendliness of the country as well as my discomfort with this friendliness. As I wrote, I realized how selfish I was being. How can I say I felt anxious in a situation that was meant to express pure happiness and authenticity? I was upset that I let my anxiety and discomfort with one situation shut me down. This country welcomed me into their home, and I was uncomfortable with the way they interact; yet this is what they know."

Diane let Sarah's story resonate for a minute before asking, "So, Sarah, what have you learned about yourself as well as the process of traveling?"

Her reply was fairly quick.

"I've realized that by no means were the individuals trying to make me uncomfortable like I may have thought at first. Instead, the Ghanaians were simply welcoming me and excited to show off their country. I've learned that anxiety goes away the more you expose yourself to the things that make you anxious. The longer I was with the family and the more that was explained to me, the less threatening everything seemed.

"Anxiety, although not a welcomed feeling for me, is something I've found that is inherent in travel—it is natural to feel some anxiety in a new place. And while I didn't want to feel it, I also didn't intend for it to get the best of me or control my experience. It's just something I have to learn to overcome—and I think this whole experience is helping me to do so. The longer I expose myself to the things that initially may make me uncomfortable, the more familiar they will become, the more accepting I will be, and the less anxiety I will feel."

Diane's facilitation partner, Derek, asked whether anyone else had experiences related to anxiety while in any of the ports. Amber, a junior from Arizona State University, was quite animated as she shared one of her experiences in India.

"When our tuk-tuk driver, Rafi, didn't recognize the restaurant that we wanted to get to, I wasn't too worried [a tuk-tuk is a small motorized three-wheel taxi used for everyday transportation by many in India and elsewhere in Asia]. But then, when my phone read no service, I started to get a little concerned that Sue and I might not reconnect with the others we'd planned to meet. Then, when we'd been driving for about twenty minutes with Rafi promising to take us somewhere better for dinner, I was full-on anxious. Why hadn't we asked where we were going or negotiated the fare beforehand? What if we weren't actually headed to a restaurant? My head was just spinning with all kinds of possibilities.

"With Bollywood music blaring through the speakers, I heard Ken's voice reminding me that good cross-cultural travelers have a high tolerance for ambiguity. Once out of the port area and into the heart of Kochi, I began to relax a bit. Even if I still didn't know where we would end up, at least there were other people around. Rafi eventually pulled into a restaurant and walked right in after us; he seemed to assume a role of protector. Because we befriended our driver, not only were we able to ask questions about the food, but we also learned a lot about life in Kochi.

"After dinner, Rafi took us around town to many popular areas overlooking the backwaters and even let us practice driving the tuk-tuk on an empty strip of road. The longer we spent with him, the more I understood that he did not see transportation the same way as we do at home. He really wanted to become our guide for the evening and share his love for Kochi rather than simply take us from point A to point B. Once we were able to relax, we began to trust him more and more, even laughing about our initial mistrust. We really had a good time with him and saw quite a lot that I'm sure we would have never seen on our own. We enjoyed being with him so much that we arranged for him to take us around the next day as well."

"And what did you learn from this?" Derek asked.

"My message to all is simple," Amber responded. "Work through your anxiety and strive to develop a trust in others."

"Anyone have a similar experience to share?" asked Diane.

"Well, I also had an experience in India that led me to rethink how I perceive others," chimed Andrew. "This concept of being an 'academic adventurer,' as we've been hearing in our Global Studies class, has been rather troubling for me. I understand the general idea—going somewhere to experience and learn about a place firsthand is very different from visiting someplace and simply posting cool Instagram photos or Facebook posts. I honestly do try my best to be more than a tourist, yet I find myself often asking if I'm exhibiting stereotypic tourist behavior nonetheless.

"Does going to the Taj Mahal make me less of an academic adventurer and more of a tourist? Does driving around in a tuk-tuk all day with the same driver take away from my ability to gain greater meaning from a country? I'm still reluctant to participate in most tourist activities as well as hesitant to engage with most of the people I encounter when on a tour. It's a problem I'm still working on. When I think of stereotypical tourist activities, I think of locals knowing how to take advantage of touristy, college students like us who don't know any better. The concept of a personal prejudice involves acknowledging that one has predetermined, most likely judgmental and unquestioning, thoughts or beliefs about a group of people. For me, the judging comes rather easy—I assume that any taxi driver or street vendor who picked me out as a tourist and tried to talk to me was by nature a bad person. Confronting and questioning this prejudice took hard work and effort.

"My revelation came in India, and I'm not really sure if it reflects anxiety or ambiguity, or perhaps a bit of both. A young Indian woman approached us trying to sell us some bags. This has happened to us dozens of times before, not only in India but almost everywhere we've traveled. We were used to having to say no ten times before people would finally leave us alone. However, this girl was different. I was so busy trying to dismiss her as simply someone trying to sell us something that I didn't realize she was actually trying to help us. She went up to my friend, who had bought a flower lei, and showed her that she was wearing it wrong. She then began to braid it into her hair. This woman, who was about seventeen years old and pregnant, continued to be incredibly interested in our lives, and she never asked us for money. When we asked her about her baby, she glowed with excitement.

"In retrospect, the thought that I would originally shun a young, sweet girl who had no intentions but to help us and who wanted to talk with us about her future and her baby makes me a little embarrassed. It is this embarrassment that has encouraged me to try to get rid of some of the other prejudices I might unconsciously hold. I talked to my tuk-tuk drivers after that, I didn't dismiss street vendors, and I learned to try to understand everyone's views a little better. Looking toward the future, I hope to let go of more of my prejudices and be more open to everyone, especially those in the tourist industry who may just be helping me become a better academic adventurer."

Diane chimed in at that point, "So it sounds as if Andrew has confronted some of his own prejudices or preconceived notions about others, and like Amber who had to overcome some of her initial anxiety, both learned that people can generally be trusted and even helpful—once you get beyond the anxiety-driven preconceived notions we may hold."

From this group, I moved on to another part of the ship. It was a rather warm day, and I found Brian and Sue's group outside on the starboard side sitting just beneath one of the lifeboats—something I hoped we would never have to experience firsthand. They were in the midst of breaking their group of twenty-five into two smaller groups of twelve and thirteen. I arrived just as Sue was setting the context.

"If you recall from the lecture earlier today, Ken talked about the fact that most people encounter a certain amount of ambiguity when they are engaged in intercultural experiences. When faced with ambiguous situations— meaning when things are not very clear—most people try to understand them by applying their own culturally familiar criteria, which oftentimes is incorrect. People who have a high tolerance for ambiguity are those who do not get too flustered when they don't quite understand everything; they feel confident that with time things will become clearer and that they will better understand the situation. Can you share a time when you found things rather ambiguous and did not fully understand what was going on? How did you react in this circumstance?"

Madison was the first in Sue's group to respond. "Boy, I sure had an experience that at first I found really confusing. I was on our tour bus from Delhi to Jaipur, watching the passing landscape, when something caught my eyes. I saw a swastika symbol boldly painted on the top of a tall, light pink building that I really found disturbing. My initial reaction was one of shock because I immediately put the symbol into the context I was most familiar with, the use of the symbol as an emblem for the Nazi Party. I saw the symbol many other times after this, including engraved on a brick wall, displayed on a poster, and painted on the back of a truck. I was really confused and to be honest, a bit scared.

"I grew up Jewish in New Jersey," Madison continued, "and this certainly was something I had learned to associate with hate and genocide. I finally asked our tour guide about this. He explained to our entire group that although much of the Western world has condemned the use of this symbol since World War II, the swastika has been in common use in Indian culture for some 3,000 years. It is still used as a symbol today to represent health and good luck.

"Once I learned this interpretation of the symbol, I relaxed a bit and was better able to understand its purpose and meaning to the Indian people. Rather than feeling offended by the symbol, I found myself eventually accepting it as a part of the Indian culture. It really surprised me how a simple symbol can generate such a reaction in me and yet have such a different meaning in another culture. By clearing up the ambiguity and overcoming my initial reactions, I gained a deeper understanding into the culture of the Hindu people in India."

Allison jumped right in, eager to share what she found to be ambiguous in India. "Being Vietnamese and coming from a diverse community back in California, I never felt out of place anywhere I went. Traveling through Europe before the voyage as well as in Ghana and South Africa I never got more than the occasional stare from people. This happened to most of us on the ship because we were all foreigners who looked different from most of the locals wherever we went. But it wasn't until I got to India that I really began to find myself in many ambiguous situations.

"It seemed that almost everywhere I went, people would constantly yell out, 'China,' 'Ching-Chong,' 'ni hao,' or 'konichiwa' to me. I just couldn't understand how I would stand out more in an Asian country, of all places, as an Asian American? I somehow, and perhaps foolishly, thought that only my Caucasian and African American friends would stand out but not me! As I traveled throughout India, these phrases would constantly be thrown at me, and I found myself asking, 'What are they assuming about my ethnicity? Are they making fun of me?' Here I was, trying so hard to fit in, yet constantly being called out for my unchangeable physical characteristics.

"The feeling of ambiguity and uncertainty seemed constant, and for the first time on the voyage, I was genuinely confused as to why I was being treated this way and struggling to better understand the reasoning behind it. It was not until I talked to one of the Indian students I met at the university welcome reception in Cochin that I better understood the situation. I complained to him, saying that I felt like I was constantly being made fun of. His response surprised me. He said they were not making fun of me, but that most people from India rarely see foreigners so they were very interested in me. He assured me that their intentions are well meaning and that they yelled those phrases at me only because they were trying to put me into a category that they could relate to, even if they obviously misjudged and generalized me with cultures that I am not part of.

"This made me feel a little bit better and got me thinking. I reflected about all the times I saw foreigners in the United States and I would stop and stare and whisper into the ears of my friends as we would gossip about how totally obvious it was that they were tourists. It made me realize that this occurs everywhere and stems from pure curiosity. Although I am careful not to yell racial slurs at tourists that I encounter, I realize that each country is different and has different societal standards.

"After talking to my new Indian friend and spending some time reflecting on the cultural differences and similarities between India and the United States, the ambiguity I felt slipped away and was replaced with a better sense of understanding how all people might react to difference. This just reinforced the idea of cultural diversity, that every culture and country in the world is different from each other and that I should go in with an open mind in order to grasp each culture and country as a whole."

"Boy, it sounds as if India presented many of us with many ambiguous situations," added Nancy, a junior from Kansas. "Let me share my story.

"I was hesitant at first to accept my tuk-tuk driver Wahab's offer to accompany me on my walk around Munnar. Quite frankly, I was afraid. I didn't know what to expect, nor did I have an inkling as to what he expected from me. But I took a chance after reasoning that I wouldn't really know until I found out. As I stepped away from the familiarity of my friends at the Airbnb and onto the highway, a rush of uncertainty—I guess you could say ambiguity—swept over me. I was alone with Wahab. And he was much older and much bigger than me, and he knew the area.

"My understanding of Indian culture regarding the interactions between men and women was limited to the aversion to public displays of affection, so I really had no clue what kinds of signals I might have inadvertently sent to him. But at the same time, I didn't want my fears to interrupt an opportunity to learn and make a new friend. Keeping in mind the cultural and language barriers that stood between us, I decided to ask him a number of questions as a way to engage him in conversation.

"Quickly, our conversation began to blossom. The message was clear, even in simple or broken English—all he wanted was for us to share our worlds with each other. We were both from what felt like different worlds, in two very different places in our lives, but managed to connect over many aspects of our lives. I quickly realized that although my fears were understandable, I would be cautious in a similar situation in my own culture. I am so grateful that I didn't let that fear of what could be stop me from getting to know Wahab. My willingness to embrace that ambiguity ended up being my ticket to not only getting to know an incredible individual but also meeting Ledha.

"During our walk, we stopped along the side of the road to get a cup of tea when we were suddenly beckoned by an older woman from across the street. Although speaking the regional language, through Wahab's translation, I learned that her name was Ledha, and we were able to have a conversation.

This ended with her inviting us both into the house she had lived in for sixty years. She showed us her entire home, from her wood-fired stove, to her bedroom, to her collection of newspapers that dated back to the sixties.

"The only way I can describe the way she looked was that she had joy written all over her face and she glowed so brightly as she floated from room to room showing us her home. She was so happy to share her life, to let us in, and to teach us both. I realize now, looking back on it, that she mirrored myself at the end of the experience—I too was beaming from ear to ear, so happy to have shared in this experience. She, as I, welcomed the ambiguity or uncertainty, knowing there is no greater joy than in sharing your world with another human being. At first, I didn't know what to do. But by trusting in this ambiguous situation, I was carried to places I could have never imagined, and I am forever grateful."

Once again, I moved to another group on the ship, this time to Ricardo and Samantha's group that met on the balcony of the main lecture hall, or Union. The group was smiling and laughing away. They were discussing the notion of disconfirmed expectations, that is, when things don't unfold the way in which you'd expected them to. I'd introduced this as one of the eighteen culture general themes earlier during my lecture, suggesting that because of a variety of reasons, this is something that's frequently encountered when crossing cultural boundaries. I knew that it would lead to lots of discussion because all of the students had experiences that didn't quite end the way they'd anticipated. This is, after all, what prompts much culture learning—when one begins to inquire about why things didn't quite pan out as expected.

Alan was the first I heard tell his story. "I was surprised on many levels during my time in Ghana. I learned quite a bit not only about another person, but to tell the truth, I'm not necessarily proud of what I learned about myself. Before my arrival in Ghana, I found myself mentally preparing for a great deal of culture shock and perhaps some conflict and confrontation resulting from potentially tense and stressful travel situations. I knew that my travel plans were somewhat ambitious and that to safely accomplish everything I wanted to, I would have to be careful, watch my back, and look out for others at all times. These expectations were probably there because of many of the stereotypes I held as well as some of the warnings we'd received during our preport orientation session. I expected absolute chaos and constant harassment from vendors, taxi drivers, scam artists, and everything in between. Much of this turned out to be true, but my overall impression, particularly in my interactions with locals, was disconfirmed in the most positive of ways.

"During my first day of independent travel in Accra, my senses and my nerves were absolutely on high alert! I did in fact encounter some of what I had expected, but the overwhelming majority of my encounters were positive, heartfelt, and genuine. The one encounter that stands out the most for me was the friend a few of us made while walking the side streets and alleyways in Accra. As our taxi driver dropped us near a market, I began to notice that we had ventured far away from any area where tourists were present. The more we walked up a dirt road surrounded by local merchants, chickens, goats, and bicycles, the more out of place we felt.

"After deciding we were most certainly lost, we were approached by a guy about my age who introduced himself as a local hotel staff member and aspiring tour guide. He asked us a bit about our background and informed us that we were definitely not in a tourist part of town. He also assured us many times that his intentions were purely to help us friend to friend and not to scam us in any way. Initially, I deflected most of his offers of assistance because I expected that we would inevitably be hassled into paying for some sort of tour or would end up bargaining our way out of an overpriced taxi ride or store visit of some sort. However, as the day progressed and our new friend delivered on all of his promises without bringing us to a tourist trap of any sort, I began to lose the initial apprehensions and judgments I had.

"I found myself wondering why a local would want to help me if money was not part of the bargain, and then I realized how dismissive such an assumption would sound if directed at my own culture. As we got to know our new friend, Kwasi, I learned that not too long ago he had been living a rather privileged life. His father, it seems, was a prominent local politician but had unfortunately passed away some months ago. Now, he was living with some friends in an apartment in the city and working at a hotel to support himself, all while attempting to make a start in the tourist industry by offering his services to foreigners like us.

"As our relationship progressed from the distrust that typically characterizes overly friendly offers in unfamiliar countries to a true sense of camaraderie and mutual understanding, I began to realize how close-minded and dismissive I had been from the very beginning. In an effort to avoid unnecessary risks, I had prevented myself from giving anyone I encountered the benefit of the doubt, expecting that most overly friendly interactions would be less than sincere and that anyone who wanted to be my friend after having just met me was not to be trusted. However, this just was not the case; it was a disconfirmed expectation to say the least, especially when Kwasi told us that he was really going to miss us and that we should come visit his family any time we return to Ghana. I never thought that the man about my age who I thought was hassling us for money in the morning would become a Facebook friend by the end of the day."

Ricardo asked, "So, Alan, what's the take-away from this? What can others learn from what you experienced?"

Alan was quick to respond. "Don't be too quick to judge others. For the most part, people can be good, probably even those we might be put off by at first. And once you get past the initial hesitation, there are lots of meaningful encounters you can have."

"I had a similar experience I'd like to share," Sara added. "For some reason I thought that a global citizen was one who saw people as similar to one another. I thought that even though people came from different places and may have different religions, beliefs, and values, that we should ignore those differences. I think Ken referred to this as Minimization when he taught us last time about the intercultural continuum [see chapter 5].

"After our time in Ghana, I realized that trying to reduce the level of my anxiety was really counterproductive to the impact travel could have on me and that it could significantly impact my relationships with others. Instead of noticing and valuing the differences between my culture and the one I was visiting, I kept searching for common characteristics in an attempt to connect with the people and place I was in. After a few weeks, I realized that this resulted in a reduction in my curiosity and sensitivity. It was then when I changed my behavior and started reflecting on how to transform myself into a global citizen who tried to better understand and value the cultural and religious differences I was encountering without letting them be an obstacle to my interactions.

"I kept this new realization in mind during my stay in India. My intention was to implement it in two ways. First, I tried to put myself in new and perhaps even uncomfortable situations and then to ask as many questions that came to my mind. That is to say, when I found myself in a situation I wasn't completely comfortable in, I forced myself to overcome the negative feelings until I understood why I had them and to learn from that experience.

"The most profound example of this was during my first morning in Agra. I decided to walk around a nontouristy part of the city. I immediately found myself being stared at by the local men and approached by countless tuk-tuk drivers asking me over and over again if I needed transportation and vendors trying to sell me all kinds of things I didn't really want. I wasn't too bothered by this at first until a local person about my age approached me in the middle of the chaos. I thought for sure that he expected money from me for something. I gave the encounter and him a chance instead, trying hard to ignore my initial perception. We started talking about all kinds of topics, living in a Muslim majority city in a Hindu majority country, the holiness of cows, the customs of this particular place, and all kinds of other interesting topics. As time passed, I felt more comfortable. We became friends and spent the afternoon together in the Taj Mahal and then the Red Fort. By the end of the day, I had learned a lot about the local way of life and about him as a person. The most touristic landmark of India suddenly had turned into one of the most authentic experiences I've had on my voyage up until now. I worked hard to get past my initial anxiety and apprehensions.

"In the second situation, I eliminated some sightseeing I'd planned to do and instead intentionally searched for experiences in which I had to confront uncertainty and ambiguous situations. For example, in Jaipur instead of visiting all the beautiful palaces there were, I found the time to go with a local to his home village forty-five minutes outside the city. Our first stop was at a school. The children didn't speak English, but instead of asking my companion to translate conversations for me, I confronted the ambiguous situation and tried to communicate with the kids using body language and the little Hindi I had learned in my four days.

"The successful connections I felt with them proved to me that I had made the right decision about my priorities during my travels and the way I wanted to approach future destinations. As we've heard many times in class, this experience is really all about the people. In my experience, it is impossible to perceive and analyze a new place accurately and with meaning unless you overcome your anxiety, welcome the ambiguity, and seek out what's unique in the local area. Now, I think I'm learning what it means to become a global citizen."

"I too had an experience I'd like to share," Reilly interjected. "It was the day I was to visit a UNESCO World Heritage Site, the jewel of India, a place almost everyone around the globe knows of, the Taj Mahal. Visiting this famous landmark had been something I've always wanted to do. When I first learned that we would be going to India, the first thing that came to mind was seeing the Taj Mahal. I eagerly awaited what I anticipated to be an incredible experience. I had dreamed of this trip for ages, and the big day finally arrived.

"I had envisioned, or some might say romanticized about, the Taj Mahal so much that when at last I stood in front of the monument, the experience was not what I expected. The Taj Mahal itself was beautiful. But I was overwhelmed by the vast number of people at the site, and my expectations were immediately disconfirmed. I anticipated the day to be flawless, yet I found myself sweaty, dehydrated, flustered by the chaos and noise, agitated by the crowds pushing past me, and frustrated that it wasn't as surreal as I had imagined it to be in my head. After pushing my way through the entrance, I found it impossible to simply take in the moment because I was so consumed by my frustration of not getting a good view or even a decent picture of the infamous place. Additionally, I was disappointed because I was hoping to learn more about the history behind the Taj Mahal. My tour guide, however, gave us about a three-minute history of the place and nothing more.

"Midway through the visit, I realized just how miserable I was making myself, so I tried my best to fix the problem. Because I had Internet access, I searched for information on the Taj Mahal and read up on the history. I tried to escape the crowds by sitting on a bench in the gardens on the side of the monument that was much quieter. After a few minutes, I calmed down, adjusted to the reality of the circumstance, and rejoined my group. The situation was a challenge, but I learned that traveling isn't always what one expects it to be. But I also learned that I can do something to change the situation. I also learned that I must be flexible."

Hana was the next to join in. "I had a most interesting realization in Myanmar that in many ways reflects disconfirmed expectations, especially after all the discussions we'd had about the situation the Rohingya are facing in the north of the country. As most of you know, I'm from Bosnia. The term ethnic cleansing that we've recently been hearing in regard to the situation in Myanmar was initially coined and used during the 1990s war in Yugoslavia, a country that my parents saw fall apart and splinter into what is now eight distinct countries. In Bosnia, war marks and impacts everyone's life, whether you were born before 1992 or today, many years after the war ended.

"I read the news rather avidly, especially in the months before we departed on this voyage. I saw all the reports of people being killed again, somewhere in Southeast Asia, in a country I was soon to visit. I cannot say that I never heard of Myanmar or Burma before, but I can say I had absolutely no knowledge about the place. It seems to be another of those countries that are shadowed by the many ethnocentric views I see perpetuated by many of the world's leading countries. In other words, the lives 'over there' don't matter enough for the world to take any action. The events that are happening make for good news reports, but at the end of the day, it is only a Burmese problem, just like it was only a Bosnian problem when 8,372 Muslims were killed by Serb forces in front of a UN base five months before our war officially ended."

All eyes were on Hana as she continued to share her own personal story. "Before I ever stepped foot in the country, whenever I would think about Myanmar, images of refugees, burned buildings, and people running in convoys would emerge—similar to the images that were ever present at home. I was aware that it was not happening in the whole country, but I thought that some evidence of this as well as feelings of distress would be present. I thought that even if it does not impact the whole of the country directly, it will at least impact it indirectly.

"Do you recall the panel discussion we had the night before we arrived in Myanmar when we discussed the ongoing problems, the ethics of travel, and what our response should be? Many of us thought that we should not visit, thus indirectly showing our support for this action. I was frustrated. I knew that whether we went or not that we were not about to change anything. For years, I was angry at the world for ignoring and not helping my country when it was falling to pieces. Now, I was a part of that same world, and I felt guilty and helpless. Even if I learned something about the country from the people, I would not contribute to changing the problem; I would simply gain more knowledge and understanding, and that was selfish. I know that people's opinions about war don't change easily; it is a complex and sensitive topic governed by fierce opinions. Also, because Myanmar is a mostly Buddhist country and their religion advocates peace, calmness, and well-being of everyone around, I thought this would mitigate the ongoing conflict.

"I was really conflicted once we actually arrived in Myanmar. My imaginary pictures and my preconceived notions were literally torn apart. It seemed like there was no war and that people did not care. I could not believe that I was visiting a country that is in the midst of the war. What war? I didn't see it; everything looked peaceful. I found this absolutely fascinating and extremely sad.

"Then, after speaking with local people, I heard a completely different view of the Rohingya people and the ongoing conflict. According to at least one person I spoke with, *rohingya* means people who are from Bangladesh. She added a few more details about how and why, at least in her view, they go back to Bangladesh. Just like that, the single story that I had in my head exploded. I did not know what to think anymore. Is it really ethnic cleansing? How badly do the Rohingyas want to stay in Myanmar? Why is war happening, and is it really a war after all?

"Following this explanation, she told us that we should not worry because we are completely safe. And I was mad because I was safe, freely walking without any danger while so many of those in the north of the country were fearing for their own safety. To make matters worse, ironically this was the country in which I felt the safest on the entire voyage. What a sad irony that I should now begin to behave no differently from all those people outside Bosnia while our own people were being killed. I am similar to most of the people in the capital city of Yangon who don't even think about the ongoing conflict.

"Now that I am back on the ship, I'm aware of how little I can contribute. I hate that now I sound like a helpless utopian. I don't want to be like many of the volunteers who came to Bosnia to hand out Snickers bars in a war zone. I might never go back to Myanmar again. I don't know what to do to help. I don't trust the world, and I know that the United Nations will arrive here too late to solve problems that are not theirs in the end. I'm really conflicted. Thanks for listening to my experience."

Reilly stood up and faced Hana. "I want to thank you for sharing your story. There's so much I need to understand, and you've helped open my mind to so much that I'd never really considered. I appreciate that. I'm also learning about how complex some situations really are."

I had time to sit and listen in on one more group, this one located in a classroom on deck nine in the front of the ship. The Lido Terrace is a large, brightly lit room, offering two kinds of spaces—about thirty-five chairs facing toward the fairly large computer screen and a similar number of seats scattered around small tables along the front windows. As I entered the room, I heard Max, one of the facilitators, pose the question, "So what are some of the major insights you have gained so far on this experience?"

Brittany was the first to offer her thoughts. "Ghana has been the most impactful country for me so far on this voyage in terms of personal growth. The four days we spent in Ghana affected me in ways that I had hoped this entire experience would. I was forced to confront personal prejudices that I honestly didn't even realize I had and that I now realize skewed the way I viewed much of the world.

"I've grown up in the United States in a culture and society that tends to teach that our American lifestyle is the ideal lifestyle and that other people should aspire to live like us. And if they aren't living like us, they are somehow 'less developed' and we must fix them and teach them how to live the same way that we do. Before arriving in Ghana, I never thought much about how harmful that perspective of other cultures could possibly be. After all, who wouldn't want the comfort of reliable transportation, free Wi-Fi almost everywhere, air-conditioning, and well-maintained plumbing systems? What I didn't consider was that these are luxury items to most people around the world and that they only seem ordinary or necessary to me because I was lucky enough to be born in a place where they are common if not expected.

"I went into Ghana expecting to see people living lives drastically different from my own. And I thought I'd leave Ghana inspired to fix the problems I saw there. I was correct in thinking that the difference in lifestyles would vary. But what I realized through reflecting on my entire visit to Ghana was that just because a person lives a life different from my own does not mean that there is something wrong with it or that it needs to be altered or fixed in some way.

"On my second day in Ghana, I participated in a naming ceremony at a village called Torgome. It was hot, about 90 degrees with about 90 percent humidity. We were there for a few hours in long sleeves and long pants well protected from any mosquitoes. We were all sweating profusely, and I was so ready to cool off. When we finally departed and headed off to lunch, we arrived at an air-conditioned restaurant, and I remember thinking, 'Thank God! Air-conditioning!' And then it hit me! All the people I had just met at the village were still there in the blazing heat and sunlight. They were not here. They were not going to feel the relief of the air-conditioning like I was. I suddenly felt so guilty. Why did I get the privilege of sitting in an air-conditioned space and they did not?

"It wasn't until I was back at the ship participating in our first reflection group that I realized how privileged I sounded—feeling bad that these people wouldn't get to cool down like I would in the refreshing AC. I had to step back and realize that when I visited that village I was not visiting a town in the United States; I was visiting a village in Ghana. I couldn't possibly have the same expectations for two completely different places. The pity I was feeling at the moment for these people was not the same thing they felt for themselves. They don't look at themselves and see poor villagers with little electricity, no running water, and no access to AC to escape the heat. They look at themselves and see wealth in each other, water that quenches their thirst regardless of whether it came from a tap or not, and that the heat is simply a part of the Ghanaian experience!

"Home for me is the northeastern part of the United States. I don't live year-round in the blazing heat; I have four seasons. It's important to remember that when you visit new places, even something as simple as climate can change the way you view people's experiences. I made the assumption that just because I felt that I was dying in the heat that these villagers must be as well. But just because I was comfortable in cooler air, does not mean they would be. And I was wrong to think that this was a problem that needed to be fixed.

"Humans have lived thousands and thousands of years without the luxury of air-conditioning, so clearly, we can get by just fine. At home, we treat luxuries like air-conditioning as though they are completely necessary for our survival. We've forgotten that technologies like these are relatively new in the entire span of human history and that people did and can survive without them. We must remember that there are people in this world who don't have access to luxuries like that and that's perfectly okay. They know how to live without them because they've done so their entire lives.

"And in fact, their way of life may be much healthier for the planet at large. Sure, there are problems in this world, and some of them may need to be fixed. But there are also a lot of problems that aren't real problems at all—some have called them 'first world problems'—and we don't need to swoop in and save the day. Maybe instead of trying to make others live like us, we should try to live like they do and remind ourselves that our way of life is not the only way, nor necessarily the best way of life. I'm grateful to have this realization, but as yet I am not sure how I will translate it into new behavior. But I am thinking a lot about this."

"Talk about the single story," Cameron chimed in. "We've all seen television infomercials asking people to donate money to help starving children in Africa. We've all seen posts all across Facebook with pictures of people sitting on dirt roads who are so malnourished that you can see their bones. And we've all heard of the tales of people in other countries putting their children to work instead of receiving an education because that was the only way for the family to survive. Those images and sayings were all I'd heard before I arrived in Ghana, so that is all I expected to see. I couldn't have been further from the truth.

"My first day in Ghana proved to be so much different from what I had expected and forced me to dismantle all the preconceived notions that I had about the country. Once I set foot in the country, I saw an unusual beauty that the media seems to deem as ugly, I assume because it was different from their usual Western standards. I saw people laughing and enjoying life as if they didn't have a worry in the world.

"I really knew that all of my previous conceptions of the country were wrong when I was talking to Kwame, a local resident I met in a shop. He and I had an extensive conversation about the state of the government, education, and life in Ghana. I asked a lot of questions that were hard to ask, some of which I'm sure came off as rather ignorant, but Kwame was happy to answer them. Ultimately, this helped me understand the country better, challenged many of my preconceptions, and took away a lot of the prejudices I had.

"What really helped me understand the danger of a single story was not necessarily that many of my preconceptions about Ghana were disconfirmed, although that was profound in many ways, but when Kwame started asking about the lives of Blacks in the United States. He asked, 'Why are Black people so dangerous in the United States?' That question really caught me by surprise, especially as an African American myself.

"We had an extensive conversation about how the media portrays Blacks in the United States and that although shedding light on some communities, it didn't define everybody—just look at me! It was difficult for me learning that he had these notions about the country and people that I call home. And based on the questions I had asked him about Ghana, I suspect that this was difficult for him as well. Living life with a preconceived notion in your mind—essentially a prejudice you have about a place—can be dangerous and reinforces the idea of a single story. Everyone should know that everything presented in the media isn't the whole truth and that there is no way that one situation can represent an entire group. Recognizing this and then asking appropriate questions instead of accepting as accurate the initial ideas one may have will help create more understanding and a balanced environment."

Before bringing the session to a close and with about ten minutes remaining, Max asked everyone to stop and think for a moment about one thing that stood out for them so far. He asked them to try to express that thought in a tweet—a concise statement under 140 characters. After a few minutes, he asked for volunteers to share their tweets.

Sue was the first. "I started this voyage thinking I needed to learn about other cultures. What I am finding out is that I also need to learn about myself within those other cultures."

Dave followed. "I felt like I wasn't really in India. Then, I realized I just wasn't in what I thought India was going to be."

Angie quietly added, "I am learning that it is okay to make mistakes within a culture as long you are willing to learn from those mistakes."

Andrew was next. "I lived in the moment and took in the Taj. Later, I realized I hadn't taken any photos of myself! I was really living in the moment, and it was wonderful!"

Mandy added, "Pursue your passion and try to go without a tour. Go to places you're interested in, and you're more likely to have a deeper experience."

Max thanked everyone for their willingness to share their insights and learnings and urged them to continue to reflect upon the experiences they were having. "It is through the act of reflection coupled with the content you are learning in classes that will help to move you along the intercultural continuum and to become more interculturally competent."

And this is what is covered in greater detail in the next chapter.

Chapter 11

Beyond Tourism: The Role of Experience in Intercultural Learning

Keep your hands open, and all the sands of the desert can pass through them. Close them, and all you can feel is a bit of grit.

—T. Deshimanu

It is the structured experiences and intentional opportunities that teachers develop that are designed to bring young people into close interpersonal interaction with those different from themselves that are key to intercultural development and growth. This chapter surveys the research literature, highlighting what we are learning about how to design educational experiences that have the greatest impact on intercultural growth.

"I'll bet you don't recognize me," the bartender said with a slight smirk as he handed me my drink, "but I know you."

Now, my curiosity was peaked. I had stopped at a local bar to meet a few colleagues before all of us headed off to a university function. I studied the face of this young man who appeared to be in his late twenties. He could have been a former student of mine, and I'm usually good at remembering faces. But a lot of changes occur between the ages of ten and thirty.

My colleagues stared in my direction, wondering how I would respond.

"Gee, I'm sorry, but I just don't recognize you," I said, somewhat embarrassed. "Were you a student of mine at the university school?"

"Now, you're getting somewhere. I will say that it is because of you and the trip we took to Belize when I was ten years old that I am the kind of person I am today. We had such an incredible experience there. And you really did a fine job of taking what could have been a two-week trip and turning it into an experience that lasted the year for the class and then a lifetime for me. I remember that when I first came back from Belize, I felt quite different from

those who did not go with us. And it took me a while to understand this and the impact that the experience had on me. But I can tell you that, even though the trip was not necessarily easy, I am not a prejudiced person as are so many others I went to high school with. And I want to thank you for that."

My colleagues were suitably impressed. Teachers seldom have the privilege of knowing the impact of their work because it is the rare student who comes forward with thanks and appreciation for the impact they may have had earlier in the student's development. This was proof enough for me that something quite powerful had gone on in the lives of these young students many years earlier. "Thank you, Brad, for coming forward and sharing your experience with me—and with my colleagues. You just demonstrated the importance of firsthand experience on the development of an intercultural perspective."

To further illustrate, here's another example from my own experience. It is one thing to read or hear from others that in some parts of the world it is common for men or women to hold hands with one another in public, not necessarily as a display of a same-sex relationship, but merely as a sign of friendship. I learned this piece of information when I was young and first traveling, and I found it quite intriguing and would use it liberally in orientation sessions for would-be travelers. It was something quite different, however, when Mohammed, my Israeli Arab colleague and friend introduced in chapter 7, suddenly took my hand as we walked along the streets in his village of Iksal. I just was not prepared for this act of friendship. But here he was, letting others in his village know that I, an outsider and an American Jew no less, was a trusted and true friend and should be welcomed in the community. Unfortunately, that was not the attribution I made the first time it happened. This just was not a behavior I was accustomed to, and I quickly removed my hand from his.

Thus, it was that although I may have learned this fact cognitively from a book or lecture years before and could readily share this fact with others, it meant something quite different to me when it happened in real life. It was then that I truly learned what this meant. Although it took a while, after some time I could comfortably walk while holding hands with Mohammed, and it was others who had to find their own meaning in our behavior.

Such is the crux of experiential learning—it is characterized by experiences that are holistic, affective, and personal in nature. And it is critical to intercultural learning. Although we have numerous books, films, knowledgeable speakers, and increasingly sophisticated technology that makes it possible for people to be in almost instantaneous communication with one another, research increasingly points to the critical role that firsthand, person-to-person immersion experience plays in advancing people along the intercultural continuum. Experiential learning involves both the right and left hemispheres of the brain, holistically linking encounter with cognition. And the international travel experience can play a major role in the success of this effort—there is just no substitute for the real thing.

Two other characteristics are associated with experiential intercultural learning. Distinct from a simple cross-cultural encounter or international experience, intercultural experiential learning is planned and reflected upon. An increasingly important task for educators today is to encourage and provide significant intercultural experiences for their students, be they children or teacher education students, who typically are not experienced in cross-cultural matters. Teachers are a critical link in structuring the educational experiences that assist students to reach out to the international community, be they at home or abroad, with the aim of forging significant personal relationships based on deep and meaningful understandings of people's similarities as well as differences.

If teachers are truly the architects of educational experiences and opportunity, they must understand how closely intertwined the relationship is between cognition and affect—they are just inseparable when it comes to culture learning. A deep understanding and commitment to living and working with others is not achieved in a cognitive-only approach to learning—it develops only with attention to experience and the affective domain. It is through experiential, immersion experiences that people are challenged to make sense of their new environment and accommodate any changes required for them to function better, ultimately gaining a feeling of being at home in a new context and more knowledgeable about other people.

THE IMPACT OF LIVING AND STUDYING ABROAD

What happens as a result of an overseas or domestic intercultural experience? What changes are evident in people's lives, in their thinking, attitudes, and behavior? What educational interventions help account for these changes? This chapter will look at the impact of intercultural immersion experience and the role of experience in the attainment of new knowledge and skills.

There have been increasing efforts over the years to understand the impact that an international, or even a domestic intercultural experience, has on young people. Although studies investigating this have primarily been undertaken with university-aged students, there has been increasing interest on the impact on younger students. But this has been and will continue to be a difficult line of research to carry out because much of the impact is not really realized nor measurable until many years after someone has had an experience.

The experience abroad involves both physical and psychological transitions that have the potential to impact the cognitive, affective, and behavioral domains. And as was presented in chapter 6, these transitions occur twice, once during entry into the host culture and then again upon return and reentry into the home culture.

One of the goals of study abroad has always been to impact students' knowledge base, and several studies report an impact in the cognitive domain (for comprehensive overviews, see Cushner & Karim, 2004; Vande Berg, Paige, & Lou, 2012). The majority of students who live and study abroad report that their intercultural sojourn challenged their perceptions of themselves as well as their perceptions of others. Those who have studied abroad for a semester or longer tend to demonstrate an increase in cultural and political knowledge and have more critical attitudes toward their own as well as the host culture. Upon their return, these students tend to enroll in a greater number of foreign language classes and to study them for a greater length of time, they tend to spend a greater amount of time studying in college, and they tend to be higher-achieving students than those who do not go abroad. And students who study overseas demonstrate higher levels of cross-cultural interest and cultural cosmopolitanism than do those who remain at home.

We are also beginning to document the long-term impact of the international experience. The largest retrospective look at the impact of study abroad, the SAGE Study (Study Abroad for Global Engagement; Paige, Fry, Stallman, Josic, & Jon, 2009), surveyed 6,391 participants years after their study abroad experience. This study revealed that study abroad impacts at least five dimensions of global engagement—civic engagement, knowledge production, philanthropy, social entrepreneurship, and voluntary simplicity—as well as having an impact on subsequent educational and career choices.

Additionally, years later, people who had studied and lived abroad report having a greater understanding of the intellectual life and traditions of their host country in addition to an increased awareness of the differences between nations. Former study abroad participants tend to become involved in more international activities; have more friends, professional colleagues, and acquaintances in other countries; and read more books and newspapers in foreign languages than do those who remained at home.

There is an impact on the affective domain as well. Early studies looking at the impact of study abroad suggest that participants report growth, independence, self-reliance, and an increased ability to make decisions on their own. Significant changes in people's acceptance of cultural diversity as well as others' perspectives and beliefs also occur as a result of study abroad. There is also evidence of an increase in self-confidence, adaptability, flexibility, confidence in speaking to strangers, and gathering information in new and unfamiliar settings.

Those who participate in study abroad programs also demonstrate greater levels of cultural sensitivity and racial consciousness, thus making them more effective at addressing domestic diversity issues. Thomas Pettigrew (2001), one of the most influential researchers in the field of prejudice formation and reduction, reviewed more than 200 studies of ethnic contact, one-fourth of which involved international contact through travel and student exchange. Excluding the relatively restricted encounters that are typical of most tourist experiences, international contact was shown to have a greater impact at reducing prejudice than does within-nation interethnic contact. Thus, student exchanges, especially those a semester or longer in duration, appear to be especially effective at achieving this end.

Behaviors may also change as a result of an international experience. For many, the overseas experience sets new direction and focus to their career paths. Some may wish to prepare for a career working with other sojourners, and they find themselves working as international student advisors or in the growing field of study abroad. Others may seek out careers that allow for subsequent international experiences, perhaps in international business or tourism. Some find that the overseas experience has sensitized them to issues and values they never knew they held, and they become more active and engaged with environmental or political issues. And others work to internationalize whatever career they choose, such as becoming global or multicultural educators, culturally sensitive health care providers, or foreign service officers. Others simply become good cultural mediators in their schools and communities, bringing their overseas experience to the domestic front for the benefit of others.

Numerous scholars have identified the value of increased international experience specifically in the preparation of globally minded teachers (Cushner & Brennan, 2007; Kissock & Richardson, 2010; Malewski, Sharma, & Phillion, 2012; Ochoa, 2010; Quezada, 2004; Walters, Garii, & Walters, 2009). Some studies document the impact of overseas student teaching on instructional practice and improved employment opportunities (Alfaro & Quezada, 2010; Bryan & Sprague, 2012; Gaudino, Moss, & Wilson, 2012; Gilson & Martin, 2009; Shively & Misco, 2012), and others report positive impact on such aspects as global knowledge, increased sensitivity to second language learners, and growth in cultural competence (Batey & Lupi, 2012; Cushner, 2009; Landerholm & Chacko, 2013; Malewski & Phillion, 2009; Marx & Moss, 2011; Phillion, Malewski, Sharma, & Wang, 2009; Quezada & Alfaro, 2007).

CHECKING OUR ASSUMPTIONS

Professionals working in the field of study abroad know that it is far too easy for students to have an international experience that focuses on surface-level, or objective, aspects of culture (e.g., monuments, mansions, and museums or food, festivals, and fashion) without having acquired deep intercultural impact. Some programs are designed in such a way that participants spend far more time with their own peer groups than in having new cultural experiences and intellectual engagement with host nationals. Given that we are not simply travel agents trying to fill as many seats as possible but are really in the business of education, we are obliged to ensure that effective and comprehensive intercultural learning occurs during these experiences. We must therefore examine our assumptions in this regard, being careful that we do not simply assume that more is taking place during such an experience than is actually occurring.

Vande Berg, Paige, and Lou's recent volume, *Student Learning Abroad: What Our Students Are Learning, What They're Not, and What We Can Do About It* (2012), raises important issues and questions concerning the assumptions often made about the impact of study abroad on student learning. Of special relevance here is what has been referred to as the "immersion hypothesis."

The assumptions made along with the subsequent follow-up actions often taken are summarized by Vande Berg and his colleagues in the following way: (1) students learn effectively while abroad simply by being exposed to new and different cultures; (2) reports from returning students that they have been "transformed" provide the evidence that having had this experience is in fact effective; and (3) because most students say they are learning effectively while abroad, it makes sense to focus more on getting larger numbers of students overseas than working to improve the teaching and learning that takes place during the experience.

This in large part explains the meteoric rise witnessed in recent years in the number of students studying abroad that we have witnessed—especially on short-term faculty-led or teacher-led programs. Again, we must check our assumptions and take a closer look at what occurs during these experiences.

Relatively recent investigations into the impact of study abroad attest to the complex nature of cultural learning. The Georgetown Consortium Study, a comprehensive analysis of more than 1,000 participants in sixty-one different study abroad programs, demonstrated insignificant gains on intercultural development (as measured by the Intercultural Development Inventory; Hammer, 2011) for participants in sixty of the sixty-one programs investigated (Vande Berg, Paige, & Lou, 2012). Only one program that strategically addressed intercultural concepts and learning throughout the experience demonstrated significant intercultural gain.

Gmelch's (1997) study of fifty-one American students in a European university semester program sheds some light on what happens during the experiences of students who spend most of their time with their peers. This particular study documented students' activities during the days when they left their program site to travel, typically via a Eurail Pass on Fridays through Sundays.

When asked, students believed that they learned more from their travel experiences on weekends than from their formal educational program at their study site. What they actually experienced, however, was quite different from what they thought. Hoping to see as much as they could in the brief time available to them, the typical student tended to hop around the continent, spending more time traveling in trains than doing anything else, averaging 1.72 countries and 2.4 cities per weekend over the six-week program. On an average weekend, students spent 18.7 hours on trains and 3.0 hours in stations waiting for them—instead of staying in one place for the entire time and gaining any in-depth understanding of a particular area. Train schedules often dictated where students went next, especially if they were not happy with a current destination. Sometimes, whichever train left earliest was the one that was chosen, regardless of where it was headed! Even at the base study sight, students often went out in large groups, limiting their interactions to shopkeepers and taxi drivers and thus having little meaningful contact with any locals. As was evident in this particular study, students who do not make the effort to separate themselves from the larger group may not learn as much about local culture as is assumed by their parents and instructors.

Cushner and Chang's (2015) study of sixty-two student teachers participating in an international student teaching program that placed students overseas without offering an explicit intercultural curriculum supports the results of the Georgetown Study. Ninety-one percent of the subjects in this study were on the ethnocentric side of the intercultural continuum at the start of their overseas student teaching experience with a Group Mean Developmental Orientation score on the IDI of 89.85. Participants were assessed again at the completion of their experience, that is, after eight to fifteen weeks of living with host families and teaching in local schools. Results demonstrated a postexperience Developmental Orientation score on the IDI of 92.75—no insignificant gain evident simply as a result of being immersed in another culture.

Vande Berg and his colleagues (2012) were clear when they stated that the majority of students will not develop interculturally merely because they are "immersed" on their own in another culture. If intercultural development is an expectation and desired outcome of any educational intervention, then specific criteria, as were evident in the one program that demonstrated significant gain, seem to be essential.

The following criteria seem to facilitate intercultural growth in study abroad:

- intentionally focused and active intervention throughout the immersion experience giving attention to intercultural concepts and content that is informed by theory and supported by research;
- predetermined learning outcomes that are specific to concepts related to intercultural interaction and the enhancement of intercultural competence;
- cultural mentoring throughout the experience provided by on-site local individuals emphasizing the role culture plays in the classroom and host community; and
- regular reflection and debriefing.

The message for educators in general and teacher educators more specifically is clear—if we are serious about our desire to enhance the intercultural competence of students at all levels, we must be strategic and mindful that we make culture and intercultural concepts a priority.

What can we learn from those deemed successful at teaching from an intercultural perspective? Merryfield (2000) interviewed eighty teacher–educators recognized by their peers as being successful in preparing teachers in both multicultural and global education. She discovered significant differences between the experiences of people of color and Whites (the majority of teachers in the United States and elsewhere) that reflect the importance of impactful, experiential learning.

Most American teachers of color have a double consciousness (DuBois, 1989). That is, many have grown up conscious of both their own primary culture and having experienced discrimination and the status of being an outsider by encountering a society characterized by White privilege and racism. Middle-class White teacher–educators who were effective at teaching for diversity had their most profound and impactful experiences while living outside their own country as an expatriate. These teachers had, in a sense like the teachers of color, encountered discrimination and exclusion by being an outsider within another cultural context.

As Merryfield's study suggests, those who leave the comfort of their home society for an extended period of time come to understand what it is like to live outside the mainstream and to be perceived as the "other." It is the impactful international experience that has thus facilitated many European American mainstream teachers to become more ethnorelative in their understanding of others, more skilled at crossing cultures, and committed to bringing about change through their work. Travel and living outside one's own culture can for many lead to firsthand understandings of what it means to be marginalized and to be a victim of stereotypes and prejudice and how this might affect people.

A strong rationale for integrating international travel in education can be found in the context of situative theory (Putnam & Borko, 2000). Because so much of learning occurs within the confines of a typical classroom setting, behaviors of both teachers and learners often become routine and automatic. In situative learning, the context in which the individual learns is seen as integral to one's cognition. It is the outside experiences encountered through international educational travel that facilitate the individual development of alternative perspectives, thus helping people see themselves as global citizens and others as potential partners.

Traveling as a tourist—be it individually, in small groups, or even in the more common large groups by which school groups often travel—is qualitatively different from the kinds of experiences that are possible in carefully guided culturally focused travel. And although casual travel through tourism can involve an educational component, it is rarely achieved (Li, 2000). Tourists traveling in groups may travel in a world unto their own, surrounded by, but not necessarily integrated within, the host society. The casual tourist experience is typically understood through the eyes of tour guides, tourist brochures, commercial guidebooks, and programmed performances that often sanitize and generalize the local culture as if tourists are spectators, visually consuming their destination rather than fully engaging with it. Meaning is generally made and communicated by others, not by the self.

Humans as social beings learn best in situations when the complexity of social reality is encountered, examined, and understood. Such is the nature of constructivist learning. In the situated learning that occurs in a well-structured international travel experience, the context enables learners to participate in the social milieu of the host setting, thus enabling people to build rapport with locals, interpersonal relationships with host families, and identification with a local community. Mass tourism does not allow this to occur and may simply distort and reinforce stereotypic images of many of the world's peoples.

Culturally focused travel sets the stage for people to engage in meaningful relationships and thus opens up opportunities that may otherwise not occur. Through interpersonal dialogue and personal encounters, people have the opportunity to learn to see others as well as themselves through new eyes. It is just not possible to re-create the critical relational interdependence of the learner, the activity, and the world in the formal classroom setting.

The lived experience is thus the critical element in gaining a meaningful understanding of other cultures as well as one's own place in an interconnected world. Learning a second culture, although having some similarities to how people learned their original culture, is significantly different in many respects. When learning one's original culture, the entire surroundings, including family, community, and institutions, generally support such efforts with little discontinuity in what one already knows and what one is expected to learn. In learning a second culture, one comes into immediate conflict between the culture of self and the new culture to which one is exposed. Reconciling these differences is critical to successful adjustment and subsequent learning.

In any new cultural setting, the individual is confronted with continuous tensions between previously learned knowledge that must be eliminated or temporarily ignored and new information and behavior that must be accommodated. Suddenly, in the new setting, new categories of information must be identified and understood, and in many cases, finer differentiations must be made in categories that were once not seen as important or that may not have even existed. Problems must be solved in settings that are new to the individual, without the supports one has typically come to depend upon. Thus, large-group travel cannot be a substitute for independent travel. Students should be encouraged to travel in small groups because it increases the likelihood of interacting with local people and having to solve daily problems.

As emphasized by the eighteen-theme culture general framework (Cushner & Brislin, 1996), one's emotions, although initially unanticipated, are oftentimes highly engaged in a new cultural setting. When strong emotion is encountered, people can respond in one of three ways: they can retreat to their own culture by returning home; they can segregate themselves from the local people and spend their time in cultural enclaves separate from the local community; or alternatively, they can begin taking the risks necessary to learn new behaviors that will facilitate their integration into the local context. If one chooses to remain and learn in the new setting, especially with the guidance of a good educator, it becomes impossible to maintain an emotional distance from the surroundings.

Emotional engagement is thus a critical element in the learning process because it prompts one to pause, observe, hypothesize, reflect, and inquire. Sikkema and Niyekawa (1987) underscore this when they state that it is the "emotional ego-involving experience of success and failure as well as the temporary loss of role identity that makes the learning from living in another culture different from learning about the culture from lectures, books, films, and simulated experiences" (p. 43).

But it is through reflection that people make meaning of what it is they have encountered. Thus, although experiences outside one's own culture provide the necessary foundation from which further learning can occur, they cannot stand alone. Each stage of the educational travel experience— the planning and preparation, the travel to the destination, the in-context experience, the return home, and the reflection and evaluation—becomes an essential element of any learning that takes place. But different from a tourist experience, where learning if it occurs is incidental and haphazard, facilitation of learning by a teacher must take place at each step along the way. The teacher thus becomes a critical dimension of effective culture learning in all stages of travel. Guiding observation, reflection, interpretation, and application is a critical dimension the teacher can provide.

Appendix

Making It Work for You and Your Students: Travel Tips and Resources

Now, it's your turn. As you consider an overseas venture for yourself, your students, or perhaps your own children, there are a variety of issues to consider and resources you can use to make your trip planning and execution as rewarding and impactful as possible. Go prepared, be safe, and enjoy, but more importantly, connect with and learn from others.

PREDEPARTURE

Predeparture Teacher Tips:

- Obtain required travel documents early in the trip planning. All travelers require a passport that officially identifies them as a citizen of a particular country. US passports, issued by the Department of State, are good for ten years (five years for people under eighteen years of age) and can be obtained at any US Passport Agency or by mail through certain US post offices that are designated to accept passport applications. Apply for passports as early as possible because they can take between four and six weeks to process. Contact the US Department of State at their website at https://travel.state.gov/content/travel/en/passports.html for comprehensive information and downloadable forms for applying for passports. Each applicant will require proof of citizenship (birth certificate or naturalization papers), two color passport photographs (be sure to review current photo requirements), proof of identity, and an application fee. Passports must be valid for at least six months after the expected date of return, so keep them current.

- Certain countries require an official visa issued by their government that grants the traveler permission to enter the country. Although many countries do not require US citizens to obtain visas ahead of time (some are issued at the border as you enter the country), some do require advance processing and fees. In such instances, the tour operator or travel agency will be able to advise as will private visa service agencies with which you can work. Some visa service agencies specialize in certain countries, so review their website carefully. Different visa requirements will apply for non-US passport holders, so consider such cases early in your planning if so required.
- Visit the US Department of State website for a variety of resources and information to assist you with your travel planning, including up-to-the-minute travel advisories that may be in effect for your destination (http://www.state.gov/travel/). Register your trip prior to your departure with the State Department Smart Traveler Enrollment Program (STEP; https://step.state.gov/step/). This alerts the local US Embassy of your whereabouts so they can reach you in case of an emergency. You may receive periodic updates from them during the time of your visit.
- Check to see whether any specific vaccinations or other health precautions need to be addressed well in advance. In the past, travel vaccines were often available through local health departments. In recent years, however, many have stopped offering this service. Passport Health (www.passporthealthusa.com), a private agency, is available in some areas to those who require vaccinations and have other travel medical needs. You can also check with the Centers for Disease Control and Prevention (CDC; https://www.cdc.gov/travel) for updated information on travel health needs.
- It is advisable to consider health and travel insurance early in program planning. In addition to having medical information on any student who has a medical condition that may be of concern during the program, you should strongly recommend that each participant obtain health insurance that is fully applicable overseas in case of emergency. Although you may have to pay for any medical emergencies out of pocket while traveling, having insurance will make it easier to obtain reimbursement upon your return. Travel insurance is also advisable in case trip cancellation is necessary at the last minute for some unforeseen reason.
- Carry a photocopy of all participants' passport pages and emergency health information with you at all times in case of emergency. Leave similar copies with someone at home as well.
- The Council on Standards for International Educational Travel (CSIET) publishes a directory of international exchange programs that have been evaluated and found to be in compliance with their standards. Schools can

use their Standards for International Student Exchange programs to assist them in administering successful international exchange programs. Find them at www.csiet.org.

- Students of all ages might benefit by having an International Student Identity Card (ISIC). Recognized throughout much of the world, this card verifies student status, thus enabling card holders to obtain discounts with some airlines and insurance providers as well as discounts or free admission to many museums and other cultural sites around the world. The ISIC may also provide supplemental insurance coverage, including emergency medical evacuation in case of illness and repatriation in case of death—something most other policies do not include. The card is available at https://www.myisic.com/isic-card/.
- There is much overlap between the goals and objectives of cross-cultural training and good multicultural education programs. If your school is already actively addressing multicultural education, look to integrate some concepts that cut across diversity throughout your teaching.
- Comprehensive sources of cross-cultural training materials are increasingly available from a variety of publishers. Early books in the field published by the groundbreaking Intercultural Press are now available from Hodder & Stoughton (https://www.hodder.co.uk/search.page?SearchText=interc ultural+press). For a comprehensive academic treatment of intercultural training issues, see *Handbook of Intercultural Training*, available from SAGE Publications (second edition, 1996, by Landis and Bhagat; third edition, 2004, by Landis, Bennett, and Bennett).

Predeparture Student Tips:

- Make friends with people from as many different backgrounds as you can. This will help you learn to be comfortable with a wide range of cultural differences.
- When you find yourself judging others in a negative way, stop and ask yourself why they may be behaving in the manner that you are observing. Don't be afraid to ask others about the reasons they do things in particular ways.
- Expect there to be differences in such things as foods, weather, daily schedule, and supervision. At times, your teachers and chaperones will expect certain behaviors or patience from you. Understand that while traveling, the demands on everyone will be different. Some of these will be because of cultural differences, and others may be dictated by the fact that you will be traveling in a group. The more flexible you can be, the easier your overall adjustment will be.
- Be aware and understanding of your own as well as your fellow students' feelings before and during travel. Some may find certain aspects of travel

adjustments more difficult than others at certain times and in certain circumstances. Some may be surprised that they become homesick or have difficulties that they did not anticipate.

Predeparture Parent Tips:

- Retain a photocopy of your son's or daughter's passport at home in case it is lost during travel. Students should also travel with a photocopy.
- Help your children experience other cultural settings so they become increasingly comfortable in diverse contexts and less judgmental about others. Travel at home by visiting other communities and religious settings, and vacation with this in mind.
- Encourage children to study a foreign language as early as possible in their schooling.
- People who tend to be effective in intercultural settings are eager to try new foods. Help children develop this by taking them to ethnic restaurants and introducing them to new foods on a regular basis.
- Consider currency needs prior to your departure. Travelers should not carry large amounts of cash, but each student should have a small amount of local currency prior to his or her departure, which can be obtained from most banks a few weeks before departure or at the airport, hotel, or bank upon arrival. Most ATM cards now work well overseas, thus limiting conversion fees.
- Each individual has certain needs and desires as he or she travels that may need to be tempered or postponed in lieu of the needs of the group. Talk seriously with your son or daughter about the necessity to be flexible as well as cooperative during group travel.

WHILE TRAVELING

Teacher Tips:

- Once you arrive in your country of destination, immigration officials will ask to see all passports and any necessary visas as well as inquire about the purpose and length of stay in their country. This will take place before you obtain your luggage. Be sure all students have basic information about where they will be staying and for how long they will remain in the country. You may have to assist students in completing any paperwork on the plane or before they reach the customs hall.
- After passport control or immigration and upon collecting your luggage, you will be asked to declare whether you are carrying certain items with

you (large sums of money, any restricted agricultural items, cameras and computers, and so forth). Luggage may also be opened and checked by government officials. Be certain that students take this exercise seriously because the local officials certainly do. Discourage any wisecracks or joking about anything, especially bombs or illegal drugs.

- For the first few days after arrival, you and your students may experience jet lag. Jet lag is nothing more than your body clock trying to synchronize itself with the local time zone. Do not be surprised if people feel disoriented, wake up in the middle of the night, or fall asleep midafternoon for a few days. Although jet lag is an inevitable part of travel, it can be minimized by avoiding alcohol and caffeine while traveling, setting your watch to the local time as soon as you depart, and adopting the local meal schedule as soon as possible.
- Soon after arrival, you will want to do an on-site orientation to familiarize participants with specifics of the local program, including any rules and local laws that may be new or unfamiliar to students. Any special health or safety precautions should also be covered at this time as well as culturally appropriate behavior people should be certain to adopt. Any basic survival language education, if not already under way, should begin at this time.
- Encourage participants to communicate with home soon after arrival so people do not worry in these early days of the experience.
- Take time each day to help students reflect upon what they are experiencing. Focus special attention on cultural differences—the way people communicate with one another and the things that seem important in conversation, in the news, and on the streets. If staying with host families, what differences are students beginning to notice in the manner in which adults interact with children or the expectations parents have of children? If in schools, what differences stand out in the way teachers teach, in the interactions between teacher and student, or in the general behavior of students?

Student Tips:

- It is in the early stages of a travel experience that you can begin to "learn how to learn." That is, adjusting to the local culture requires new sets of skills that you may not have used for some time. In the early days of your experience, you will probably be excited. After some time, however, the excitement may wear off and be replaced with frustration because things you encounter on a regular basis may be quite different from what you have become accustomed to at home. Learn as much as possible from locals, keep your eyes and ears open, and ask as many questions of others as you can. If you have learned some basic cross-cultural concepts, pay particular attention to these aspects. You can use this information as a starting point to begin to ask specific questions about how things are done locally.

- Maintain a journal or blog about your experiences. What have you observed? Whom have you met? What significant differences seem to stand out to you? What questions do you have? What have you learned about yourself or another culture? How can you find out the answers to your questions?

- If you plan to be in one country for an extended period of time, keep your long-range goals in mind. Early on, you may be afforded special status as an outsider, and people will be especially interested in you. Eventually, you will want to fit in like the locals, and others will begin to expect certain "local" behavior from you. Most locals have stereotypic images of Americans (or wherever you are from), based upon what they see in popular media and culture. Remember, you are an individual, and work to dispel the stereotypes people may have of you. You can become an effective culture teacher in this regard.

- If you are staying with a family or if you have met people you wish to get to know better, offer to make a favorite meal for your hosts. This is a wonderful way to share some of your own culture and to become involved with locals in a meaningful way. Or offer to make presentations at local schools and community organizations.

- Women traveling in some countries may wish to be especially cautious. Appropriate behavior for young women varies from country to country, with some nations having strictly defined gender roles. Although it may be uncomfortable, learn how local women are expected to act and dress, and try to do accordingly. You may wish to dress modestly to reduce the likelihood of any unwanted sexual advances. Likewise, in some countries, girls' and young women's behavior may be more controlled by the family, and this includes host families. You may be expected to conform as anyone else in your family might. Try to view this as a compliment and a sign that you are being accepted as a local.

- Although your stomach may take some time to adjust to local foods wherever you may be, there may be certain things you want to avoid. Find out whether there are any restrictions on eating or drinking to which you should be attentive and especially whether the local tap water is safe for you to drink. Ask whether you need to be certain to wash, peel, or boil fresh fruits and vegetables.

- Do not be surprised if you experience an upset stomach and/or diarrhea early in your experience. This is the most common form of traveler's illness, and it will be almost impossible to avoid. In most cases, it should last only a few days. During this time, be sure to replace lost fluids, eat carefully, and use medications wisely. If it lasts more than four or five days or is accompanied by extreme pain, see a physician.

- Remember, ignorance of the law is no excuse. You are subject to all local laws and regulations, and your own government officials will not be able to intervene should you break the law. Be knowledgeable and wise.
- In some countries, you will be perceived as rich and seen as an easy target simply by the very nature of who you are. Think safety when you are out, especially at night. Use common sense—don't walk alone at night, don't wear expensive jewelry, and don't flash expensive cameras; be cautious of road rules when walking or jogging; find out from locals how to best use taxis, Ubers, and public transportation; know where high crime areas are and avoid them; avoid large crowds, which are big draws for pickpockets; and protect your passport at all times.

Parent Tips:

- CSIET publishes a directory of international exchange programs that have been evaluated and found to be in compliance with their standards. Parents can use this as a guide to determine which international student exchange programs meet their child's needs and have met their high standards. Obtain a copy through CSIET, 212 South Henry Street, First Floor, Alexandria, VA 22314, or at www.csiet.org.

UPON RETURN

Teachers Tips:

- When you and your students return home, you will have to clear local customs, and you will again be asked to declare the value of any items purchased abroad. At the time of this writing, each returning American is allowed to bring back up to $800 in gifts and souvenirs without having to pay any tax or duty. Expect to pay a tax on purchases made over this amount.
- If you are enriched and invigorated by the international experience, consider teaching overseas yourself, even if only for a year. More than 1,000 English-language schools exist overseas to serve the needs of Americans and others who wish to have an American-oriented education. Organizations such as International Schools Services (ISS) or the European Council for International Schools (ECIS) offer placement services to assist schools and teachers in making an appropriate match. Subscribe to The

International Educator, available at www.tieonline.com, to learn about international school issues and to keep abreast of international teaching vacancies.

Student Tips:

• Reentry back home, especially if you have been away for a significant period of time, can be as severe and as surprising as one's initial culture shock or adjustment. Expect there to be some period of readjustment, and begin to plan early what you will do upon your return to integrate your intercultural experience into your day-to-day life or how it will impact your future decision making.

• Participate in any reentry workshops that may be offered. It may take time to go through your own reentry experience. Be patient, and learn throughout the process.

• Upon your return, it may be helpful to think of yourself as entering a new culture. Like you were advised in your initial entry, ask questions when you do not know what is going on. How will you integrate the new knowledge and skills you have acquired?

• Sharing your international experiences with others is often a good way of helping you to work through some of your own reentry issues. Seek out audiences that would welcome you to make a presentation about your experience, such as foreign language classrooms at school, elementary, or middle school social studies or language classes, local civic groups (Rotary Clubs, Boy and Girl Scouts, etc.). You should also continue meeting and talking with others who were on your trip. Sharing your feelings and frustration with others while seeking out ways to integrate your new knowledge and experience is often a help.

• Ask your family and friends to keep your letters, e-mails, and postcards and use them to remember and reflect upon your experience at a later time.

• Become active with a local international student club, or encourage your family to host an international student for a semester or a year.

• Retain your international contacts by keeping in contact with the friends and families you cared about from overseas. Stay current with news and other events from the country you left. Online versions of many newspapers from around the world are available via the Internet.

Parent Tips:

• Be patient with your son or daughter. Breakdowns in communication are often at the heart of reentry difficulties, so listen and try not to judge. Your son or daughter may be experiencing a multitude of conflicting feelings, from being excited to be home while also missing friends from abroad. They do not mean to hurt anyone's feelings.

- Help your son or daughter find others who have had similar experiences. Encourage others to listen to their adventures and to help them discuss the significant things they experienced and to explore how they may have changed.
- Don't take it personally if the returnee does not seem interested in some of the activities or people you think he or she should be interested in or he or she does not seem thrilled with a meal or an activity you have planned.
- Seek out ways that your family might become more engaged internationally. Consider hosting an international student or becoming active in international community events.

References

Alfaro, C., & Quezada, R. (2010). International teacher professional development: Teacher reflections of authentic teaching and learning experiences. *Teaching Education, 21*(1), 47–59.

Allport, G. (1954). *The nature of prejudice*. Reading, MA: Addison-Wesley.

Amir, Y. (1969). Contact hypothesis in ethnic relation. *Psychological Bulletin, 71*(5), 319–343.

Austin, C. (1986). *Cross-cultural re-entry: A book of readings*. Abilene, TX: Abilene Christian University Press.

Batey, J. J., & Lupi, M. H. (2012). Reflections on interns' culture developed through a short-term international internship. *Teacher Education Quarterly, 39*(3), 25–44.

Bayles, P. P. (2009). Assessing the intercultural sensitivity of elementary teachers in bilingual schools in a Texas school district (Doctoral dissertation, University of Minnesota). Retrieved from: http://proquest.umi.com/pdqweb?did=1684138321&Fmt=7&clientId=4653&RQT=309&VName=PQD

Bennett, M. (1993). Towards ethnorelativism: A developmental model of intercultural sensitivity. In M. Paihe (Ed.), *Cross-cultural orientation* (pp. 27–69). Lanham, MD: University Press of America.

Berardo, K. (2012). Framework: Four key components of transition planning. In K. Berardo & D. Deardorff (Eds.), *Building cultural competence: Innovative activities and models*. Sterling, VA: Stylus.

Bransford, J. (1979). *Human cognition: Learning, understanding and remembering*. Belmont, CA: Wadsworth.

Bryan, S. L., & Sprague, M. M. (2012). The effect of overseas internships on early teaching experiences. *The Clearing House: A Journal of Educational Strategies, Issues, and Ideas, 70*(4), 100–201.

Chatwin, B. (1987). *The songlines*. New York: Penguin Books.

Coon, C. (2000). *Culture wars and the global village: A diplomat's perspective*. Amherst, NY: Prometheus Books.

Cosineau, P. (1998). *The art of pilgrimage*. Berkeley, CA: Conari Press.

Covey, S. R. (1989). *The 7 habits of highly effective people: Powerful lessons in personal change*. New York: Free Press/Simon & Schuster.

Cushner, K. (1992). Creating cross-cultural understanding through internationally cooperative story writing. *Social Education, 56*(1), 43–46.

Cushner, K. (2009). The role of study abroad in preparing globally responsible teachers. In R. Lewin (Ed.), *The handbook of practice and research in study abroad: Higher education and the quest for global citizenship* (pp. 151–169). New York: Routledge.

Cushner, K. (2014). Strategies for enhancing intercultural competence across the teacher education curriculum. In S. Sharma, J. Phillion, J. Rahatzad, & H. L. Sasser (Eds.), *Internationalizing teacher education for social justice: Theory, research, and practice* (pp. 139–162). Charlotte, NC: Information Age Publishing, Inc.

Cushner, K., & Brennan, S. (Eds.). (2007). *Intercultural student teaching: A bridge to global competence*. Lanham, MD: Rowman & Littlefield Publishers.

Cushner, K., & Brislin, R. (1996). *Intercultural interactions: A practical guide*. 2nd ed. Thousand Oaks, CA: SAGE Publications.

Cushner, K., & Chang, S. (2015). Developing intercultural competence through overseas student teaching: Checking our assumption. *Intercultural Education, 26*(3), 165–178.

Cushner, K., & Karim, A. U. (2004). Study abroad at the university level. In D. Landis & J. M. Bennett (Eds.), *Handbook of intercultural training* (pp. 289–308). London: SAGE Publications.

Cushner, K., & Landis, D. (1996). The intercultural sensitizer. In D. Landis & R. Bhagat (Eds.), *Handbook of intercultural training* (2nd ed.; pp. 185–202). Thousand Oaks, CA: SAGE Publications.

Cushner, K., & Mahon, J. (2002). Overseas student teaching: Affecting personal, professional, and global competencies in an age of globalization. *Journal of Studies in International Education, 6*(1), 44–58.

Cushner, K., & Mahon, J. (2009). Developing the intercultural competence of educators and their students: Creating the blueprints. In D. Deardorff (Ed.), *SAGE handbook of intercultural competence* (pp. 304–320). Thousand Oaks, CA: SAGE Publications.

Cushner, K., McClelland, A., & Safford, P. (2018). *Human diversity in education: An integrative approach* (9th ed.). Boston, MA: McGraw-Hill.

Darwin, C. (1874). *The descent of man and selection in relation to sex* (2nd ed.). London: John Murray: Abermarle Street.

Deardorff, D. (2009). *SAGE handbook of intercultural competence*. Thousand Oaks, CA: SAGE Publications.

Dewey, J. (1938). *Experience and education*. New York: The Macmillan Company.

DuBois, W. E. B. (1989). *The souls of Black folks*. New York: Bantam Books.

Fussell, P. (1987). *The Norton book of travel*. New York: Norton.

Gaudino, A. C., Moss, D. M., & Wilson, E. V. (2012). Key issues in an international clinical experience for graduate students in education: Implications for policy and practice. *Journal of International Education and Leadership, 2*(3), 1–16.

Gilson, T. W., & Martin, L. C. (2009). Does student teaching abroad affect teacher competencies? Perspectives from Iowa school administrators. *Action in Teacher Education, 31*(4), 3–13.

Gmelch, G. (1997). Crossing cultures: Student travel and personal development. *International Journal of Intercultural Relations, 21*(4), 475–490.

Grossman, D., & Yuen, C. (2006). Beyond the rhetoric: A study of the intercultural sensitivity of Hong Kong secondary school teachers. *Pacific Asian Education, 18*(1), 70–87.

Gullahorn, J. T., & Gullahorn, J. E. (1963). An extension of the U-curve hypothesis. *Journal of Social Issues, 19,* 33–47.

Hammer, M. (2011). Additional cross-cultural validity testing of the intercultural development inventory. *International Journal of Intercultural Relations, 35,* 474–487.

Hammer, M., & Bennett, M. J. (2003). Measuring intercultural sensitivity: The intercultural development inventory. *International Journal of Intercultural Relations, 27,* 403–419.

Inhelder, B., & Piaget, J. (1958). *The growth of logical thinking from childhood to adolescence: An essay on the construction of formal operational structures.* New York: Basic Books.

Kissock, C., & Richardson, P. (2010). Calling for action within the teaching profession: It is time to internationalize teacher education. *Teaching Education, 21*(1), 89–101.

LaBrack, B. (2015). Re-entry. In J. Bennett (Ed.), *The SAGE encyclopedia of intercultural competence* (pp. 723–727). Thousand Oaks, CA: SAGE Publications.

Landerholm, E., & Chacko, J. (2013). *Student teaching abroad: An experience for 21st century teachers.* Washington, DC: ERIC - Institute of Education Sciences.

Lee, J. (2011). International field experiences: What do student teachers learn? *Australian Journal of Teacher Education, 36*(10), 1–21.

Lemonick, M. (2000, May 22). Two skulls help explain when and why our ancestors left Africa. *Time,* p. 62.

Li, Y. (2000). Geographical consciousness and tourism experience. *Annals of Tourism Research: A Social Science Journal, 27*(4), 863–883.

Lysgaard, S. (1955). Adjustment in a foreign society: Norwegian Fulbright grantees visiting the United States. *International Social Science Bulletin, 7,* 45–51.

Mahon, J. (2002). *Intercultural sensitivity development among practicing teachers: Life history perspectives* (Unpublished doctoral dissertation). Kent State University, Kent, Ohio.

Mahon, J. (2006). Under the invisibility cloak? Teacher understanding of cultural difference. *Intercultural Education, 17*(4), 391–405.

Mahon, J. (2009). Conflict style and cultural understanding among teachers in the western United States. *International Journal of Intercultural Relations, 33*(1), 46–56.

Malewski, E., & Phillion, J. (2009). International field experiences: The impact of class, gender, and experiences of pre-service teachers. *Teaching and Teacher Education, 25*(1), 52–60.

Malewski, E., Sharma, S., & Phillion, J. (2012). How international field experiences promote cross-cultural awareness in preservice teachers through experiential learning: Findings from a five year collective case study. *Teachers College Record, 114*(8), 1–44.

Martin, J., & Harrell, T. (2004). Intercultural reentry of students and professionals. In D. Landis, J. M. Bennett, & M. J. Bennett (Eds.), *Handbook of intercultural training* (pp. 309–336; 3rd ed.). Thousand Oaks, CA: SAGE Publications.

Marx, H., & Moss, D. M. (2011). Please mind the cultural gap: Intercultural development during a teacher education study abroad program. *Journal of Teacher Education, 62*(1), 35–47.

Merryfield, M. M. (2000). Why aren't teachers being prepared to teach for diversity, equity and global interconnectedness? A study of lived experiences in the making of multicultural and global educators. *Teaching and Teacher Education, 1*(16), 429–443.

Oberg, K. (1960). Culture shock: Adjustment to new cultural environments. *Practical Anthropology, 7,* 177–182.

Ochoa, A. (2010). International education in higher education: A developing process of engagement in teacher preparation programs. *Teaching Education, 21*(1), 103–112.

Paige, R. M., Fry, G., Stallman, E. M., Josic, J., & Jon, J. (2009). Study abroad for global engagement: The long-term impact of mobility experiences. *Intercultural Education, 20,* 529–544.

Pearce, R. H. (1965). *The savages of America: A study of the Indian and the idea of civilization* (p. 155). Baltimore, MD: Johns Hopkins University Press.

Pedersen, P. (1995). *The five stages of culture shock: Critical incidents around the world.* Westport, CT: Greenwood Press.

Pettigrew, T. (2001, April 21). *Does intergroup contact reduce racial and ethnic prejudice throughout the world?* Paper presented at the Second Biannual Meeting of the International Academy of Intercultural Research. Oxford, MS.

Phillion, J., Malewski, E. L., Sharma, S., & Wang, Y. (2009). Reimagine the curriculum: Future teachers and study abroad. *Frontiers: The Interdisciplinary Journal of Study Abroad, 18,* 323–339.

Putnam, R. T., and Borko, H. (2000). What do new views of knowledge and thinking have to say about research on teacher learning? *Educational Researcher, 29*(1), 4–16.

Quezada, R. (2004). Beyond educational tourism: Lesson learned while student teaching abroad. *The International Education Journal, 5*(4), 458–465.

Quezada, R., & Alfaro, C. (2007). Biliteracy teachers' self-reflection of their accounts while student teaching abroad: Speaking from the "other side." *Teacher Education Quarterly, 34*(1), 95–113.

Quinn, D. (1995). *Ishmael: An adventure of the mind and spirit.* New York: Bantam Doubleday Books.

Sherif, M. (1958). Superordinate goals in the reduction of intergroup tensions. *American Journal of Sociology, 63*(4), 349–356.

Shively, J. M., & Misco, T. (2012). "Student teaching abroad will help you get a job": Exploring administrator perceptions of international experiences for pre-service teachers. *The International Education Journal, 11*(1), 52–68.

Sikkema, M., and Niyekawa, A. (1987). *Design for cross-cultural living*. Yarmouth, ME: Intercultural Press.

Stephan, W. (1999). *Reducing prejudice and stereotyping in schools*. New York: Teachers College Press.

Stephan, W. G., & Vogt, W. P. (2004). *Learning to live together: Intergroup relations programs*. New York: Teachers College Press.

Triandis, H. (1972). *The analysis of subjective culture*. New York: Wiley Interscience.

Trifonovitch, G. (1977). Culture learning – Culture teaching. *Educational Perspectives, 16*(4), 18–22.

Tudball, L. (2012). Global perspectives on the internationalization of teacher education. In B. Shaklee & S. Baily (Eds.), *Internationalizing teacher education in the United States* (pp. 93–111). Lanham, MD: Rowman & Littlefield.

Vande Berg, M., Paige, R. M., & Lou, K. (2012). *Student learning abroad: What our students are learning, what they're not, and what we can do about it*. Sterling, VA: Stylus.

Walters, L. M., Garii, B., & Walters, T. (2009). Learning globally, teaching locally: Incorporating international exchange and intercultural learning into pre-service teacher training. *Intercultural Education, 20*, 151–158.

Wang, M. M. (1997). Re-entry and reverse culture shock. In K. Cushner & R. Brislin (Eds.), *Improving intercultural interactions: Modules for cross-cultural training programs* (Vol. 2). Thousand Oaks, CA: SAGE Publications.

Ward, C., Bochner, S., & Furnham, A. (2001). *The psychology of culture shock* (2nd ed.). East Sussex: Routledge.

Ward, C., Okura, Y., Kennedy, A., & Kojima, T. (1998). The U-curve on trial: A longitudinal study of psychological and sociocultural adjustment during cross-cultural transition. *International Journal of Intercultural Relations, 22*(3), 277–291.

World Travel & Tourism Council (WTTC). (2016). Travel & tourism: Economic impact 2016 annual update summary. Retrieved from https://www.wttc.org/-/media/files/reports/economic%20impact%20research/2016%20documents/economic%20impact%20summary%202016_a4%20web.pdf

Yuen, C. (2009). Dimensions of diversity: Challenges to secondary school teachers with implications for intercultural teacher education. *Teaching and Teacher Education, 26*(3), 732–741.

Zimpher, N. L. (1989). The RATE project: A profile of teacher education students. *Journal of Teacher Education, 40*(6), 27–30.

Index

About the Author

Dr. Kenneth Cushner is an emeritus professor of International and Intercultural Teacher Education, has served as executive director of International Affairs, and has been associate dean at Kent State University (1987–2015). Prior to his university appointment, he taught in schools in Switzerland, Australia, and the United States and completed his doctoral studies at the University of Hawaii at Manoa while a degree scholar at the East-West Center. Dr. Cushner is a founding fellow and past president of the International Academy for Intercultural Research; has been a Fulbright Scholar to Sweden (2008) and Poland (2016); has been a visiting professor at Shanghai International Studies University, the College of the Bahamas, University of Newcastle (Australia), and the University of Nis (Serbia); has taught with Semester at Sea on four voyages (Summers 2010 and 2011, Fall 2017, Spring 2019); and has twice served as director of COST—The Consortium for Overseas Student Teaching. He is author or editor of several books and articles in the field of intercultural education, including *Human Diversity in Education: An Intercultural Approach* (9th ed., 2019), *Intercultural Student Teaching: A Bridge to Global Competence* (2007), *Beyond Tourism and Intercultural Interactions: A Practical Guide* (2nd ed., 1996). He has traveled with young people and teachers on all seven continents. Since retiring from Kent State University, Dr. Cushner has consulted with ECIS, a network of 400-plus international schools in ninety countries, and with NAFSA: Association of Intercultural Educators and has instituted a professional development program for teachers in a Maasai community school in northern Tanzania (www.ieftz.org). In his spare time, Dr. Cushner enjoys playing music (guitar and percussion), traveling, and photography.

Lightning Source UK Ltd.
Milton Keynes UK
UKHW041015210719
346380UK00018B/45/P